On Foot Through History

BY MARTIN COLLINS

Scottish Walks by Rennie McOwan

The Oxford Illustrated Press

I would like to thank Rennie McOwan for his authoritative and entertaining forays into Scottish history, and Kev Reynolds for describing two long-distance routes in the south-east of England with customary enthusiasm. My colour film was processed impeccably by Richard Kreutzmann of Colwyn Bay, Clwyd.

'To walk into history is to be free at once, to be at large among people.'

Elizabeth Bowen, from *The House in Paris*, 1935.

Photographs by the author unless credited otherwise.
Maps © Martin Collins

©1991, Martin Collins, unless credited otherwise.

ISBN 1 85509 214 X

Published by:
The Oxford Illustrated Press, Haynes Publishing Group, Sparkford, Nr Yeovil, Somerset BA22 7JJ, England.

Printed in England by:
J.H. Haynes & Co Limited, Sparkford, Nr Yeovil, Somerset.

British Library Cataloguing in Publication Data:

A catalogue record for this book is available from the British Library.

Contents

INTRODUCTION

Man and his ape-like ancestors have existed for no more than 2 million years. We should not forget that the planet Earth had already existed for over 4,600 million years without him and that in global terms the sum of all human activity did little more than scratch the surface of the land until the emergence of industrialised societies two centuries ago.

Man's story in Britain has no easily identifiable beginning. As we trace its course back through time, evidence to substantiate our assumptions about how man lived becomes increasingly sparse. At the most distant point in our history, the human presence itself is represented by no more than a fragment of bone or a primitive flint tool.

Although we are a small island nation off the north-west edge of Europe, our temperate and fertile land drew in early incursions by tribes from the continent, became part of the Roman Empire, suffered invasions by Vikings and Normans, and subsequently played out its role in the tangled web of European and world history. Signs of these diverse influences abound in our architecture, patterns of farming, ancient earthworks, old roads and trackways, place names and customs.

In recent centuries, Britain became a cauldron of invention, enterprise and creativity. The Agricultural and Industrial Revolutions of the eighteenth and nineteenth centuries did much to set the developed world on its present course. It was here that new machinery and methods of transportation evolved, paving the way for mass production and rapid communications—the very cornerstones of a consumer society.

It is a sad fact that history can be destroyed more rapidly than it is made. Most of the natural habitats in which early civilisations flourished—forest, marsh and fen, and grazed downlands rich in wild flowers and insects—have gone, destroyed by man's insatiable appetite for timber, a burgeoning population and, not least, modern agricultural practice.

Prehistoric tumuli and standing stones, Roman fortifications, great castles and abbeys have all been subject to the vagaries of British weather and to plundering or thoughtless damage in less heritage-conscious times than our own. Many buildings from the 1700s and 1800s—industrial dinosaurs from another era—lie in ruins, though increasing numbers now enjoy listed status and are being converted to new uses or protected from further decay. Perhaps the greatest losses of all, however,

have occurred piecemeal during the relentless spread of new building development and the construction of new highways. As we overlay the past with the present, it is often inconvenient to preserve what we remove or obscure. There will always be those who argue in favour of providing car parks, shopping precincts and new motorways at the expense of small but appreciable pieces of our historical inheritance. But these pieces can never be reclaimed and their loss is not ours alone. If the modernisation of Britain's towns and countryside continues without a sensitive regard for the historical foundations upon which our culture is based, future generations will find it increasingly difficult to make meaningful connections with the past.

There is, after all, a spiritual dimension to the tangible remains from previous ages—a sense in which those very remains trigger imaginative leaps back in time. Combined with the necessary background knowledge, direct encounters of this kind provide vivid insights into the lives and endeavours of people long dead but whose footsteps we follow on mankind's unfolding journey into the future.

We should never undervalue the magnificent work done by museums in preserving and interpreting the past. I do believe, however, that where possible museum visits should precede exploration 'in the field', for the discovery of relics *in situ* yields a very different order of experience from that gained by viewing displays. However imaginatively designed, no static exhibition can compete with crossing a wild hill on old drovers' roads, or wandering beneath the crumbling masonry of a medieval castle, or confronting prehistoric dolmens on some remote, misty moor.

Ours is a tiny nation but it possesses one of the most richly varied and accessible histories of all countries on Earth. Despite being densely populated, with all the environmental threats that this imposes, much of our history can be traced in the landscape provided you know where to go and what to look for. The walker is at a tremendous advantage, for not only are many sites reachable only on foot, but you really need the mobility and contemplative pace of walking in order to appreciate the broader context into which details fit.

About the Walks

This book sets out to sample as varied a cross-section of British history as space allows. At the same time, it also addresses itself to the walk-

ing fraternity and therefore combines discovering sites of historical interest with the delights and challenges of pedestrian travel. The actual selection of walks reflects both the need for a reasonable geographical spread and the authors' own recommendations.

It is virtually impossible to travel far in the landscapes of Britain without encountering structures from the very dawn of history: the sarcen stones of Avebury, Dorchester's Maiden Castle earthworks, the Cerne Abbas Giant and Uffington White Horse are notable examples.

The Roman occupation of Britain had a profound and lasting effect upon our country's development and left in its wake such astonishing features as Hadrian's Wall and the Roman road over Lakeland's High Street fells. No less imposing are the extraordinary remains of Offa's Dyke delineating the old frontier between Wales and England.

Medieval castles and coastal fortifications bear witness to centuries of struggle for power and to the need to defend our shores against invasion. By way of a counterpoint, religious buildings, stately homes and the gradual transition of farmstead to hamlet, hamlet to village and village to town reflect periods of economic and social stability. For centuries, farming methods remained constant and little changed in the rural landscape.

A growing network of rough roads and paved packhorse ways across hill and moor improved trade and communications, but long before they appeared man had already established trackways along ridges of high land, linking settlements and sites of religious significance. Canals, turnpike roads and railways eventually superseded many of the earlier thoroughfares, though some of those, in turn, were rendered obsolete by later technology or abandoned for other reasons. A large number survived and have been adopted as walking ways. In addition, we owe a debt of gratitude to our pedestrian predecessors for the countless miles of footpaths which, through habit of use, provide public rights-of-way across the countryside.

Of many diverse industries, mining, quarrying and textiles in particular left an indelible mark; a poignancy hangs about the ruins as we come to realise how the investment of so much human effort and the suffering of such grinding hardship yielded only transient rewards. There is irony, too, in the way these enterprises often sprang up in areas of abundant natural beauty, to which we walkers naturally gravitate—the Cornish and Pembrokeshire coasts, Yorkshire's dales and moors, the Pennines and Snowdonia, to mention but a few.

As Rennie McOwan explains, walks in the Scottish section touch on the Celtic races of ancient centuries, on the native Picts who left us a legacy of intricately carved stones and a puzzling language, and on the incoming Scotti from Ireland who were to fight and intermarry and eventually (and jointly) produce the nation we call Scotland.

Invading Norsemen raided and settled and left their mark on many of the hill and place names of the islands and western seaboard, these mingling with the more widespread names in the Gaelic tongue.

The clansmen of old were superb hillmen and women, tough and tenacious. By the eighteenth and nineteenth centuries, the old cattle economy of the Scottish hills had evolved into a thriving droving business with huge cattle drives from the Highlands and Islands converging on markets further south.

The legends of the people, their belief in a living 'spirit' in nature and in supernatural beings—witches, water-horses, sprites, sea-people and others—as well as their belief in talismans and charms, are a subject worthy of the most serious study. Such convictions often existed alongside the Christianity of the Celtic saints.

The old shieling pattern, whereby temporary homes were built in the hills for spring and summer occupation, is also covered in these chapters. Many of the ancient routes of the cattle drovers were, in time, replaced by eighteenth-century military roads, designed to curb the activities of clans who supported the exiled House of Stuart. In many Lowland areas and in the Southern Uplands are secret glens and hollows—gathering places for Scots who refused to allow monarchs to dictate their religious beliefs. This was a complex period in Scottish history, which produced the Covenanters.

The book is divided informally into three sections—Wales, Scotland and England—with routes arranged from north to south in each section. Walks vary considerably in length and difficulty, from strolls suitable for all ages and abilities to demanding treks in remote hill country or multi-day hikes on long-distance footpaths. Most routes fall between these extremes, however, and represent ideal day or half-day outings well within the range of the majority of walkers.

Whilst it is impossible to make recommendations about clothing, gear and footwear that apply equally to all the walks (some, indeed, could be undertaken in everyday clothes), commonsense decisions do need to be taken before setting out. In rough country, requirements include all the usual items for a hill or coastal expedition—stout footwear, functional clothing, waterproofs, map and compass and a rucksack containing food, first-aid kit, spare sweater, etc. Much will depend upon the time of year and the prevailing weather (always try to obtain a forecast), but remember that winter brings with it increased risks from exposure to the elements as well as from shorter daylight hours. Even modest itineraries are transformed into potentially serious propositions at the onset of storms, mist or nightfall. The 'fact box' provided for each walk and the relevant OS map, however, will give an indication of the route's nature, while any specific difficulties are mentioned in the text.

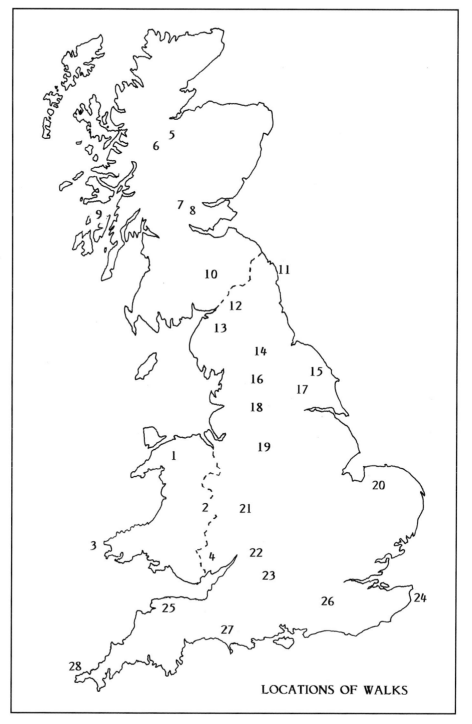

LOCATIONS OF WALKS

WALK 1: *GWYNEDD—Welsh Copper Mines and a Mountain Railway*

Remains of old copper mines beside a rugged path crossing a mountain pass culminate in workings open to the public. The return leg is through tunnels along a disused narrow-gauge railway track. **Start/Finish:** Car park near Pont Aberglaslyn (or any other suitable point on the circular route). **Distance:** 4½ miles (7km). **Location/Access:** Beddgelert lies south of Snowdon, at the junction between the A498 from Capel Curig and the A4085 from Caernarfon. Nearest railway station—Porthmadog. **Map:** OS Landranger Sheet 115.

*Facing page **Aerial ropeway pylons lead down from workings near the head of Cwm Bychan.***

The history of copper mining in Snowdonia dates back over 2000 years. Throughout the span of centuries, where attempts to extract the metal either failed or were abandoned, spoil heaps, adits, old trackways, machinery and building ruins have been left for today's observant passers-by to contemplate.

Although documentation of mining activity is scarce—returns of ore production did not become compulsory until 1872—the area's mountainous nature has tended to protect what relics still exist from those who consider them 'untidy' and would have them removed. On this walk you will enjoy a veritable feast of industrial archaeology combined, coincidentally, with some of the finest mountain scenery in Britain.

Copper mining in North Wales reached its zenith with the discovery of rich deposits at Parys Mountain on Anglesey in 1768. Over the ensuing years, the fishing hamlet of Amlwch swelled into a boom town of Klondike proportions. Men, women and children were engaged in open-cast extraction, aided by windmill-driven pumps—the stump of a tower still crowns Parys Mountain. Amlwch's little harbour, destined to become the world's largest copper port for a time, was enlarged to accommodate ore-carrying vessels. As if to underline its own significant contribution to the nation's wealth, the Parys Mountain Copper Company even minted currency tokens when copper coins of the realm were in short supply during the late eighteenth century.

Against this background, it is interesting to reflect that well before the great Amlwch boom, miners were already prospecting busily for copper in the mountains of Snowdonia. Not only were their efforts poorly rewarded—the small-scale search for metals has always been a speculative venture akin to gambling—but daily life must have been uncompromisingly rigorous. Two hundred years ago, before the advent of turnpike roads and railways, wheeled transport was virtually non-existent in these remote parts and men would routinely walk half a dozen miles to and from work on sheep tracks over rugged terrain. Mountain weather can be arctic in severity and is often inhospitable for weeks on end. Some workings had barracks attached, where miners lived while optimism in their undertaking remained, but men were worn out at 40 by the physical privations they endured.

The brassy, almost gold-like copper pyrites yielded the richest ore, lodes sometimes occurring as solid ribs, sometimes as tenuous threads. Extraction was frequently complicated when lodes of lead ore, itself a valuable commodity, coincided with copper ore and required separation. Quantities of rock and quartz, too, had to be removed by crushing and dressing before the final product was marketable. Smelting became centred on Swansea owing to its cheap sources of coal and its docks, but Welsh copper production was always eclipsed by the prodigious output of more richly endowed mines in Cornwall.

Despite limited success—it is estimated that Snowdonia yielded a total of some 160,000 tons—copper mining here led to more frustration, disappointment and debt than prosperity for those engaged in it. The eternal springs of hope sustained many an adventurous spirit whose morale depended more upon the chance of sudden wealth than upon the bleak realities of actual production. Armed with this realisation and a little imagination, the sites of the old mines take on a new poignancy.

In truth, you could start the walk almost anywhere on the circuit, but I have chosen the car park near Pont Aber Glaslyn because I believe it offers the best sequence of events: an ascent when you are fresh, mining relics in the hills seen before the Sygun Mine and Visitor Centre, a possible refreshment stop at Beddgelert and an easy final stage along a disused railway trackbed.

As you drive south from Beddgelert, the A498, the River Glaslyn and the old Welsh Highland Railway are all held cheek by jowl in a deep, romantically wooded gorge, carved out since the ending of the last Ice Age 10,000 years ago. From the bridge at the Pass of Aberglaslyn, views back to the Snowdon massif are memorably dramatic. There is a seasonal café at the road junction and this walk begins at the car park about 300m along the A4085 towards Barmouth. A small crushing mill was sited nearby, associated with the workings higher up Cwm Bychan.

With no gentle preamble to ease you into the effort of walking, the waymarked path attacks steep wooded slopes with some determination. Beyond a handgate, however, the gradient relents and as you follow the stream up, marvellous views of the Cnicht ridge unfold to the east across a foreground of rock outcrops.

Meandering onwards up natural steps in the valley floor, you cross the stream and are suddenly confronting the steel towers of an old aerial ropeway, originally almost a mile long and supplied by R. White and Sons of Widnes around 1925. This enterprise represented the

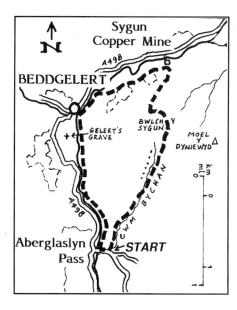

last and least successful working of deposits in Cwm Bychan (or Nantmor, after the village at its base) and produced almost no ore. In fact, mining here dates from 1720 and was most profitable during the last two decades of the eighteenth century; further work on a north lode began in 1870 but lasted less than five years.

The pylons are impressive structures, especially when seen in line marching down the valley from the upper terminal. Not only have they escaped being dismantled but, at my last visit, there were signs that preservation work had been carried out.

You continue up past ruined buildings and heaps of spoil, aiming towards a grassy swath which rises to the skyline, dominated on the right by the rocky eminence of Moel y Dyniewyd (1253ft/382m). At the top, veering left, you find yourself at Bwlch y Sygun, an exciting lip of land overlooking the beautiful Vale of Gwynant. Opposite soar the convoluted flanks of Yr Aran, overtopped by summits on the famous Snowdon Horseshoe; the north-western horizon is formed by the extraordinary profile of the Nantlle Ridge.

From a broken wall, a clear descending path zig-zags down over brackeny mountainside: faced with such breathtaking scenery, it is not easy to concentrate on placing your feet! Lower down, amidst rampant rhododendrons, you pass the Victoria tunnel and a spoil heap associated with the Sygun Copper Mine. Started about 1830, the yield from this mine proved disappointing and it changed hands several times until entering its final phase in 1896 with a momentous technical discovery. Quite by accident, Stanley Elmore and his brother Frank noticed how copper pyrites adhered to surfaces which happened to be

7

smeared with grease or oil. This chance observation led to the development of the flotation process, a much more efficient method of separating sulphide ores than conventional dressing by machine. Little remains of the Elmores' research and development work, but their achievement in pioneering the new process represented a technical innovation of major significance.

Despite estimates of generous reserves waiting to be brought out and the erection of a costly steam-powered mill on terraces cut into the hillside, Sygun was a financial disaster. Even the new Elmore separation process was no match for persistently low-grade ore and plummeting copper prices; by 1903 the plant had ceased production and four years later had been decommissioned.

Today you can explore the tunnels and chambers of Sygun Mine, with their stalactites, stalagmites and veins of copper ore, in 40-minute guided tours. Since 1986 the mine has earned a well-deserved place on the North Wales tourist circuit and has attracted a prestigious British Tourist Authority award. Open from March to October and on winter weekends, it provides much to fill out the picture you may already have of copper mining in these hills.

As an adjunct to the mining theme, the old Sygun mill was transformed into a Chinese village for the filming of *The Inn of the Sixth Happiness* in 1958. Hillsides in Cwm Bychan above Nantmor, chosen for their resemblance to the North China landscape mentioned in the story,

became the site of Wangeheng, a walled city fabricated from scaffolding and acres of plasterboard!

The mile-long stroll along to Beddgelert past woods and the occasional building is an easy one and will lead you to a choice of eating and drinking places in this popular mountain village if needs be. Otherwise, you take to a path along the east bank of the Glaslyn, crossing to the west bank near the church. The flat riverside fields you now skirt once supported a sixth-century Celtic monastery and a twelfth-century Augustinian priory, to which the present church was attached.

Nearby, set in a small enclosure to the right, stands Gelert's Grave. In the thirteenth century, Prince Llewelyn the Great returned from hunting—so the story goes—to find his infant son missing and his dog, Gelert, whom he had left on guard, covered with blood. Assuming the dog had killed his son, Llewelyn drew his sword and slew the hapless animal, only to discover the child hiding beneath his cradle and a dead wolf nearby; clearly Gelert had saved his son from the wolf's attack. Distraught, Llewelyn ordered the faithful dog be buried and a monument erected in his memory. Absorbed into popular Welsh legend, the story is almost certainly bogus, concocted by local innkeepers to drum up custom at the end of the eighteenth century!

The walk's final leg follows the trackbed of the Welsh Highland Railway, a narrow-gauge line intended to link the towns of Caernarfon and Porthmadog via Beddgelert. At first, the

line only extended from Dinas, near Caernarfon, to Rhyd-ddu, $3\frac{1}{2}$ miles ($5\frac{1}{2}$km) north of Beddgelert and later re-named South Snowdon. For a time the service was popular but the more dramatic attraction of the Snowdon Mountain Railway, inaugurated in 1896, killed off trade and it closed in 1916.

In 1922, the newly created Welsh Highland Railway Company revived the idea of a 22-mile (35km) through-line to Porthmadog and work was completed by 1923. Once again, demand failed to meet expectations and trains ceased running in 1937. Hopes of resurrecting much of the line for use with steam engines are kept alive by the Welsh Highland Light Railway (1964) Ltd. which, since 1980, operates on $\frac{3}{4}$ mile of track from Porthmadog to Pen-y-Mount.

As you might expect, the walking is straightforward along the trackbed, though there is a surprise in store! Crowded by precipitous crags near the Pass of Aberglaslyn, the railway builders were forced to blast their way through solid rock. Two short tunnels are followed by a very long one which those who suffer from claustrophobia or fear of the dark will not relish! No daylight at all penetrates to the dank, echoing middle section, but the ground underfoot—and presumably the rock above your head!—is safe enough. You emerge, blinking, just short of the car park where the walk began.

On the old railway trackbed near Beddgelert.

Offa's Dyke on Llanfair Hill.

WALK 2: *WELSH BORDERS—Montgomery to Knighton along Offa's Dyke*

A long and quite strenuous hike following the famous earthwork at its most impressive from the historic county town of Montgomery to the Offa's Dyke Heritage Centre at Knighton. **Start:** Montgomery Castle. **Finish:** Offa's Dyke Park, Knighton. **Distance:** 19 miles (30km)—a full day's walk preferably in good weather. **Location/Access:** Montgomery lies on the B4388 south of Welshpool, south-west of Shrewsbury. Knighton is on the A488 between Bishop's Castle and Llandrindod Wells, or west of Ludlow on the A4113. Nearest railway stations—Welshpool and Knighton. **Map:** OS Landranger Sheet 137.

The history of Offa's Dyke is inextricably bound up with political developments in Welsh border country some 600 years after the withdrawal of Roman rule. During the fifth, sixth and seventh centuries, the Celtic language and culture, along with Christianity, spread right through the west of Britain, from Devon and Cornwall north to Cumbria and Strathclyde and it was not until the end of that period that the first English kings were able to make significant inroads into this territory. That they eventually did, however, splitting away the north-west and south-west from what we know now as the separate country of Wales, or Cymru.

Anglo-Saxon England, initially composed of many smaller kingdoms, moved gradually towards unification, although powerful individuals and alliances continued to compete for supremacy. The English limit of influence pushed inexorably westwards, but its progress was stubbornly resisted by the Welsh in well-defended hill country.

Mercia—the kingdom embracing all central and southern England—was reigned over for 30 years by Aethelbald, but he was murdered by his own bodyguard in AD 757. From the ensuing civil conflict, Offa emerged as king, developing into an effective and durable leader: his rule of 39 years was unprecedented in those times. His administration established dialogues with the Pope and Emperor Charlemagne, the first coins of the realm since the Roman era were minted and an audacious earthwork was built from the Wye to hills above the Dee. Defining the 150-mile (241km) western boundary of Offa's kingdom, the Dyke probably dates from after AD 784, following the great campaign against the Welsh Kingdom of Powys which yielded a period of relative calm along the border.

The Dyke, some 80 miles (129km) in length, averaging 6ft (1.8m) in height and in breadth almost 60ft (18m), was not militarily defensible in the way that, for example, Hadrian's Wall certainly was. Neither could it have been constructed without a level of agreement between Welsh and English. Principally a political and territorial frontier, the Dyke did control trade and movement across the border but it was imposed after cultural and settlement patterns had become established and did not in itself create significant change. Nevertheless, the Dyke's striking alignment across often difficult land, its command of views to the west and its close-up profile of bank and ditch represented a very tangible—not merely a symbolic—obstacle.

Today where sections of the Dyke are extant it still has the power to astonish. Its construction and sheer length would create immense

logistical problems even in our age of powerful earth-moving machinery. That it was dug by hand—probably in the space of a few years by neighbouring Mercian landowners each allotted a marked-out section—is scarcely imaginable! In fact the Dyke never reached its planned conclusion at the River Dee, possibly owing to Welsh harassment or perhaps to a fall-off in commitment following Offa's death in AD 796.

Inevitably, erosion by the elements and from ploughing, roadbuilding, quarrying and housing development over ensuing centuries has softened the Dyke's form and in a few places has destroyed it altogether. Yet in many locations—particularly in limestone country—it has survived remarkably well. The England/Wales political boundary has changed since Offa's day, but there remains a sense in which the Dyke delineates the underlying human and geographical transition from lowland England to highland Wales.

The notion of an Offa's Dyke Path took root following publication of Sir Cyril Fox's celebrated archaeological survey of the earthwork between 1926 and 1931 when he was Director of the National Museum of Wales. After official designation of the path in 1955, much work remained to be done establishing rights-of-way and devising a path line that would follow the Dyke wherever possible yet also provide varied and interesting walking. Progress seemed slow, even after the Countryside Commission had taken over from the National Parks Commission, and the Offa's Dyke Association was born in 1969 from an action committee of enthusiasts keen to complete the path and provide information for walkers. The way opened officially on 10 July 1971 at Knighton, now the Association's headquarters.

Of the path's 176 miles (283km) only 67 (108km) are along the Dyke itself. But much of parallel or incidental interest is passed along the way and for lovers of true hill country there are the Black Mountains and the Clwydian Hills to savour, with their challenging terrain and magnificent views.

It is generally accepted that the Dyke is at its most impressive over the rolling hills of Clun Forest—the Shropshire Hills Area of Outstanding Natural Beauty. Here the going can be surprisingly strenuous and the countryside, though farmed, lacks settlements of any size. That very remoteness, however, and the Dyke's forceful presence switchbacking over ridge and valley invest this walk with purpose and offer what I consider to be the definitive experience of the Welsh Marches.

The journey begins not on the Dyke but a mile to the west at Montgomery, Britain's

smallest county town. To the north stretches flat farmland, but the Kerry Hills beckon in the south. It is always a good idea to start a walk where you have a chance to take stock of your surroundings, to gather resources and sharpen the senses. There is no better place to do that than Montgomery Castle.

Built by Henry III on a virtually impregnable rocky ridge strategically positioned to attack Welsh territory, it was completed by 1225 and a town soon grew up naturally at its base. Though besieged more than once, the castle never fell to the Welsh, despite the sacking of Montgomery by Owain Glyndwr in the early 1400s. From the time of Henry VIII, Montgomery has been associated with the powerful Herbert family. It was Lord Edward Herbert—author, adventurer and Montgomery's MP—who played a decisive role in the castle's final scene. Threatened by a Parliamentary army at the outbreak of the Civil War in 1644, Lord Herbert surrendered the castle; despite Royalist opposition which led to a bloody battle, it was finally lost to the King and was demolished in 1649. Excavation and strengthening of the surviving masonry has been carried out and, although only a shadow of its former self, the ruin is well worth visiting and views are wonderfully wide-ranging.

There is more history to Montgomery than its castle, but with many miles to tread it is time to leave the sleepy little town with its Georgian market hall and head for Offa's Dyke. You temporarily take the B4385 Bishop's Castle road before turning left into Lymore Park with its lake and fine trees. The roadway passes through gates and a plantation, depositing you right on the line of Offa's Dyke not far from Whitley Farm and, coincidentally, on the present England/Wales border where Shropshire meets Powys.

Striding out south along pasture fields, you pass a good section of earthwork below Gwarthlow. Beyond Ditches Farm you reach the A489 (you can see the Dyke in the garden of the Bluebell Inn here at Brompton) and cross the River Caebitra on the approach to Mellington Hall. For over a mile the Dyke forms the park's western perimeter and it is superbly preserved in Mellington Wood—some 20ft (6m) high and 54ft (16m) wide. (This section can be badly overgrown in summer, and a detour through the caravan park is recommended).

In a perfectly straight line, partly built over by the road, the Dyke reaches Cwm hamlet at the start of an ascent to the Kerry Hill Ridgeway. As you climb the steep hillside, views open out back over the Plain of Montgomery to Long Mountain and the Vale of Severn and you may be glad of a breather to admire them, for 600ft (183m) of height are gained within less than half a mile!

Although damaged by cultivation around Crownest, the Dyke rises as a high bank over upland pasture to the Ridgeway itself, a centuries-old, high-level route between Wales and England. Across the country road into Shropshire, the ditch and bank are well defined but you soon drop through Nut Wood into the Unk valley where undergrowth can hinder progress.

After either fording the river or crossing the footbridge, loins are girded for another ascent—this time beside the splendidly high bank and ditch onto Edenhope Hill which some consider the best viewpoint on the entire walk, taking in Clun Forest and, in the east, the Long Mynd and Stipperstones. A steep descent brings you past the simple, isolated church of St John the Baptist—a full mile from Mainstone village. If you expected civilisation here at Churchtown, you would be disappointed by the diminutive hamlet! It sits in a narrow valley 300ft (91m) below flanking hills where two arms of Churchtown Hill divide Mainstone Brook, a tributary of the Unk.

More legwork is called for as the way rises abruptly through a conifer plantation above Cwm Ffrydd. Beyond a ridgetop lane, the Dyke is followed down through fields past Middle Knuck Farm to Hergan where two sections constructed by different gangs of workers join uncomfortably at right angles. Fox judged the Hergan section along the hill's west flank to have been built first; the second section along east-facing land fails to meet up and is connected by a weak bank.

Fields, woods and streams in undulating countryside lead onwards, the Dyke an intermittent feature but occasionally massive, until the scrubby descent into the broad Clun valley. (The Crown Inn could be visited at Newcastle, 15 minutes along to the west.) Down towards Bryndrinog Farm the earthwork assumes impressive proportions. At Lower Spoad the now expected regaining of height begins, but take a few moments to admire this fascinating and handsome old farmstead. Accompanying you, the Dyke marches to the top of Spoad Hill, intact, in very good condition and ditched on the west side, as is customary, all the way up.

Beyond Springhill on the ancient Clun-Clee Ridgeway, in the absence of a right-of-way, the country road towards Llanfair Waterdine has to be tramped for about half a mile. This is a great shame considering the proximity of one of the finest stretches of all through a little valley and onto Llanfair Hill. The Dyke is soon regained, however, by forking left on a farm track.

Llanfair Hill, a grassy upland ridge drained to east and west by numerous stream valleys, carries the earthwork to its highest elevation—1408ft (429m) above sea level. In an unbroken line, clear of hedges or trees and crossed by only one or two wire fences, the Dyke sweeps majestically across an open landscape like a green ocean swell not yet steep enough to crest. Buildings of any kind are conspicuous by their absence; only sheep, cattle

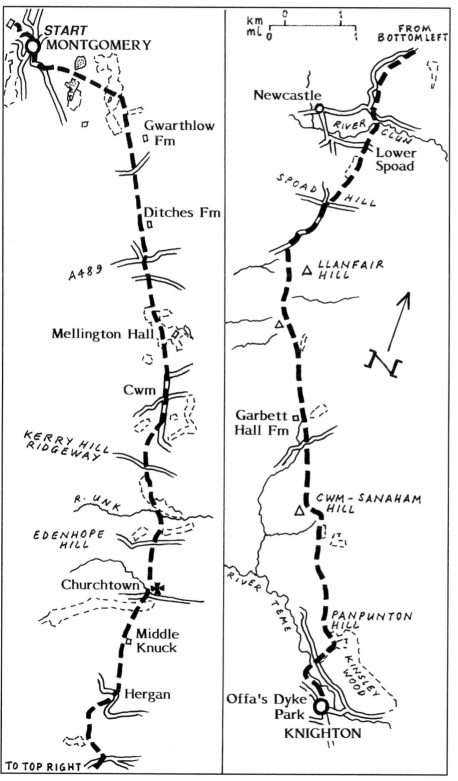

and the occasional horse inhabit the empty, rolling miles.

On either side or along its top, you follow the bank past a Dutch barn and down through larches to Garbett Hall Farm (drinks and snacks for walkers). Climbing directly over a rocky spur created by Selly Brook, Offa's Dyke runs remarkably straight, though of lesser stature, taking you steeply up through gorse onto flat-topped Cwm-sanaham Hill (1343ft/409m). This is another viewpoint par excellence—especially west over the meandering Teme valley. Sharp gradients to the south round the head of the gorge-like Cwm Sanaham give out to an easy onward path along or just back from the scarp slope, the Dyke little more than a bank between arable fields. Relaxed progress on this final leg will doubtless be appreciated, for the walk's switchback nature will have taken its toll! As if in sympathy, the Dyke too is dimished.

The cairn on Panpunton Hill was erected by locals when Offa's Dyke Path opened and there is a fine view down to Knighton, though of the Dyke hardly a trace. Half a mile on and 600ft (183m) lower down, you cross road, river and railway and enter Knighton on a riverside path. If the hour is right, an appropriate ending would be at Offa's Dyke Park just up from the path where the Memorial Stone, set beside a good section of earthwork, could be touched to signify journey's end. The Park was created in 1970 by the Tref-y-Clawdd Society (named after Knighton's old Welsh name) and includes a heritage centre and youth hostel housed in the old primary school which was rescued from demolition.

The Offa's Dyke Memorial Stone at Knighton.

Facing page **Careg Sampson, near the start of the walk, is one of the finest 'cromlechau' in Wales.**

WALK 3: *PEMBROKESHIRE—Prehistory, Industrial Archaeology and Britain's Smallest City*

From *cromlechau* to Iron Age hut circles, from a nineteenth-century quarrying port to remarkable religious buildings—all along a ruggedly beautiful coastline. **Start:** Abercastle. **Finish:** St David's. **Distance:** 17½ miles (28km)—a full day's hike, best in spring or early summer. **Location/Access:** Abercastle lies north of the A487 Pembrokeshire coast road, St David's 8 miles (13km) farther west along it. Nearest railway station—Haverfordwest. **Map:** OS Landranger Sheet 157.

It is a rare pleasure indeed to discover a delectably beautiful coastline liberally imbued with historical interest. Pembrokeshire's westernmost tip is worth exploring on foot for all manner of reasons—its geological land forms, its beaches and cliffs, the wild flowers and seabirds with which it abounds, and a coastal path whose quality is second to none. As if all this were not enough, a web of old and occasion-

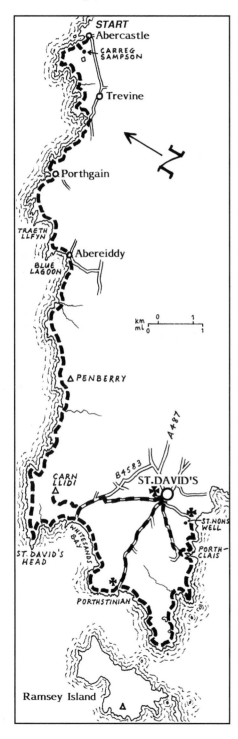

ally ancient structures speak eloquently about man's past occupation of this remote area and of his industrial endeavours when coastal trade and communications were developing from the sixteenth century onwards. The walk's undoubted climax at St David's occurs at the end of a long day: best, perhaps, to earmark a few hours separately to view the cathedral, Bishop's Palace and other nearby antiquities.

Trevine, with its youth hostel, campsite, pub and modest amenities, may be your preferred starting point. However, its location is somewhat inland and Abercastle does set the scene for this walk through coastal history rather more convincingly. As far back as the mid-1500s, Abercastle was an established harbour, well protected by the cliffs of Cwm Badau (Bay of Boats) and the island of Ynys-y-Castell. Ships were even built here and in the early nineteenth century sloops carried corn and butter to Bristol, returning with general cargo. Up until the 1920s, oats were being shipped up the Bristol Channel, while anthracite and culm from Hook or Saundersfoot was imported to fire the harbour-side limekilns which still stand in remarkably good condition. Before the turn of the century, limeburning was an integral part of the rural scene and kilns were built in every suitable spot along the coast and across the countryside.

Like most Pembrokeshire ports, Abercastle suffered a lingering death after 1852 as trade gradually transferred to the railways and later to lorries which could deliver door to door. Even so, the hamlet's older inhabitants recall steam coasters and sailing craft still using the harbour well after World War I. These days there is little activity off season, but during the summer the inlet is frequented by scuba divers, dinghy sailors, fishermen and holidaymakers. Not one of the three original inns has survived, though the old granary has been renovated for craftworking and there are public toilets; there is no shop.

The path sets off along rock ledges above the grey-sand harbour and soon reaches a little grassy valley. I strongly recommend a short detour left here to view Carreg Sampson, an exceptionally fine dolmen in a magnificent hilltop situation. It is not in sight until you have gained some height and entered a track leading past a marshy pond towards Longhouse Farm.

Probably the best known of all Pembrokeshire's *cromlechau*, Carreg Sampson was a burial chamber for Bronze Age man, though the mound of earth which would have covered it has long since eroded away. The capstone is supported by three of the six uprights to form a roughly polygonal interior space. There are stunning views along the coast to Strumble

Head but they are eclipsed by the marvel of the engineering skill of the Megalithic period 5000 years ago—a skill that allowed the transportation and placement of such massive stone monoliths. Legend has it that Sampson lifted the mighty capstone using just his little finger which was then severed and buried within sight on the harbour island of Ynys-y-Castell.

Hugging the seaward edge of farmland outide field walls, the coastal path to Trevine provides a wonderful—if at times rather precarious—foretaste of what lies ahead. Coves are all but inaccessible, the clifftops high and subject to cracking around Pen Castell Coch.

Within half an hour you have reached the lane end below Trevine—a quintessentially Welsh village it has always seemed to me, and the largest settlement between Fishguard and St David's. A detour for a meal or refreshment so early in the hike will probably not appeal and the onward cliff path leads west past small bays and headlands before swinging down to Porthgain.

Confronting you is one of Pembrokeshire's most evocative industrial ruins. Between 1878 and 1914, Porthgain Village Industries (also known as London Crushed Stone and United Stone Firms of Bristol) established a thriving quarrying and brick-making enterprise here. Sailing ships called regularly and the company operated a fleet of 6 specially built steam coasters of around 350 tons each. Between 1902 and 1904, new, larger quaysides were installed to accommodate the increasing number and size of vessels taking on Porthgain stone, as well as slate from nearby Abereiddy. The years from 1900 to 1914 were heady ones during which many millions of tons of crushed roadstone were exported—some to surface the streets of London—and the brickworks was in full production using local crushed slate shale.

Porthgain was a 'company' village with a distinctly paternal ethos and offered the only work in the area other than farming. The Street of 5 cottages—once condemned but now scheduled as worthy of preservation—typifies the village's down-to-earth Welsh architecture. The long-established Sloop Inn and a few modern houses back the harbour but it is the great redbrick quayside ruins that command attention.

After World War I trade declined, as it did all across the land during the Depression years. By 1929 business was low and the plant in need of repair; even the harbour was silting up. Output varied from 200 to 1000 tons in a good week, but the writing was firmly on the wall and that year the company was declared bankrupt. Despite the manager's efforts to delay closure, installations were dismantled. During the 1930s and 1940s, individual lorry

loads of stone were taken out but the enterprise as a whole was finished.

Today the crushing plant, with its sloping storage hoppers from which graded igneous rock from local cliffs was shovelled down chutes into berthed coasters, stands gaunt and silent. Signs of the elaborate tramway systems used to shift stone and spoil are few, the brick-making and brick-drying sheds have disappeared, workshops lie derelict and the tall chimneys were demolished in 1954. The site office, however, is now a café and there is a large limekiln above the slipway. Few visitors will be unimpressed by what remains.

Sensitive measures are necessary to preserve such industrial relics for future generations to appreciate and it is to be hoped that neither undue 'tidying up' nor sheer neglect will prejudice Porthgain's future as an ancient monument of considerable significance.

Beside the small pilot hut, steep steps lead up to clifftop level and for a while you are following the line of an old quarry tramway, short-cutting several minor promontories past various ruins. Glancing back you will see the navigation beacons on Porthgain's flanking headlands which, painted white, aided the passage of many a ship into the awkward harbour entrance.

Traeth Llyfn sands are held between high rock walls and once round the bay you come quite suddenly upon the disused Abereiddy slate quarry. Extraction was relatively small-scale and took place mainly in the last half of the nineteenth century. Most of it was hauled along a narrow-gauge railway for shipment from Porthgain. Abereiddy's slates split less cleanly and were more absorbent than those from many other locations; this may explain the quarry's failure to compete with the extensive Caernarfon workings further north and its consequent closure (after flooding by the sea)

The substantial and evocative remains of Porthgain's stone-crushing industry.

in 1904.

Connected to the open sea by a channel blasted through the rock, Abereiddy's 'harbour' is used by a few local fishermen and is known as the Blue Lagoon after its deep, slate-reflected hues. Little is left of the original hamlet which has been supplanted by modern holiday homes. The bay's black sand, the result of marine erosion excavating Ordovician shales, strikes a distinctly Stygian note!

A gate and stile to the south lead back to clifftop walking which begins to take on a more rugged aspect as you draw closer to the swelling cones of Penberry and Carn Llidi. These hills of volcanic origin seem to slip into the edge of so many views across the flat, marine-scoured Pembrokeshire landscape. Rearing up to 600ft (180m), they would have been islands (*monednocks*) when sea level was 200ft (60m) higher. Despite their modest elevation, there is an unexpected wildness about these miniature mountains which draws the eye upwards and the feet too if you have time and energy to spare. Your effort will not be wasted! From Carn Llidi in particular there is a grand panorama over the entire St David's peninsula and Ramsey Island.

Pathside banks are starred with wild flowers in springtime as you approach St David's Head. The OS map shows an anvil-shaped wedge of land and the path makes a beeline for the headland tip above sea cliffs of rough gabbro, the haunt of climbers. Puncturing the sea's surface as an archipelago 4 miles (6km) offshore, the same resistant rock appears as the Bishops and Clerks, known to early mariners as the Promontory of the Eight Perils.

Although the coast path actually cuts across the point, be sure to detour out onto it. Its Iron Age promontory fort was defended by the Warrior's Dyke and a formidable drystone wall some 15ft (4.5m) high and about 12ft (3.7m) thick at its base. Within the fort area are seven or eight circles of stone and rock—the remnants of huts from that time. Beads and loom weights discovered here (now in Tenby Museum) point to a mixed economy and stock-breeding figured prominently.

It is fascinating to pause here and reflect that although the headland is named after the saint who spread the Christian gospel throughout Wales in the sixth century, it was known to Greek navigators exploring islands off northwest Europe 400 years before. For the medieval English, St David's was the end of the then-known world and it became a centre for Christianity long before Canterbury.

Porthmelgan is the first of three sandy beaches to be passed before you are returned to the twentieth century with a jolt! As its name suggests, Whitesand Bay (Porth-mawr) is a splendid bathing beach, attracting holiday-makers galore during the season—and rightly so! A rather inexpertly carved stone tablet behind the dunes just before you reach the car park commemorates St Patrick's Chapel (Parc y Capel). The diminutive building—only 30ft (9m) long by 13ft (3.9m) wide—was built between the sixth and the tenth centuries and was used by sailors and Irish pilgrims, though of the structure no trace remains.

If legs are weary, a short cut could be taken inland, first along the B4583 then branching right on a country lane to St David's, which lies but 1½ miles (2½km) away. However, a little more coastal walking brings you along the back

of Whitesand Bay and round Point St John.

Ramsey Island (Ynys Dewi), with its twin *monednock* hills, lies less than a mile offshore across the often fearsome Ramsey Sound—a tidal race that can reach 6 knots. The island's 600 acres were farmed until the 1960s but are now an RSPB nature reserve whose seabird and grey seal populations are admired by boatloads of summer visitors from Porthstinian. There is much coming and going by pleasure craft from the exposed little anchorage, but the lifeboat station provides a reminder, if one is needed, that sea conditions are not always benign.

Not far from the small lane-end car park stands the overgrown ruin of St Justinian's Chapel. A Breton hermit and martyr, St Justinian withdrew to Ramsey Island where, so the story goes, his followers, unable to tolerate his unforgiving and disciplinarian ways, beheaded him. The saint is said to have picked up his head and walked across the water to the mainland where he was buried. A chapel built on the spot became a place of pilgrimage but the existing ruin dates from a sixteenth-century reconstruction by Bishop Vaughan.

Heading resolutely inland now, less than 2 miles (3.2km) of country lane separate you from St David's. (If desired, the walk could be extended further round the peninsula, picking up any of several paths and lanes which lead like spokes in a wheel to St David's centre). The settlement seems hardly larger than a good-sized village but enjoys city status by virtue of its magnificent cathedral. By keeping left you will arrive above Cathedral Close and can appreciate to the full this famous ecclesiastical precinct, set unexpectedly in a protective hollow formed by the River Alun.

The history of St David's (Tyddewi) begins with a monastic foundation by the missionary saint himself in the sixth century. Viking raids and the Norman Conquest influenced the settlement's development and ultimately led to the end of the Welsh monastery here. But it was during the late twelfth and thirteenth centuries that major building work took place, first on the cathedral then the Bishop's Palace, the latter finally reaching completion in the late Middle Ages.

Pilgrims by the thousand travelled from Ireland via St David's, Cornwall and Brittany to Santiago de Compostela in Spain. In many ways the city would have been busier then than after the Reformation in 1538 and certainly more lively than over the last two centuries. The railway never penetrated this far, ensuring St David's obscurity until the advent of motor transport and the growth of tourism.

Originally surrounded by a wall (still largely intact), Cathedral Close holds much of

architectural and religious interest. The cathedral must rank as the most visited in Wales and although down the centuries it has been vandalised, repaired, rebuilt and added to—particularly in the late 1860s—it remains a hugely impressive, if rather dourly coloured, edifice. Astonishingly, the nave floor rises a full 3ft (1m) from the west front to the High Altar. Of detail there is a great deal and I recommend the purchase of a guidebook or attendance at one of the conducted tours (summer Mondays at 11am).

There is an admission charge for the Bishop's Palace—money well spent if you wish to savour this noble ruin built, like the cathedral, from purple-red Caerfai sandstone. Erected between 1280 and 1350, the Palace is usually attributed to Bishop Henry de Gower. Richly embellished parapet walls which crown all the buildings, along with the Great Hall, are unmistakably his, but at least half the structure was the earlier work of Bishop Thomas Bek and Bishop Martyn.

Decay and neglect began following the Reformation. Bishop Barlow, the last incumbent, stripped lead from the Great Hall roof around 1540; the last known use of the Palace was in 1633; a hundred years later it had all become a romantic ruin. Only in the nineteenth century were essential repairs carried out to conserve what still stood then and today the majestic complex is managed by Cadw: Welsh Historic Monuments.

Before leaving the St David's area, try to see St Non's Chapel and Well, ¾ mile (1km) to the south. St Non was the mother of St David, to whom she gave birth during a great storm in AD 462 in a cottage on the present chapel ruin site. Soon afterwards St Non went to Brittany and became the patron saint of Dirinon in Finistère where a chapel contains her celebrated tomb.

After the Reformation when pilgrims ceased travelling to St David's, St Non's Chapel was converted to a dwelling, eventually becoming a leek garden. The ruin, with its cross-incised stone slab once built into the walls, is cared for by the Welsh Office. Nearby will be found the Holy Well of St Non, in earlier times a popular wishing well, healer of eye complaints and baby dip. The well enclosure and steps were restored by the Passionist Fathers in 1951 when they also built the adjacent shrine.

Facing page **Porch to the Great Hall, Bishop's Palace.**

WALK 4: *GWENT/HEREFORD AND WORCS*
South Wales Border Castles

An undulating route on field paths, farm tracks and country lanes, linking historic Monmouth with four superb castle ruins (admission free). Careful navigation required at times. **Start:** Agincourt Square, Monmouth. **Finish:** Longtown. **Distance:** 22 miles (35km)—a long day's hike! **Location/Access:** Monmouth lies on the A40 between Ross-on-Wye and Abergavenny near Gwent's boundary with Hereford and Worcester. Nearest railway stations—Chepstow and Abergavenny. **Maps:** OS Landranger Sheets 162 and 161.

Between the Wye valley to the south and the Welsh hill country to the north, the Monnow valley provided a natural route for the Norman conquest to extend westwards into an already strife-ridden Wales. A few months after the Battle of Hastings in 1066, William the Conqueror appointed William FitzOsbern, of Breteuil in Calvados, Earl of Hereford and it was he who established a number of castles in this southern border region—including Chepstow, one of Britain's first stone-built castles. Initially these fortifications were of the motte and bailey type—earthwork and timber defences—though later many acquired stone keeps or halls, with towers and curtain walls being added as Welsh attacks strengthened.

By the end of the eleventh century, the Welsh Borders had seen sweeping political changes. Norman Lords Marcher ruled with virtual autonomy over the fertile lands they had won and their castles became fortified centres of administration. The Norman feudal system based on castle, manor and borough dominated life in these lowland areas, with tenant farmers paying for their land and homesteads and trading through weekly markets and twice-yearly fairs. In hillier country the Welsh managed to cling on to their own traditional ways.

Subsequent changes of power in this border region after the twelfth century are complex indeed. Wave after wave of uprisings characterised the struggle to unite Wales and culminated in the emergence of that great leader Owain Glyndwr in 1440. During this period the border lands were opened up as woodland was cleared for agriculture and used to provide valuable timber for houses, shipbuilding and fuel. Townships sprang up around the Norman castles, leaving us today with an interesting range of border settlements at various stages of development.

By the time of the Wars of the Roses, the strategic importance of the Welsh Borders had diminished significantly and the great castles fell into decay. By the sixteenth century most had become ruinous.

This walk links together four border castles on a meandering cross-country route from Monmouth to the threshold of the Black Mountains. In fact, it forms part of the Castles Alternative on the long-distance Offa's Dyke Path and could be extended into a 2-day hike by crossing high ground to Hay-on-Wye. Equally feasible would be to stop overnight at

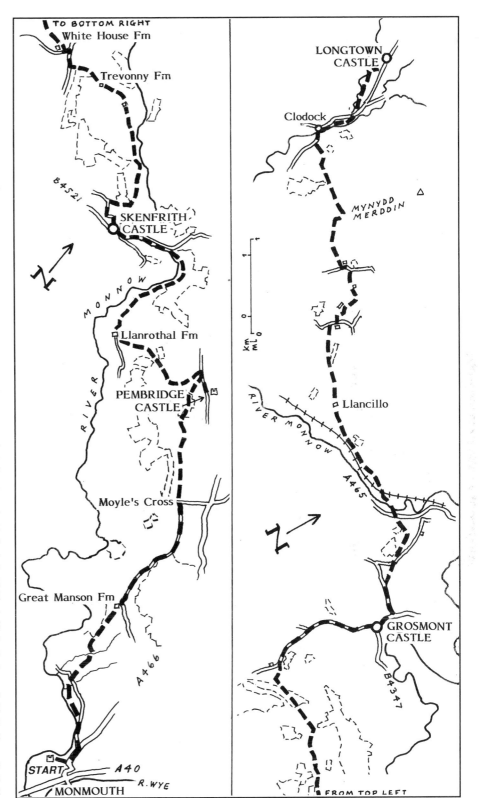

one of the wayside inns, though forward booking is advised. Waymarking tends to be sketchy, so great care needs to be exercised when following the route over farmland. Detailed route instructions make tedious reading in a work of this kind which does not purport to be a guidebook as such. For that kind of information—and it is useful on this particular route—send for a copy of the *Castles Alternative Route* to: Offa's Dyke Association, Knighton, Powys LD7 1EW. Walkers wishing to return to Monmouth at the end of the walk will need to arrange private transport.

Monmouth itself is worthy of exploration. Its history dates back to the construction of a Norman castle by William FitzOsbern in 1071. By the time of the Domesday Survey 15 years later, it was held by William FitzBaderon whose family remained in occupation for a further 170 years. Eventually the castle and town passed to Henry III's second son on his creation as Earl of Lancaster and Monmouth's long association with the royal duchy began.

During Tudor times the castle suffered neglect but still played an active part in the seventeenth-century Civil War during which it changed hands three times. The victorious Parliamentarians destroyed the remaining fortifications but in 1673 the third Marquis of Worcester built the Great Castle House close by so that his daughter might bear her first child next to the castle site where Henry V had been born in 1387. The building's imposing Renaissance façade dominates the meagre castle ruin and is today the headquarters of the Royal Monmouthshire Royal Engineers.

Other notable sights in the town include the famous and striking thirteenth-century Monnow Bridge Gateway—one of the few surviving examples of a fortified bridge gate in Britain. Agincourt Square—the old Market Place—is overshadowed by Shire Hall built in 1724, where assizes were held until 1939. A statue of Henry V appears in an alcove above the clock face and a bronze of the Hon. Charles Stuart Rolls stands in front of the building. Rolls, a pioneer of aviation and motoring, joined Mr Royce in 1904 to form the now celebrated Rolls-Royce Ltd. The museum in Priory Street is worth looking round, both for its Local History Centre and for a fine collection of Admiral Lord Nelson memorabilia.

From Agincourt Square the walk commences by turning left by Woolworths and dropping over the Monnow footbridge to playing fields. A riverbank path leads along to the Vauxhall Training Camp but this can also easily be reached by road. From Osbaston, field paths lead on to Great Manson Farm whence a country lane is followed north via Oldshop to Moyle's Cross.

More field walking continues north-west, passing to the left of Parkside Farm and to the right of Upper Skenchill Farm. A rather overgrown woodland path brings you up towards the road at Pembridge Castle. This is perhaps the least impressive of the four to be encountered, but is nevertheless a good example of

a small, private border castle. Held by the Wake family up to the fourteenth century, its gatehouse and curtain wall are thirteenth century, pre-dated by some 50 years by the north-west tower.

Skenfrith is our next objective—an hour or so distant. To reach it you strike off west down a stream valley, joining an access lane to Llanrothal Farm. A short way to the left stands Llanrothal Church with a Norman nave and some thirteen-century features—all that remains of a village in this location.

Field tracks take you north beside the River Monnow—the present-day border between Gwent and Hereford and Worcester—over streams through Daren Wood and along the riverbank into Skenfrith. The castle is reached by passing the Bell Inn and turning right.

Skenfrith and Grosmont castles, along with White Castle which stands on the main Offa's Dyke Path to the south-west near Llantilio Crossenny, formed a trio of castles set up by the Norman Lords Marcher to secure their hold on the Welsh borderland of Gwent. Occupying the three points of a triangle, these fortifications were known as the Castles of the Trilateral.

Early earthwork and timber defences on these sites may well have been the work of William FitzOsbern who overran eastern Gwent from his castles at Chepstow and Monmouth. However, during the twelfth century all three were given stone keeps or halls. Hubert de Burgh, Earl of Kent, was granted the trilateral by King John in 1201 but lost them four years later. He regained them after John's death and before he finally fell from power in 1232 built the existing stone castle at Skenfrith, along with the towers and curtain wall at Grosmont.

Skenfrith's moat was fed by the River Monnow and when you enter the castle through the much ruined gatehouse area you are confronted by a massive circular keep, three storeys high and built on a mound, or motte, 100 years older. The foundations of a large hall range indicate its use as a nobleman's domestic residence—a feature Skenfrith shares with Grosmont but not with White Castle, which housed a military garrison. The corner towers have raised doorways, once reached by wooden stairs, deep circular basements and batteries of arrow-loops to trap attackers in cross fire.

Skenfrith's church across the way is likely to attract your attention; its perpendicular tower bearing a lovely timbered belfry reflects some of the best qualities of Early English architecture.

Adjacent to the castle are a small general store and a tea room and it is from here that

the onward route resumes, turning right in front of Drybridge House on a lane towards Birch Hill Farm above the Monnow. Down alongside the river, the field path makes for Trevonny Farm and along its road past Box Farm. Three hundred and fifty yards (325m) north on the B4347, you branch sharp left to White House Farm then uphill beneath an old quarry and into an overgrown hollow. Graig Farm is in ruins; soon you reach a saddle in the long, curving ridge of Graig Syfyrddian. Bearing west then north on a lane, zig-zags lead past barns on a beeline down over a tributary of the Monnow and up into Grosmont.

The little hilltop upon which the castle stands was ditched and steepened to enhance its defensive effectiveness (hence *gros mont*, French for big mound). Set at the hub of radiating roads, Grosmont typifies the kind of small boroughs that grew up around these Norman border castles; clustered together are the Market Hall, the Angel Inn, a shop and the large cruciform church.

A timber footbridge crosses the castle moat and drawbridge pit, allowing access to the inner courtyard. Though it is a crumbling ruin of warm-coloured stone, some of the walls are still sturdy enough to support the trickle of visitors who climb them for a bird's-eye view of both castle and village, seen against a backcloth of verdant, rolling countryside.

The first-floor great hall and the curtain wall to its south-west date from the thirteenth century, replacing earlier perimeter palisades of timber. Ground-floor entrances are later alterations, the hall having originally been reached by external wooden stairs. Hubert de Burgh built the gatehouse and three four-storey drum towers between 1220 and 1240, but much of his work disappeared when further residential apartments were added around 1330. The remarkably elaborate, octagonal chimney on the north block dates from then. Grosmont Castle became a favoured residence of Henry, Earl of Lancaster, whose son Henry of Grosmont was born within its walls. Fourteenth-century building modifications reflect well the castle's dual role as private home and defensive stronghold.

Leaving Grosmont on the final leg to Longtown, you continue on the main road to the village school, turning left up a minor road signposted 'Abergavenny'. After 600 yards (550m), field paths and tracks lead north-west down to the A465 just south of Llangua church. An iron footbridge spans the Monnow and a field later you cross the railway line, approaching it again by an embankment before heading off to Llancillo Farm. Through Llancillo churchyard, the way proceeds uphill above a stream towards the road near Arcadia Farm.

As you pass Upper House and Pen-yr-Heol farms, good views are opening out ahead to the Black Mountains' Hatterall Ridge and the Skirrid.

Still climbing, you follow an ever more complex succession of gates and stiles to emerge at a country road near the summit of the Mynydd Merddin ridge at 984ft (300m) (though the OS pillar stands almost a mile north on slightly higher ground at 1060ft/323m). Fields stretch downhill past deserted Garngaled Farm and a grassy path takes you to the road at Clodock hamlet near the pub. Over the bridge you turn right on to a riverside path, through the churchyard and onwards over a series of stone stiles through fields. The approach to Longtown is somewhat inauspiciously past a sewage plant,

but for the post office/stores and the pub you turn right to the road, then left. With few complications remaining, you will soon arrive at the road near Longtown's church, its shop and an outdoor education centre. Longtown Castle stands a short distance to the left.

Another ancient borough, Longtown was the domain of the de Lacies until 1240 and the old market place can be found in front of the church. The castle may well be the earliest of its kind in England, being late twelfth or early thirteenth century. It clearly stands on a Norman motte of greater age and occupies one side of a large rectangular enclosure. Doubt exists as to the enclosure's origins which may be Roman or Saxon, but its adaptation produced an inner and outer bailey separated by a cross wall containing a gatehouse. Today,

the massive round keep—gauntly ruinous and partly screened by trees—seems the most romantic of all four castles seen on this route.

NB: A further $11\frac{1}{2}$ miles ($18\frac{1}{2}$km) separate you from Hay-on-Wye. Should this extension of the walk take your fancy, go prepared for true hill-walking for the path traverses Cat's Back Ridge to Black Hill and Pen-y-Beacon at an altitude of 2221ft (677m) before making its long descent into the Wye valley. From a walker's standpoint it is a marvellous tramp in good weather.

Views from Grosmont Castle walls are of a verdant, rolling countryside.

WALK 5: *HIGHLAND REGION—General Wade's Road over the Corrieyairack Pass by Rennie McOwan*

The highest and most evocative of General Wade's military roads in Scotland. Mainly a rough track, the route rises to over 2500ft (762m) but is nowhere difficult and has no navigation problems. Go equipped, however, for a full hill day. Weather at the crest of the pass can be fierce. The old road is a right-of-way but do not stray from it during the deer-stalking season. **Start:** Melgarve bothies (cottages), 5 miles (8km) west of Garva Bridge on the River Spey. **Finish:** Fort Augustus, at the southern end of Loch Ness. **Distance:** 12 miles (19km)—allow 5–6 hours. **Location/access:** Garva Bridge is 6 miles (9½km) west of Laggan village on the A86—7½ miles (12km) north of Dalwhinnie and 6 miles (9½km) west of Newtonmore. Road access is by car. Nearest railway station—Dalwhinnie. **Maps:** OS Landranger Sheets 35 and 34.

In different parts of the Scottish Highlands the remains of old roads can be seen, some buried for ever under modern highways or railways and others still easily discernible amid the heather and grass.

They date from the eighteenth century and are generally known as Wade roads, after Major-General (later Field Marshal) George Wade, Member of Parliament for Bath and Commander-in-Chief of North Britain in 1724, who launched the road-building programme.

Strictly speaking, many of these roads were built by his subordinate and successor, Irish-born Colonel William Caulfeild, who actually built more roads than Wade, but the name 'Wade roads' has stuck, as he began the roads project.

An old jingle, possibly coined by Caulfeild, runs:

*'If you had seen these roads before they were made,
You would hold up your hands and bless General Wade.'*

But not all Scots wanted the roads. Some hated them and did everything in their power to halt their progress.

Wade is remembered for another reason: he figures in a verse in Britain's modern National Anthem, a verse which is *never* sung in Scotland nowadays, in which he is thanked for crushing 'rebellious Scots' in torrent-like activity.

With the exception of one in Dumfries and Galloway to ease the passage of troops to and from Ireland, all the eighteenth-century military roads are in the Highlands or border them.

When James VII (II of England) went into exile and was replaced by the incoming William of Orange (and, in turn, by the House of Hanover), many Scots, in a complex mix of nationalism, religious fervour and an apprehension that the Gaelic and Highland way of life was under threat, felt that the exiled House of Stuart was still the legitimate ruling house of Britain. They became known as Jacobites, from the Latin word for James, Jacobus.

The Government passed disarming Acts, but the clansmen hid their weapons and straight-faced entrepreneurs shipped in worthless swords and broken muskets from the Low Countries and Spain, handed them over to a believing Government, received good-conduct payment for them and had the heat taken off the searches.

The Jacobites gave the new monarch and his successors a hard time. The Rising of 1688–9 fizzled out after Viscount Dundee, John Graham of Claverhouse, known as Bonnie Dundee, was killed during the moment of victory at the battle of Killiecrankie. The 1715 Rising should have succeeded, such was the support from France, the numbers involved and the strength of pro-Jacobite feeling in parts of England, but it petered out amid bad leadership.

There was a short-lived rising in 1719 which ended in the Battle of Glenshiel, in Kintail, and which gave us one of our most interesting hill names, Sgurr na Spainteach, the peak of the Spaniards, named after a sizeable Spanish contingent which fought on the Jacobite side.

Forts and barracks were built or extended in the Highlands by an alarmed Government. Bodies of militia, known as watches and under the control of 'loyal' chiefs, had the dual role of trying to stop cattle-reiving (stealing), regarded by many as more of a manly sport than a crime, and being the eyes and ears of the Hanoverian authorities.

It was because of one of these chiefs that we now have a pattern of military roads in our hills and glens, including the gem of them all, the high pass of the Corrieyairack, linking the village of Dalwhinnie (where the modern A9 road runs) and the village of Fort Augustus, in the Great Glen.

Simon Fraser, Lord Lovat, had his watch

disbanded because he was considered unreliable and in a fit of pique he sycophantically wrote to George I in 1724 saying that the situation in the Highlands was still politically lively, that the Jacobite clansmen were still well armed, that the Government troops were ponderous compared with the fast-moving Gaels and that a network of roads might be the answer.

In July 1924 Wade was sent to Scotland to investigate the position and he reported by December. Over 22,000 men in the Highlands were able to bear arms, of whom about 12,000 had been in the Risings and were ready to rise again.

Wade urged that the disbanded watches be re-formed, but under Highland officers and martial law. A new fort should be built at Inverness, and another at Kilcumin (the old name for Fort Augustus), 'the most centrical part of the Highlands'. A ship was needed on Loch Ness to supply Kilcumin from Inverness and to carry troops, and a new Disarming Act should be passed, with penalties.

Wade acted with energy when he was appointed Commander in North Britain on 24 December 1724. He was given funds and men, the Highland companies had some success in finding arms, some work was done on the foundations of the new forts and he set parties of regular troops 'in making the roads of communication between Killichuimen and Fort William'. The first such road was built in 1725 and his plan for a system of Highland roads evolved from that. Wade was promoted and fears of further Jacobite risings led to the forts being strengthened.

Wade was to leave Scotland in 1740 and he was made a Privy Councillor in 1742 and appointed a Field Marshal in 1743. He became Commander-in-Chief of the Low Countries and England and was later to preside at the court martial of Sir John Cope who commanded the Hanoverian army which was outwitted and outfought by the Jacobites in the 1745 Rising. Cope was cleared. Wade died aged 75, left a fortune of over £100,000 and is buried in Westminster Abbey.

But there is another side to this story. The Highlanders in their own terrain, accustomed to using weapons, to campaigning and sleeping out of doors, to moving speedily in their own hills and glens, saw the new roads as a major threat. They knew they could take cavalry, baggage, and cannon and improve marching times.

Author Neil Munro in his magnificent historical novel *The New Road* described by John Buchan as the best historical novel since Sir Walter Scott, has Duncan Forbes of Culloden, a Hanoverian supporter, saying to the scout-

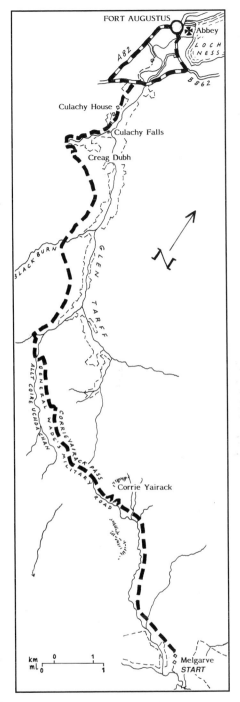

agent Ninian MacGregor Campbell: 'Do you see the road? The Romans didna manage it. Edward didna manage it. But there it is, right through to our vitals.'

The new roads, well constructed of a stone base and hard gravel on top, skilfully drained and engineered, lay like red sword slashes through the hills. Some were not used for domestic purposes in later times because they were military roads and often took their lines from military and not commercial needs.

The counties sometimes loaned money for their construction and the sweating soldiers got extra pay. Stones and gravel were plentiful. First foundations were dug, then big stones broken by gunpowder were levered into the bottom of the trench. Smaller stones were piled on top followed by two feet of packed gravel, which often had to be repaired yearly. On boggy ground the road was 'floated' on a raft of brushwood and timber.

Wade respected his roadbuilders and often held feasts of oxen for them or supplied beer. There is an account of a man called MacLeod, possibly one of the MacLeods of Dunvegan, on Skye, crossing the pass in 1731 and seeing six great fires at which oxen were being roasted whole as a treat for the 500 soldiers who had that summer completed 'the great road for wheel-carriages between Fort Augustis and Ruthven, it being October 30, His Majesty's Birthday'.

High on the ridges and the hills the clansmen watched gloomily. They ambushed supply parties and disrupted the road building. They pushed boulders down the hills so that they landed on the roads. They dammed the burns so that they flowed across the road and removed the gravel. They considered the roads to be for softies and refused to walk on the surface, striding along on the grass and heather verges. Their womenfolk were equally contemptuous and waded the rivers and burns rather than use the new bridges. The cattle drovers, too, were uneasy and as some of the roads were laid over ancient and grassy drove routes they feared the effect on the feet of their cattle.

As an engineering feat, the roads are remarkable and nowhere is this more evident than on our walk over the Corrieyairack. Eighteen traverses or zig-zags were put in over the highest section of the pass. Masons and pavers constructed the well-drained traverses, supported by bulwarks of stone and mortar.

The route over the Corrieyairack pass was linked to Ruthven Barracks, near Newtonmore, to the east and north, but the route suggested in this book is from the Dalwhinnie side on the south and the modern A9 and over the hills to the north-west.

Leave the A9 and drive to Dalwhinnie village, where there is a modern distillery and a rail halt, and then drive 4 miles (6.4km) north-west on the A889 to Catlodge: you are on the line of the military road at this stage. Continue on westwards to Drumgask Farm and then turn due north on the A86 across the River Spey to Laggan. Just over the bridge at Laggan turn sharply westwards on a minor road and follow that road for just over 2 miles (3.2km) until it crosses the Spey southwards again just

short of the modern Spey dam. You are now back on the line of the military road. Stay on this road on the south side of the dam until you pass the entrances to Sherramore and Glenshera Lodge. The road goes through trees and about half a mile (800m) north-west of the trees keep an eye out for Garvamore Farm, on the north side of the road, where Wade's barracks were sited, and called Kingshouse as a symbol of the forces of the Crown. Garvamore derives from the Gaelic, *Garth Ath Mor*, the big rough ford. A box bed here was taken to the West Highland Museum in Fort William and is known, probably inaccurately, as General Wade's bed. In recent times the barracks building fell into disrepair and as this book goes to press it is good to know that the estate owners are now renovating it.

Just beyond Garvamore Farm is the fine Garva Bridge built by Wade's men over the River Spey: it is worth stopping to admire this structure and as the Hydro Board's pylons are not too obtrusive at this stage it is possible to sense the atmosphere of Wade's time as the walker looks at the broad strath cradled by wild mountains.

The map shows a track running westwards from Garva Bridge, but there is a metalled road, narrow and with a rough surface on which a car can be taken with care another 5 miles (8km) to old bothies at Melgarve, a name deriving from the Gaelic for rough mound. This section of the Wade road is very straight and in marked contrast to the next section where Wade's men had the problem of taking the road up and over 2500ft (762m). Just before Melgarve a big burn, the Allt Reith a'Mhoraire (possibly the clear running burn of the lords or earl) comes down through trees, crosses the road, and links with the River Spey. Park there at the south side of the road, on a little grassy section. To go beyond that is to risk one's car.

The walking now begins: it is 12 miles (19km) from Melgarve to Fort Augustus.

The pylons, alas, take the same line as Wade's engineers and the gravel surface has long gone from the road, but the stony base is quite clear as the road goes steadily uphill, climbing about 1000ft (300m) in $2\frac{1}{2}$ miles (4km), with only about 500ft (150m) from the start of the remarkable hairpins to the head of the pass. It is worth stopping to examine the traverses and their rock buttresses and to imagine the sweating men, red coats piled at the side of the road, wielding pick, shovel and mattock. Even when night came they often carried on in the light of huge heather and brushwood fires.

The meaning of the name Corrieyairack (pronounced 'corry-ah-rack') sometimes given

as Corrieyairaich or Corrieyaireag, has puzzled Celtic scholars, but the second part of the name might be a corruption of *gearrag*, the short one, and applied to a burn. But it has been suggested it might be applied to the corrie itself, below the crest, because the climber crossing the pass from the south seems to enter the corrie very quickly. A corrie, of course, is a hollow in the hills, from the Gaelic *coire*, a kettle or cauldron.

It is ironical that after so much work, when the 1745 Rising burst upon the Highlands and General Wade had gone south, Bonnie Prince Charlie's men, at that stage brilliantly led by Lord George Murray, were quick to outwit and outmarch Sir John Cope and to seize the Corrieyairack, well known to them as a strategically important and key drovers' pass.

The prince had been told that General Cope was camped at Garvamore and was anxious to engage him as soon as possible. Two Jacobite officers were sent to the watershed, but could see no sign of the enemy. Later in the day 40 deserters from General Cope's force climbed the zig-zags from the Badenoch side of the pass and joined the Prince. But General Cope had turned and headed for Ruthven Barracks so the initiative lay with the Jacobites who, unopposed, moved south and were later to defeat him soundly at the Battle of Prestonpans, south of Edinburgh.

One of the Prince's officers, Lochgarry, commanded a detachment which lay in ambush for three days at the top of the Corrieyairack and they took prisoner a noted military engineer, Captain Swintnam, who was also commander of the Ruthven Barracks, plus his horses, baggage and servant.

It was at Corrieyairack, too, that the Prince was joined by the Stewarts of Appin, commanded by their chief, Ardshiel, and the MacDonalds of Glengarry and Glen Coe who had been unable to attend the standard-raising ceremony at Glenfinnan, on Loch Shiel.

It is odd now for modern hilltrampers to look at the line of pylons and the hydro station at the crest of the pass and to think of these momentous events. Modern roads and railways taking different routes have, of course, removed the old, strategic importance of the Corrieyairack, but it was much in the minds of people in past times.

Mrs Grant of Laggan, in her *Letters from the Mountains*, wrote in 1781 from Fort Augustus: 'This district is divided from ours [Laggan in Badenoch] by an immense mountain called Corryarrick. That barrier is impassable in the depth of winter, as the top of it is above the region of clouds, and the sudden descent on the other side particularly dangerous not only from deep snows concealing the unbeaten track of the road, but from whirlwinds and eddies that drive the snow into heaps: besides an evil spirit which the country people devoutly believe to have dwelt there time out of mind'. The Hon. Mrs Murray, who left a record of her travels in the Highlands in 1798, crossed the Corrieyairack in late summer. The Governor of Fort Augustus, who had crossed the pass on horseback the previous day, gave her a somewhat exaggerated description of the perils. She reported him as saying that the pass was 'of wild desolation beyond anything he could describe: and the whole of the road rough, dangerous and dreadful, even for a horse. The steep and black mountains, and the roaring torrents rendered every step his horse took, frightful: and when he attained the summit of the zigzag up Corrieyaireag he thought the horse himself, man and all, would be carried away, he knew not whither, so strong was the blast, so hard the rain, and so very thick the mist. And as for cold, it stupified him.'

Mrs Murray told of a woman with a baby who died trying to cross the pass. The baby, covered in snow, was still alive when found and the Governor's wife at Fort Augustus restored it to health. Mrs Murray also reported that soldiers often perished on the pass, partly because 'they over-refreshed themselves with whisky before the climb'.

From the *bealach* or crest of the pass there are fine views across to the northern and western mountains on the far side of the Great Glen, Glen Albyn or Glen More, one of the main natural features of the Scottish landscape. A gate, a relic of an old march fence, stands in splendid isolation. Wooded Glen Tarff lies below and the military road now runs steadily downhill. As the walker descends there is a military bridge over the Allt Coire Uchdachan (the burn of the steep corrie) and a Bailey bridge, built in 1961, over the Allt Lagan a'Bhainne, by 278 Field Squadron of the Royal Engineers. Lagan a' Bhainne means dell of the milk (it was a shieling area in past centuries). Government troops called it Snugborough because of the sheltered hollows. On the north side of the crest the road drops 1500ft (450m) in 5 miles (8km), and undulates gently for a time before dropping more steeply as it approaches Cullachy.

It is then a steady tramp downhill and across the Black Burn until the track swings westwards a little to avoid the knoll of Creag Dubh (black crag) and then swings back northwards again close to Cullachy Falls. From there is it less than a mile to the minor road which links the A82 and B862 roads in a rough triangle to the south of Ford Augustus. It is possible to cross the middle of this triangle by a path and a track and passing an old burial ground, but it is easy to go wrong. By swinging left (west), you pick up the A82 which leads into Fort Augustus (beware of traffic) or by swinging right (east) you reach the B862 which leads north-westwards into Fort Augustus round the south end of Loch Ness.

The original name of Fort Augustus was Cill Chuimein, the cell or ecclesiastical centre of Cummein, Abbot of Iona. The fort was built by General Wade and is generally said to have been re-named after the Hanoverian commander and King's son at the time of the 1745 Rising, the Duke of Cumberland, who was responsible for directing post-Culloden atrocities. In the early part of 1746 the fort was captured by the Jacobites. Johnson and Boswell visited it on their Highland tour. The remains of the fort are now incorporated into the Benedictine abbey which is also a boys' boarding school, and which was opened in 1878. Jacobite prisoners, alas, were shot on a piece of level ground near the abbey.

Nowadays people have taken mountain bikes over the Corrieyairack and a less welcome development has been safari-type vehicles carrying foreign visitors. The remains of the old road cannot take such pressure from the four-wheel-drive vehicles and parts of the track are becoming broken up.

It would be more appropriate nowadays to leave the Corrieyairack to the walker on foot and that, after all, was the travel pattern before military needs brought the road builders to this ancient pass.

It is worth stopping to examine the traverses and rock buttresses as height is gained near the Corrieyairack Pass itself.
(Photo Rennie McOwan).

WALK 6: *HIGHLAND REGION—Alasdair MacColla and the Inverlochy March by Rennie McOwan*

This is the wildest section of the historic 35-mile (56km) route from the Great Glen to Inverlochy (now part of Fort William) taken by the royal army of James Graham, Marquis of Montrose, and his second-in-command, Alasdair MacColla, war leader of Clan Donald, in the winter of 1645. It was a march described by John Buchan as one of the greatest feats of British arms. **Start:** Just east of the A82 Fort William to Fort Augustus road near Loch Uanagan, beginning on the minor road connecting the A82 with the B862. **Finish:** Roybridge on the A86 12 miles (19km) north of Fort William and 3 miles (5km) east of Spean Bridge. **Distance:** From the Great Glen to Roybridge—21 miles (34km); from Roybridge to Inverlochy—14 miles (22½km). **Location/access:** Road access to the Great Glen and Roybridge. Bus from Fort William to Fort Augustus and Roybridge, and from Inverness to Fort William, but check locally. Nearest railway—Roybridge. **Maps:** OS Landranger Sheets 34 and 41.

This walk includes some rough paths, but is mainly grass and heather hillwalking, with tarmac road in Glen Roy. Be equipped for a full hill day. The section from Glen Buck into Glen Turret requires hill navigation skills in bad weather. Walkers attempting to do this route in winter must be fully experienced, adequately equipped and check the weather forecasts carefully. Deep snow and fierce winds

and storms can be extremely hazardous. Walkers continuing on from Roybridge to Inverlochy, Fort William, face some walking on tarmac to Spean Bridge. The Royal army waded across, but this is not recommended unless the water in dry spells is obviously at a low and safe level. Woodland walking in this section is mainly on pleasant paths, but it is easy to go wrong and care must be taken. The

route should be avoided from mid-August to mid-October, during the peak stalking period, whilst winter or early spring crossings should be left to experienced hill walkers. If you are descending to the Fort William road at Torlundy take care on the busy road. (Note: The Inverlochy battle site is at the north side of the town, to the west of the distillery and aluminium works. There is a notice-board and a viewpoint cairn on a knoll overlooking the railway. Inverlochy Castle, near Torlundy, is *not* the site of battle. There is an older castle near the junction of the A830 and A82.)

'Through the lands of my fathers the Campbells have come
The flames of their foray enveloped my home.
Broad Keppoch in ruins is left to deplore
And my country is waste from the hill to the shore,
Be it so! By St Mary, there's comfort in store.
Though the braes of Lochaber a desert be made,
And Glen Roy may be lost to the plough and the spade,
Though the bones of my kindred, unhonoured, unurned,
mark the desolate path where the Campbells have burned,
Be it so! From that foray, they never returned.'

So exhulted Iain Luim (John Lom), bard to the chief of the Keppoch MacDonnells, after the Battle of Inverlochy on 2 February 1645. There is nothing in his verses about winning Scotland for Charles I. The main point is to gloat over the defeat of Clan Donald's enemies, Clan Campbell. But this battle was not just a clan spat. It had national and international implications.

It must be emphasised that the seventeenth-century Civil War, popularly regarded in England as Charles against Cromwell, Round-heads versus Cavaliers, had quite different, although linked, elements north and south of the Border.

James Graham, Marquis of Montrose, set out to win Scotland for Charles I. He had originally supported the political and religious alliance of the Solemn League and Covenant (see Walk 10), but felt the King's rule was preferable to the Covenant's religious fanaticism and power-seeking by supportive great families, provided that religious freedom could be assured. He was sent north with only a handful of staff officers to try and raise an army to support the King.

Meanwhile, in Ireland, religious wars raged between the native Irish, mainly Roman Catholic, and the descendants of Elizabethan and Scottish colonists, mainly Anglican and Presbyterian.

Clan Donald had spread harmoniously from Scotland to Antrim, in Ireland, through marriage, and was caught up in these wars. Descended from the great Lords of the Isles, once as powerful as kings, they had seen much of their lands in Scotland lost to the expansionist policies of the Campbells and wanted to regain what they regarded as their rightful place at the head of the Gael and to ensure the place of Roman Catholicism. These

struggles were also played out against a post-Reformation European background of religious clashes which were inextricably mixed with political issues.

An experienced army of Irishmen was sent to Scotland in the hope of meeting up with Montrose and defeating the Covenant forces in Scotland, of which Clan Campbell was prominent, and drawing off Covenant forces from Ireland.

This army was led by possibly the greatest Highland soldier of all time, the Achilles of the Gael and the most courageous of the sword-and-buckler men. He was Alasdair MacColla, which in English means Alexander, son of Coll. His father was nicknamed Colkitto, which derives from Gaelic words for left-handed (although it can also mean clever, cunning or ambidextrous). Many historians and writers, including novelist Maurice Walsh and John Buchan, whose biography of Montrose was considered the definitive work for many years, confused Colkitto with Alasdair. Alasdair was later knighted, and is also known in English as Sir Alexander MacDonald.

Old Colkitto had campaigned to regain the lost or semi-lost MacDonald lands on the western seaboard. Alasdair was born on the island of Colonsay and was later weaned on the bitter wars in Ireland. He was tall and strapping and had the reputation of an outstanding soldier. He is credited with creating the Highland charge, which was not a running rabble, but a controlled affair of great power which linked old and new weapons. A volley from muskets and pistols was fired at the enemy and then arrowheads of men, supporting each other and wielding swords and axes, crashed into the enemy lines while they reeled with the shock of the volley.

Montrose has long been regarded as a Scottish folk hero, second only to Bruce, Wallace and Prince Charles Edward Stuart, and as he was later executed by the Covenant he has martyr status. Montrose wrote the oft-repeated verse:

*'He either fears his fate too much
or his deserts are small,
that puts it not unto the touch,
to win or lose it all.'*

The military campaign of 1645–6 is studied by military historians to this day. It contains six major victories, and is called the Year of Miracles. Alasdair MacColla has sometimes, unfairly, been portrayed as a sword-swinging barbarian, strong, brave and boorish and lost without Montrose's cultivated skills. This is a calumny and the result of a misunderstanding by some English or Scottish Lowland writers of two cultures, English and Gaelic. Modern research has increasingly recognised Alasdair MacColla's worth and it is realised that much of the military credit given to Montrose should be shared with him. Montrose and MacColla were a formidable combination. John Buchan's once revered work has been replaced by David Stevenson's definitive book of this period, *Alasdair MacColla and the Highland Problem in the 17th Century.*

Alasdair MacColla landed his Irish contingent in Ardnamurchan, a wise choice because it was on the fringe of Campbell influence and close to the lands of the friendly MacDonalds of Clan Ranald. He took two castles and then forged inland. But he encountered difficulties. The clans were slow to rise and he and his men came close to exchanging blows with the Athole Stewarts because they were 'lifting'

cattle when he met up with Montrose and his staff.

Montrose had his king's commission to win Scotland. Alasdair MacColla had the men. They were to be joined by Camerons, Stewarts, MacLeans, MacGregors and MacDonalds and later by Ogilivies and Gordons, and on 1 September 1644, quickly won a victory over a Covenant army at Tippermuir, near Perth. They then captured, and alas sacked, Aberdeen, and followed that with the unthinkable. They made a winter march to Inveraray, the Campbell capital in the heart of Argyll, burning homes and killing all men under arms. Alasdair was given the terrible name of *fear thollaidh nan tighean*, the destroyer of homes. They sacked Inveraray and the Marquis of Argyll, chief of Clan Campbell, head of the Covenant alliance and enemy of the House of Graham, left in a galley, an event which drew charges of cowardice from his enemies and a defence from his friends that it was essential that he stay free to organise a counter-offensive.

Montrose and MacColla pulled their army out again and moved north up to the Great Glen. They were encamped on the flat ground close to Loch Uanagan when news came that another Covenant army, under the experienced General Bailie, was moving from the east. From the north a third army was on its way under the Earl of Seaforth and from the south came the Campbells, panting for revenge for the sacking of Inverarary. Tradition has it that the intelligence that the Campbell army was close on their heels was given to Montrose and Alasdair MacColla by John Lom, Keppoch's bard, who was later to be made Poet Laureate by Charles II, the only Gaelic-speaking poet to hold that title.

They decided to fight their strongest enemy first, but on their own terms. They took to the winter hills. Much ink has been spilled in arguments about the route of the hill march to Inverlochy, which meant two nights sleeping out in the middle of winter with little food, but there is no need for controversy. The march is well documented and the Irish had a chaplain, Father MacBreck, who kept a diary. Accounts that they went over the Corrieyairack Pass and then to Loch Treig (pronounced 'traig') and down through Glen Nevis are erroneous.

The royal army did initially go up the Corrieyairack Pass and so should the modern walker. Take the track running south which starts just to the east of the west junction of the minor road which links the A82 with the B862. Take this track uphill with Cullachy House on your left (east). The royal army then left the line of the Corrieyairack and moved

south-west where there is now another path (you go through a gate) and birch woods. Before leaving the Corrieyairack, stop to look back at Fort Augustus, known in 1645 as Kilcumin (see Walk 5).

There is delightful walking through trees on a path which shows the marks of estate workers from earlier years because there are the remains of bridges and stone 'lips' on some sections of the path. In the nineteenth century this estate was one of the last to use deerhounds during deer stalking, a practice which dated from the time when weapons lacked modern killing power and range, and wounded deer had to be brought down and when dogs alone were used to bring deer to bay.

The walker almost immediately appreciates the wisdom of Montrose and Alasdair MacColla because a line of small hills, one of which has TV and radio masts on top, now hides the walker from the trough of the Great Glen. The Covenant scouts would have expected the Royal army to have gone over the Corrieyairack, which was a key pass, or up the Great Glen, and they must have been surprised to find no sign of their enemies. It was probably, snowing which would have hidden the army's footsteps.

After this pleasant woodland section the walker emerges on flat ground, green and pleasant in summer, but boggy in wet weather as the Gaelic name for this section (not given on the map), the Lon Mor, the great boggy place, indicates. There are the remains of shielings in some sections here, the temporary summer homes of the Gaelic people of past times.

Angle over in the direction of wooden Glen Buck and then climb over steeper ground due south up the line of the glen. There are excellent views to the hills on the other side of the Great Glen and also to some unsightly modern, bulldozed estate tracks. This area is known as the Aberchalder Forest. The term deer forest does not necessarily imply the presence of trees. It comes from a Latin word used in medieval documents, which means land outside the enclosure.

There is an open bothy in Glen Buck which can be seen clearly as you toil uphill; it is locked during the stalking season.

Keep following the burn, the Allt na Larach, southwards. The name Larach is hard to translate because it can mean a farm, the site of a battle or a habitation. Keep going until you reach the crest of the high ground between two hills, Carn na Larach and Carn Dearg (pronounced 'cairn jerrack', red cairn) and then angle south-west until you can see the steep, but safe, descent into Glen Turret, passing

between the hills called Teanga Bheag and Teanga Mhor (pronounced 'chenga', big and little tongue-shaped hills). Some writers argue that because the army had a cavalry contingent they must have gone over the Corrieyairack Pass to Melgarve and then pushed westwards into Glen Roy, but this is unnecessarily long and the cavalry was only a handful of horses, Highland garrons accustomed to rough places and to being led if necessary.

The going in snow must have been very tiring and it speaks volumes for the toughness of the army that they made it. It is possible the horses made a short detour when descending into Glen Turret to avoid the steepest section of the ground.

As you reach the bottom of Glen Turret keep an eye out for a single chimney stack, the remains of a bothy used in shooting days. Glen Turret was well lived in in past times and the remains of houses, shielings and peat banks can still be picked out.

The first signs of the famous geological feature, the parallel roads, can be seen in Glen Turret although Glen Roy has the most spectacular examples. The ancient Celtic peoples believed these scorings on the hillsides, which look like roads or trackways, were carved out by the Fianne, the ancient warriors of Gaelic mythology, for their horses and chariots.

They date from the Ice Age and show the falling levels of lochs impounded by dams of ice. Darwin was interested in them and in 1839 suggested that they represented former sea beaches, but he was wrong. The Swiss geologist and glaciologist Louis Agassiz told the British Association that the barriers closing the 'horseshoes' of the lochs had been made of ice. Extensions from massive glaciers filling the Great Glen and Glen Spean had once blocked the outlet of Glen Roy, damming back its water. The cols or *bealachs* were points of overflow, maintaining a level of water long enough for a beach to form,

There is a viewpoint and display board further down Glen Roy in the Glen Roy National Nature Reserve, which was established in 1970 and is owned and managed by the Nature Conservancy Council.

John Buchan's statement that the royal army walked on the Parallel Roads is not valid—to do so one would need one long leg and one short one!

An intermittent path in Glen Turret leads to an estate track which in turn leads into Glen Roy where there is a bridge across the River Roy at Turret Bridge and then Brae Roy Lodge is reached.

Remote Arivurichardich cottage and a retrospective view towards the Bealach Dearg. [Photo Rennie McOwan].

From there, the walker is on the tarmac of the narrow public road for 8 miles (13km) down Glen Roy to Roybridge. The glen is packed with interesting sites and is scenically attractive.

Roy derives from *ruadh*, red, and in 1645 the royal army would have found it friendly territory because it lay within the lands of the MacDonnells of Keppoch. The Irish and the clansmen probably followed the line of the river. The modern road is reputedly built on a bridle track widened by General Wade's men in the first half of the seventeenth century. They were regularly ambushed and built the original track high above the woods and gullies. They also built the original Glen Turret bridge.

As you descend the glen keep an eye out for Carn Bhrunachain (or Bhrunachan) on your left, the corrie of the quern stones. People came from far afield to get quern stones, a soft silvery schist studded with hard garnets like teeth, for grinding oats into oatmeal.

The River Roy has many salmon pools, with the Gaelic names superseded by English ones given by the wealthy sportsmen of the last century who operated from Brae Roy Lodge.

Just over halfway down the glen is a ruined cottage called Achavady on the modern map, *Ach a'Mhadaidh*, the field of the wolf, where the royal army rested for the night and where they were told that Campbell patrols were burning the MacDonnell houses further down the glen. The 'wolf' in the name derives from a famous bowman, Iain Odhar (Dun John), who shot the last wolf in the area.

Author Neil Munro in his magnificent historical novel, *John Splendid*, draws a graphic picture of the royal army's gruelling march through the snows and pictures them in Glen Roy.

'*At the head of Glen Roy the MacDonalds, who had lost their bauchles of brogues [skimpy footwear] in the pass, started to trot . . . Long lank hounds, they took the road like deer, their limbs purple with the cold, their faces pinched to the aspect of the wolf, their targets and muskets clattering about them. 'There are Campbells to slay and suppers to eat,' the Major-General had said. It would have given his most spiritless followers the pith to run till morning across a strand of rock and pebble. They knew no tiring, they seemingly felt no pain in their torn and bleeding feet, but put mile after mile below them.*'

About 2 miles (3km) further on is an area known as the Briagach, green and sunny and once well populated with houses.

A century after the 1645 campaign clans were again in this glen with weapons in their hands: Prince Charles Edward Stuart hid in a cave here and there is a waterfall called Steall a Phrionnsa, the Prince's waterfall.

At Achavady a path and a pass, the Caol Lairig (narrow pass), run west and south-west through the hills and it has been suggested that the royal army broke off from the main line of Glen Roy to avoid being seen by Campbell patrols, but it is more likely that they stayed on the line of the glen as it is known that the Campbell raiding parties returned to the Inverlochy area.

Three miles (4.8km) north of Roybridge itself, at the viewpoint spot known to local people as Achadh na Beithich, field of the birches, there is room for car parking and a turning place used by many summer visitors attracted to the parallel roads. There are information display boards.

Just to the south of the viewpoint, keep an eye out on the left (east) side of the road, just to the north of the Cranachan farm turn-off, for a large stone. It is known as the Mass Stone and was used by Roman Catholics during the penal times, in the post-Reformation period and after the failure of the 1745 Jacobite Rising. The carving of a chalice and host on the stone was done a century ago by a noted Gaelic scholar, the late D.C. MacPherson, of nearby Bohenie. A silver Mass cruet was found nearby in modern times.

All of this area was well inhabited in past times and the ruins of houses and cultivation areas can clearly be seen.

Just to the north of the townships of Bohuntineville and Bohuntine Mor is a site between the road and the river called Sron Dubh an t-Sithean, the black promontory of the fairy dwellings.

Further south is a house called Coille Diamhain, where Alexander, the fifth chief of Keppoch lived. He married an Irish lady and she brought Irish retainers with her, Burkes, Boyles, Kellys and O'Brynes, who settled in Lochaber and whose descendants would surely have had a special welcome for the Irish contingent in the royal army of Montrose and Alasdair MacColla. She later disappeared in mysterious circumstances and her ghost is said to haunt the area.

Just as one leaves the glen it is worth noting that the hill to the west, Maol Ruadh or Mulroy (red mound), was the site of the last inter-clan battle in the Highlands, between the MacIntoshes and the MacDonnells of Keppoch in the time of Charles II. Then it is time to relax in Roybridge and to reflect on the first section of that magnificent march.

The second section is *not* recommended, but those wishing to do it will notice that to the west and south of Roybridge the map shows two modern farms, Killiechonate and Leanachan; both of these are named in contemporary accounts of the march, but there are difficulties in following this route. The royal army waded the River Spey. There are problems over possibly disturbing the privacy of Killiechonate Farm and in finding the old route through the modern conifer plantations of the Leanachan Forest. It is best to miss out Killiechonate and to walk to Spean Bridge village on the A82 and continue west for a mile (1½km) until a side road runs southwards below the railway to Leanachan Farm. From there forest tracks lead westwards until you reach the Allt a'Mhuilinn burn (which leads into Coire Leis of Ben Nevis) and the northern slopes of Meall an t-Suidhe. You pass the Nevis Range ski development at Aonach Mor with its gondola-line going to and from the Snowgoose restaurant at 2,000 feet.

From there descend to modern Fort William. The Inverlochy battle site viewpoint is signposted, between the road and the railway and just to the west of the aluminium works. Don't confuse the thirteenth century Inverlochy Castle, seat of the Comyns, which is marked on the map as 'castle', with Inverlochy Castle mansion which lies a mile to the north-east of Fort William on the A82. The thirteenth-century castle was on the fringes of the battle. (An earlier battle also took place on the same site at Inverlochy in 1431 when Islemen defeated a stronger army of James I of Scotland.)

The battle on 2 February 1645, was not long. The sleeping Campbell army on the flat ground around the modern road, railway and loch-shore were awakened by shots being fired by sentries as the royal army approached. Montrose and MacColla's men had spent a second night in the open, well hidden by trees and with their march through the modern Leanachan Forest hidden from the lower ground by small hills and mounds.

Initially, the Campbells thought it was only a clash between patrols, but they quickly realised a pitched battle was to be fought. Sizeable contingents of their army were elsewhere, burning and pillaging in the Cameron and MacDonald glens. The Marquis of Argyll, who had an injured shoulder, was taken off in a galley, thus renewing charges of cowardice. Campbell of Auchnabreac, an experienced soldier from the Irish wars, was in command, and placed Lowland soldiers on the wings with the Campbells forming the centre. Montrose ordered his trumpeters to play a royal salute to show their credentials and then came a fearsome charge. The Lowland soldiers on the wings immediately fled and the Campbell centre, isolated and fighting bravely, was engulfed and swamped. The very tide ran red. The heather was over the gale, as the old Highland saying has it. In other words, Clan Donald (whose badge was heather) had triumphed over the Campbells (whose badge was gale or bog myrtle). The Campbell losses were fearsome and the shock to the morale of the Covenant was great.

Other families and clans, some of whom had suffered under Campbell overlordship, joined Montrose and Alasdair MacColla. They had other triumphs, winning victories at Auldearn and Alford in the north-east, and at Kilsyth, near Stirling, and they cleared Scotland for Charles I. But it was a short-lived triumph. The king's cause went down in England and Charles was executed. Many of the great families and clans held back from Montrose and MacColla, partly because of the Roman Catholic strand in the royal army, partly because of the ferocity of the Irish contingent and partly because they sensed long-term failure. Montrose was defeated at Philiphaugh, near Selkirk, in the Scottish Borders, while Alasdair MacColla was campaigning in the west and trying to recruit more men. Montrose later went into exile, came back in a new campaign, and was defeated and executed. In the time of Charles II his body was recovered from a criminal's grave and reinterred in the High Kirk of St Giles in Edinburgh.

Alasdair MacColla fought on for nearly two years, but he too was eventually forced back first, to Kintyre and then to Ireland. His stay-behind garrisons in castles waited for new armies to come, but were captured and executed. Alasdair was eventually killed in battle in Ireland and is buried in the vault of the Callaghan chiefs at Clonmeen, in Co. Cork. Better a swift death in battle than a slow one in bed, as the Gaelic proverb has it.

Montrose has his special niche in St Giles and in Scottish history. Alasdair has no monument, but is commemorated in a pibroch, the classical music of the pipes, 'The Battle of Auldearn' (where he showed particular skill and bravery) and in two tunes originally sung in Ireland as mouth-music and now played in Ireland and Scotland on the *clarsach* (harp), or by ceilidh bands, 'The Death of Alasdair' and 'MacAllisturn's March'. He was lauded in Gaelic poetry and song as late as the 1745 rising.

Montrose and Alasdair made a great team, but in the march to Inverlochy and in their other marches—longer than those undertaken by the Jacobites or by General Monk, Cromwell's hatchetman in Scotland— the courage, hardiness and tenacity of the Gaelic soldier, both Highland and Irish, shines through and in our own day is being given the respect and attention they deserve.

Neil MacMhuirich, bard of clan Ranald, wrote:

'I had many stories to write on the events of the times if I undertook to do it, but what induced me to write even this much was when I saw that those who treated of the affairs of the time have made no mention of the Gael, the men who did all the service.'

The Inverlochy Battle site near Fort William, as it is today.
(Photo Rennie McOwan).

WALK 7: CENTRAL SCOTLAND
The Bealach Dearg and Clan MacGregor
by Rennie McOwan

A hill and glen crossing amid magnificent scenery in the former lands of the clans on an old right-of-way route, including crossing the shoulders of two mountains—Ben Vorlich and Stuc a' Chroin—at just under 2000ft (610m). The terrain is linked to one of the most gory incidents in Scottish clan history and involved one of the best-known clans—Clan Alpin, the MacGregors. **Start:** The mansion house of Ardvorlich, on the south Loch Earn 2½ miles (4km) east of its junction with the A84 (there is little room for parking and no public transport, so arrange to be dropped off). **Finish:** Callander on the A84, 16 miles (25½km) north-west of Stirling (bus service). **Distance:** 13 miles (21km)—no escape route except going back, or a long walk when halfway into the west end of Glen Artney. **Location/access:** Intermittent bus service from Stirling past the south Loch Earn road junction where it links to its west with the A84 just south of Lochearnhead. From here it is 2½ miles (4km) along tarmac to Ardvorlich mansion. (Check bus times locally). **Maps:** OS Landranger Sheets 51 and 57.

Prepare for a full day's hill outing on this walk, partly on a glen path, then on rough moorland.

At the time of writing a key burn is bridged, but it may have to be waded. There is normally no problem with this, but anyone attempting this walk out of season, when burns can be swollen by melting snow or prolonged rain, should exercise caution. The map erroneously shows a path over this entire hill route,

but it vanishes for sections of the walk.

The pull-up over the second mountain shoulder can be exasperating to some people as it comes half way through the walk, but it is not as intimidating as it looks. The last quarter of the walk is on a rough farm track and about two miles from Braeleny Farm and into the town of Callander the route is on tarmac.

Walkers considering doing this route in winter should allow for early darkness, carry torches, be adequately clad for winter conditions, with extra food and survival gear and be prepared to be held up by drifts or soft or difficult snow conditions. The weather forecast should be carefully checked.

The route is a very old hill crossing used by the clanspeople of past centuries and the later cattle drovers. It is a legal right-of-way and can be walked at all times. Care must be taken in the peak of the stalking season, normally mid-August to mid-October, to stick to the line of the route.

Both the Glen Vorlich and the Callander ends have hill farms, with cattle and sheep, and you should be careful to avoid disturbing stock. It is best not to take dogs along, but if you feel that you must then do keep it under strict control.

The name Bealach Dearg, the red pass or defile, may take its name from the colour of some of the soil, but it is more probably linked to the route members of the Clan MacGregor took after they removed the head of the King's forester in Glen Artney in an act of revenge. He had cut off the ears of some of their friends after he had caught them poaching red deer. Nearby is a lonely lochan (a small loch) which has associations with this grisly event. This area was a royal hunting forest in past centuries and deer were much scarcer then. In medieval hunting reserves they were protected from indiscriminate killing.

The modern walker will be very unfortunate if he or she does not see many red deer. Gleann an dubh Choirein, the glen of the black corrie, a halfway point on the walk, is a likely place. A corrie is the Gaelic word for a kettle, which used to be cauldron-shaped, hence its use to denote a hollow in the hills. Keep glancing up at the hillsides and make a point of stopping a lot, sitting down quietly and looking around. Most hill birds can be seen, including occasional golden eagles. Glen Vorlich, at the start of the walk from the north end, was a shieling glen in past centuries and the stone foundations of these temporary spring and summer dwellings can be seen. Up until the early nineteenth century the Gaelic people took their flocks and herds, mainly cattle, goats, and small, wiry sheep, up from the lochsides and lower straths at the start of spring to the fresh grass of the upper glens and moors. They lived in these temporary dwellings, fattened their beasts, and made cheese and butter, and hugely enjoyed themselves. They returned to the lochsides and straths and lower glens at the end of summer. Some of the most exquisite of Gaelic songs and poetry were written at or about the shieling. This pastoral pattern, known as transhumance, died out when agricultural patterns changed. The shieling

ruins are often in delectable spots. Highland games may have had their origins here, young men putting the stone or having hill races, the fastest being chosen as clan dispatch runners. The shielings were also a time for courting.

Despite the gory nature of the MacGregor's deeds, it should be emphasised that alongside such fierceness, and a respect for courage, hardiness and martial virtues, there also existed an immense treasure house of Gaelic songs, poetry, sagas and piping of a most sensitive kind and it is quite wrong to call such people barbarian or uncultured. They had a different culture from the Lowland Scots and the English, but it was most certainly not inferior.

The word clan in the Gaelic language means children, generally in the sense of family or kinship. A clan in past centuries was an extended 'family' of Highlanders occupying a piece of native territory and led by a chief. People in the same clan did not all have the same name (modern surnames were not used in past times) but they regarded themselves or their ancestors as being related to the founder of the clan or pledged allegiance to that clan. Some clans were large and could put thousands of men under arms, others were small. Some were absorbed by others. Some, like Clan Donald, split into different branches. Some were part of a federation such as the MacPhersons, MacIntoshes, Farquharsons and others in Clan Chattan (pronounced 'hatton'). Some, like the Stewarts and Camerons, supported the House of Stuart, and some, like the Campbells, supported the House of Hanover who replaced the exiled Stuarts.

At its best the clan system gave people a very real dignity. The chief and his family held the land on behalf of all and could be deposed if unworthy or ineffective. Descent could go through the female line. Later this 'trustee' pattern changed to one of near-feudalism, with the chief and family becoming aristocracy or near-aristocracy, although the clan-bond was still strong and people could say, bluntly, what they thought and act accordingly. By the nineteenth century a pattern of landlord and near servant had replaced the older pattern.

The clanspeople mainly lived by a cattle economy and on the whole, lived in harmony with the landscape.

The Clan Alpin, the MacGregors, claimed descent from Scottish kings, and once held powerful lands around the east end of Loch Awe, in Argyll, mainly in Glen Strae, Glen Lochay and the mouth of Glen Orchy. They initially co-existed with the expansionist Glen Orchy Campbells (later to be the great House of Breadalbane), with their powerbase of Kilchurn Castle at Loch Awe, but then the relationship went sour. Many MacGregors

moved eastwards and settled around Loch Rannoch in Perthshire, and Loch Katrine and the Trossachs area, and in linking Balquhidder (pronounced 'balwhidder'), near Lochearnhead. They were apt to hold their lands by the power of the sword and were not too fussy about having legal documents. Consequently, they could often be outwitted by the Campbells.

They were persecuted, and some believed in getting their retaliation in first. They annoyed James VI by slaughtering the Colquhouns (pronounced 'ca-hoons') whom the King had appointed as a kind of peace keeping force along Loch Lomond-side and they annoyed other monarchs and leaders by pugnaciously swiping at their enemies and in regarding cattle rustling and raiding as a kind of manly sport.

Ruthless legislation was enacted against them; their very name was banned, their children could be taken away and their women branded, their lands were seized, they were forbidden to assemble or hold weapons, a bounty was paid for their heads and mastiffs were imported from Italy to help hunt them down.

Some clans refused to accept all of this and the MacGregors—the children of the mist—fought back and ultimately survived. They got their name back, but not before many had taken cover names (a sore trial for modern historians trying to trace ancestry) or had gone on the run.

This walk over the Bealach Dearg tells of one of their harshest episodes.

Sir Walter Scott, who had a soft spot for the MacGregors and who wrote a song about them, 'The MacGregors' Gathering', knew this area well and in his epic poem, 'The Lady of the Lake' published in 1810, he wrote:

'But, when the sun his beacon red
had kindled on Benvoirlich's head,
The deep-mouthed bloodhound's heavy bay
Resounded on the rocky way,
And faint from farther distance borne,
Were heard the clanging hoof and horn.'

When you are on your way along the south Loch Earn road to Ardvorlich, keep an eye out for Edinample Castle on your left, near the entrance to Glen Ample, but on the opposite side of the road from that glen. It was held by the Stewarts and then by the Breadalbane (pronounced 'bred-al-bin') Campbells, formerly lairds of Glen Orchy who were to become earls and marquises. It has been restored in modern times.

Loch Earn may take its name from Erin, showing the Irish influence of the early missionaries of the Celtic Church who pushed far into the Highlands, but erne is also another name for the sea eagle which formerly nested on inland lochs as well as on sea cliffs. The bird became extinct in the last century, but attempts are being made to reintroduce it from Norway on to the western seaboard of Scotland.

You pass some cottages and the western entrance to Ardvorlich House. The eastern entrance, which is the one you want, is just past a hump bridge. Keep an eye out for an engraved stone at the south side of the road. Ardvorlich has been held by the Stewarts for centuries and this stone marks the spot where seven MacDonalds of Glen Coe were buried after raiding Ardvorlich in 1620. Scott, in his novel, *The Legend of Montrose*, called Ardvorlich Darnlinvarach Castle.

The name Ardvorlich is said to derive from Ard Mhurlaig (or Mur-Bhalg), the promontory of the sea bay and as Loch Earn is a fresh-water loch this is a puzzle. That peerless naturalist historian, mountaineer and writer, Seton Gordon, who died in 1977, said that this name was sometimes used when an inland loch *looked* like a sea loch. There is another Ben Vorlich on the west shore of Loch Lomond, and it, too, could be said to have the same kind of outlook.

At Ardvorlich a family talisman called the Clach Dhearg (the red stone), is held, which is secured with silver hoops and fitted with a chain and is reputed to have miraculous properties. If the stone is dipped in a pail of water and moved three times sunwise around the pail, the water will then have healing powers in illnesses relating to cattle. Old accounts tell of people resorting to the stone for cattle disease. There is a tradition that it dates from the fourteenth century and was brought back from the Crusades. Scotland, then an independent nation, made a sizeable contribution to the Crusades. Sir Walter Scott brought Sir Kenneth of Scotland, Knight of the Leopard, into his novel *The Talisman* and portrayed him as coming from nearby Glen Artney.

The house also contains the Glenbuckie Stone which should be dipped in water by the lady of the house or a guest who can then drink and utter a wish. A number of clans held 'magic' stones of this kind.

It must be emphasised that although the right-of-way route passes beside Ardvorlich House, the house itself is private ground and this must be respected.

The site of Ardvorlich House, but not the present building, was the location of the MacGregors' bloodthirsty deed.

In 1589 James VI was about to celebrate his marriage to Anne of Denmark and arranged a great feast to be held in royal Stirling. He asked Drummond of Drummond

Ernoch, his forester in the royal forest (or hunting reserve) of Glen Artney and Steward of Strathearn, to ensure plentiful supplies of venison. Red deer then were a lot less numerous than now: the big increase in deer numbers came with the birth of the big sporting estates in the nineteenth century.

The King's forester had cut the ears off some MacGregors whom he had found poaching and their friends later took their revenge. They captured him, cut his head off and took it to Ardvorlich where his daughter (some accounts say his sister) lived. She was married to Stewart of Ardvorlich, but he was away from home. Keeping the head hidden, they asked for food and in the manner of Highland hospitality she put cheese and oatcakes on the table and left the room. When she returned her father's head was on the table with the food stuffed into his mouth.

She was pregnant and the shock was so great that she became deranged and fled up Glen Vorlich to the mountain shielings and gave birth there to a son. There is a lochan, not named on modern maps, sited to the north-east of Beinn Domhnuill and about $\frac{3}{4}$ mile (1km) from the Bealach Dearg pass crossing, which is called Lochan na Mna (pronounced 'minn-na') the small loch of the woman, to commemorate this event.

The baby grew up to be a moody and murderous youth and hated in the area. He became one of the Marquis of Montrose's staff officers during the seventeenth century Scottish Wars of the Covenant and murdered Lord Kilpont in a camp brawl. When he died his family had to organise two funerals, one to put local people off the scent because they wanted to mutilate the body and the other for real. He is buried near modern St Fillans at the east end of Loch Earn.

After you have enjoyed the Bealach Dearg walk, or before you start, try to visit Balquhidder, just off the A84 between Strathyre and Lochearnhead.

Beside the 'modern' nineteenth-century church are the ruins of the Eaglais Beag, the little church, which dates back to the seventeenth century and which may lie on older ecclesiastical ruins. Here, too, is the grave of Rob Roy MacGregor (1671–1734), perhaps the best-known member of Clan MacGregor, war leader, cattle dealer, fugitive and cocker of snooks at central authority, and his wife and some of his sons.

The MacGregors who cut off Drummond Ernoch's head all went to the old church in Balquhidder and placed the head on the altar and they swore on their dirks (long daggers) that they would all, collectively, take the blame and try to support one another. But it availed

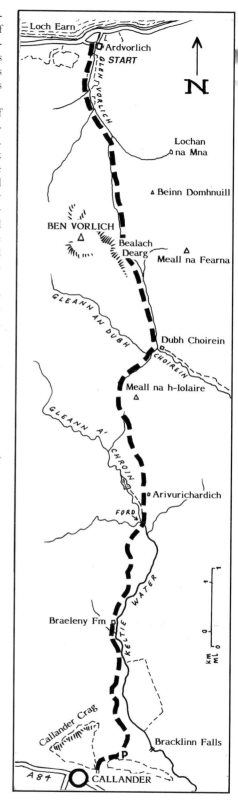

them little because they were harried and hunted and several of the ringleaders were caught and hanged.

To go over the Bealach Dearg take a broad

track at Ardvorlich with farm buildings starting to appear ahead. At a junction go right (as if going to the mansion) across a bridge, but then turn sharp left and uphill, passing through a gate. You are now following the west bank of the beautiful main Glen Vorlich burn. At one time the estate marked their preferred route on to Ben Vorlich with marker poles, but most of these have gone.

Continue up the glen, but do not go through a small gate to your left; it leads into a private section of woodland. Look out for the ruins of the old mill on your left whose machinery harnessed the power of the glen burn in past times.

Continue uphill beside attractive woodland, cross a stile and there are good views back to Loch Earn and Ardvorlich House. Ben Vorlich starts to show up ahead and the woods became more attractive.

You pass through a deer fence via a stile, but do not detour left to a bridge across the burn which can be seen from this point. (If you do decide to cross then keep uphill on the line of the main burn.) Stay on the track and cross another stile. Just past a small bridge of sleepers across a small burn a grassy side track goes off left, as the main track swings away from the burn. Take this left track. The steep east sides of the 3224ft (983m) Ben Vorlich start to dominate. Ben Vorlich is a Munro mountain, one of the 3000ft (914m) mountains in Scotland first catalogued by Sir Hugh T. Munro in 1891. He was president of the Scottish Mountaineering Club from 1894 to 1897. Munro-bagging has grown in popularity in recent years and Sir Hugh's original list has been altered by committees as map-making improved.

The ground becomes marshy, but stick to the burn and the path reappears. Old shielings are to be seen in this corner. As the trees end, make for the notch between Ben Vorlich and Meall na Fearna, the rounded hill of the alders. A tributary burn has to be crossed and the ground gets wilder and rougher as one gets up into the corrie. The ground becomes boggy and there are more shieling ruins.

Keep going until you reach the narrow pass between Ben Vorlich and the outliers of Meall na Fearna. This is an attractive and wild section. Look out for a couple of home-made howffs (shelters) made by hill walkers for sleeping overnight in the narrows of the pass.

You pass an old fence and wall and descend (south) over rough ground down the glen, with Ben Vorlich's south-east shoulder on your right, to the ruins of the old shepherd's cottage at Dubh Choirein (the black corrie) where two burns join to form the Allt an Dubh Choirein, the burn of the black corrie. It is

worth sitting down and looking around and savouring what it must have been like living in such a remote spot as a shepherd or deer stalker, cradled by hills, and with supplies brought in by pony from Glen Artney to the east or from Callander to the south. At the head of this glen the crest of another pass, this time mainly used by deer, can be seen linking Ben Vorlich with another Munro mountain,

Bracklinn Falls.
(Photo Rennie McOwan).

Stuc a' Chroin (3189ft/1972m) the sharp peak of the cloven-hoof or notch.

This is the point where some walkers mutter because another pull-up is called for between Meall na h-Iolaire and the long south-east shoulder of Stuc a' Chroin. Meall na h-Iolaire is pronounced 'mee-owl na yooler' and means the rounded hill of the eagles.

At the time of writing, there is a bridge across the burn, downstream and to your left as you stand facing the Meall na h-Iolaire ridge. Once across the bridge, turn right and follow the Allt an Dubh Choirein until you are almost opposite the ruins. Then set off uphill. If the bridge has gone—and it does happen on Highland burns—then wade the burn. It is normally not difficult, but in spate you might have to wander upstream looking for a suitable place. Caution must be exercised.

A faint path with a firm gravel base in the early sections does wend its way across the moor and goes quite high up before vanishing in boggy ground. If you fail to find it, no matter. Make your own way up to the lowest point. The slopes up to the dip are gradual and easily ascended.

At the head of this section of the pass you come across large peat banks. Go quietly in this area and scan the hillsides: it is normally a good place to see red deer.

From the south end of the ridge the bothy or small cottage of Arivurichardich and the waters of Callander reservoir can be seen below, but the best way down is sometimes hard to find. Between you and the foot of the glen below, Gleann a' Chroin, you will see a fence and a gate. Most people head for that and angle down to the bothy. It is not difficult, but can be awkward. Above the fence a path can sometimes be picked up which initially runs parallel to the fence and then cuts down. It makes for easy walking, but there are sheep tracks in the same corner which peter out. If you strike this path, then it is a bonus. If not,

you have to pick your way down.

The bothy at Arivurichardich was lived in by a shepherd and his family within living memory and was rented for a time in the fifties by the Ochils Mountaineering Club. It is now locked and used by the local estate for sheep-rearing purposes. The site is an old one and the long name intrigues many. Seton Gordon says it probably derives from Airigh Mhuir-cheartaich. Airigh is the Gaelic for a shieling and the rest is a man's name. Moriarty is a modern derivation of it.

From there, tramp southwards down the track, passing the entrance to Glen Artney, cross the Kelty Water by a bridge and continue down to Braeleny Farm. From there a metalled road runs down into Callander.

If you still feel sprightly, it is worth making a deviation about half a mile from Callander to the Bracklinn Falls. The name derives from *breac*, the Gaelic for speckled or flecked. Alan Breck in Robert Louis Stevenson's *Kidnapped* was so named because he had a pock-marked face. Linn means a pool, the speckled or flecked pool, but the speckles are foaming, flecked, roaring water or flood-carried debris. The tourist in summer does not see the best of these falls because the water is low, but in winter when there is much rain or in spring when there is melting snow the Kelty (or Keltie) water crashing through the narrow and steep rock walls can be a fearsome sight. It is a beautiful spot with woods of oak, alder and birch lipping the gorge. Take care on the edges: a couple fell to their deaths in 1844. The name Kelty derives from *coilltidh* (a wooded place).

Sir Walter Scott drew on the scene for his novel of the 1745 Jacobite Rising, *Waverley*, and

in front of some friends he rode a pony across the then flimsy bridge over the falls for a bet. The present structure is safe. Scott brought the falls into *The Lady of the Lake*—the Highland hero Roderick Dhu was 'brave, but wild as Bracklinn's thundering wave'.

'As Bracklinn's chasm, so black and steep,
Receives her roaring linn,
As the dark caverns of the deep
Suck the wild whirlpool in,
So did the deep and darksome pass
Devour the battle's mingled mass'.

Callander itself is a pleasant town, a tourist centre, and a newly created Visitor Centre in the town's main square, sited inside the former St Kessog's church, contains an exhibition about Rob Roy MacGregor. It was a frontier town in past times, one eye cocked at friendly Stirling and the safer Lowlands and the other on the Highlands where the clans could give endless headaches. It is not big, with around 2,000 inhabitants, but its initial huddle of houses was sited near strategically important glens and passes, some of which knew the tramp of the probing Roman legions and the war cries of the Caledonian tribes. Its name may derive from Celtic words for 'hard-water'. The Crown Commissioners laid out its wide squares when the Drummond estates were forfeited after the failure of the 1745 Jacobite Rising and further back the Livingstones, Earls of Callander, held sway. James VI entrusted his daughter, the Princess Elizabeth, later to become Winter Queen of Bohemia, to their care and she was partly brought up in Callander. Many of the scenes of BBC TV's serial, *Dr. Finlay's Casebook* were filmed here and Arden House can still be seen.

The serial was based on the writings of A.J. Cronin, who also wrote *Hatter's Castle* and *The Keys of the Kingdom*, and who was a doctor in Callander for a time., The town has also known other literary travellers, *en route* to the Trossachs, including J.M. Barrie, James Hogg, Jules Verne, Annie S. Swan, as well as Scott and many others.

In the time of the MacGregors the town was a small grouping of homes, a township in the Highland manner. The nearby glens, passes and straths knew their tread and the Michaelmas, autumn, moon saw their forays by night . . . and that's where we came in.

Creag an Tuire, Balquhidder.
(Photo Rennie McOwan).

Facing page **Castle Campbell in Dollar Glen.** *(Photo Rennie McOwan).*

WALK 8: *CENTRAL SCOTLAND*
A Drove Road across The Ochils
by Rennie McOwan

A glen-and-pass crossing through the Ochils—gentle, green hills—on the line of an old cattle drovers' route, a section of which spurred researches which produced the definitive book on the great days of huge cattle drives in the late eighteenth and nineteenth centuries. *The Drove Roads of Scotland* by A.R.B. Haldane was first published in 1952 and reached classic status when it was re-issued by Edinburgh University Press. **Start:** Dollar. **Finish:** Auchterarder. **Distance:** 12 miles (19km)—allow a full hill day. **Location/Access:** Dollar stands 11 miles (17½km) east of Stirling on the A91. Auchterarder is on the A824 12 miles (19km) west of Perth. **Map:** OS Landranger Sheet 58.

The drovers are an integral part of Scottish hill history and the remains of their routes and their rest stances, often grassy and green, can be seen all over Scotland and particularly in the Highlands. This big-business trade followed on the more unruly days of the clans when reiving (stealing) cattle was regarded as more of a manly sport than a crime.

This walk can begin at either end and while it is more logical to walk it from north to south because that is the way the drovers went on their way from the Highlands to the great fairs and trysts at Falkirk or Stenhousemuir, it is more scenically attractive to do it from south to north, the drovers' return journey. Start in the small town of Dollar, 11 miles (17½km) east of Stirling, on the A91 and on the southern edge of the Ochils (pronounced 'Oh-chils'), where Dollar burn runs through the centre of the town, an area known as West Burnside. There is room for parking beside the burn or nearby. The walk finishes in the royal and historic burgh of Auchterarder on the A824, on the north side of the Ochils, 12 miles

(19km) west of Perth.

The first mile from Dollar is on rocky paths through a deep-cut, ravine-type glen. Care is needed where the path lips the edge of bluffs and drops. The next 7 miles (11km) or more miles are on grassy hill tracks or moorland, part of which can sometimes be boggy. The remaining 4 miles (6½km) are on a broad farm track which leads on to narrow metalled roads. The going is not hard, but hill-walking boots, gear and food for a hill day are required. The middle section, the rise over the crest of the pass from the Borland Glen, is mainly on grass or heather. The route is clearly defined for all of the way. Allow for time to explore Castle Campbell, in Dollar Glen, as part of the walk.

The main interest of the walk lies in the memory of great herds of lowing cattle on the move, shouting drovers and barking dogs in what was once a colossal commercial business. The Ochils are nowadays very much sheep country and walkers should keep dogs tightly on a leash or, better still, not take dogs at all. Moor and hill bird life in springtime is attractive. However Glen Eagles, which links with Glen Devon, has nothing to do with birds but derives from Gaelic or Brittonic words for a church, *eaglais* or *eglis*.

The long wall of the 28-mile (45km) Ochils blocks the passage of travellers from north to south and it is not surprising that old trade routes made use of the few through-glens or the lower ground to the east. The late Dr. A.R.B. Haldane, of Auchterarder, one of the distinguished Haldane family who have long links with the Ochils, wrote that behind his family house an old road ran into the Ochils past the Haldane mansion house of Cloan and Upper Cloan and at Coulshill Farm became a grassy track.

He knew that coal and lime from West Fife were taken northwards over the Ochils to Strathearn in past centuries, and slates from Glen Almond and Glen Artney, together with grain, flax, wool and timber went south to the Forth basin.

He was intrigued to discover that this track had mainly been used by the great cattle droves of the eighteenth and nineteenth centuries, the many tributaries wending their way from the Highlands and Islands and coalescing into great rivers of cattle heading for the Perthshire town of Crieff, to the north of the Ochils, and in later times the Lowland town of Falkirk and its fringes to the south of the Ochils. Pedlars, too, known as cadgers (from where the golf term, caddie, a carrier, comes) also used this route and there is a Cadger's Yett across the track. A *yett* is a Scots word for a gate, as in Yetts of Muckhart, to the east of the town of Dollar and near the mouth of Glen Devon.

Thousands of lowing black, dun and red cattle, small, wiry and hardy, crossed the Ochils in the past—the present-day shaggy 'Highlander' is a nineteenth-century crossbred. The cattle trade's first discernible beginnings were as early as the fourteenth and fifteenth centuries and the clans 'borrowed' cattle from one another in daring raids. All understood and respected the fact that courage, cleverness, stealth, and skill in taking dozens of cattle at dead of night over Highland passes and avoid-

ing pursuit were to be admired. The Highlanders of long ago operated a cattle economy, as well as keeping many goats and some wiry sheep. The hills were lightly wooded on their lower slopes and lovelier than they are now. It was only when that devouring monster, the sheep, came in the nineteenth century that much of the grassland of the hills took on its short, cropped modern look. Constant grazing prevented the regeneration of scrub woodland.

The autumn moon was long ago known as MacFarlane's Lantern, an allusion to the time when the Clan MacFarlane, based around Loch Sloy and the east shore of Loch Lommond, and one of the most notorious clans, used the moon to go raiding. The autumn moon in North America was known as the Comanche moon for similar reasons: enough light to see by, not enough to make concealment difficult. It was said of the MacFarlanes that they paid their daughters' tochers by the light of the Michaelmas moon: in other words, they paid for their daughters' dowries by taking someone else's cattle in the autumn.

The same zest for raiding applied to many other clans and the word blackmail was coined in the Highlands. The MacGregors and others told Lowland lairds that if they paid them a certain sum, then they wouldn't steal their cattle and they wouldn't let anyone else do so either. The word black derived from nefarious deeds, and from the colour of many of the cattle long ago, and *mail* is an old Scots word for rent or payment. The practice is not as bad as it sounds; it could be seen as a kind of primitive insurance or policing. The famous regiment the Black Watch had its origins in this time. It comprised officially approved bodies of clansmen or militia set up by the Government to curb cattle raiding and the adjective black derived either from the dark colour of their tartan or from the deeds they were trying to stop or a mixture of both.

When the 1745 Jacobite Rising failed many drovers managed to persuade the Hanoverian government that they should be exempt from the ban on carrying arms. They also managed to hang on to the bagpipes as well, successfully arguing that they used them for calls, signals or recreation, rather than as a weapon of war.

From these raiding activities the legitimate sale of cattle evolved. Dealers collected small herds, sold them at localised fairs or trysts, bought more and when a large herd of several hundred was gathered they set out for Crieff or Falkirk or Stenhousemuir to sell them. Herds on the march sometimes had to be guarded against raiders, but a very high standard of honesty operated at the trysts and huge sums were pledged and honoured on no more

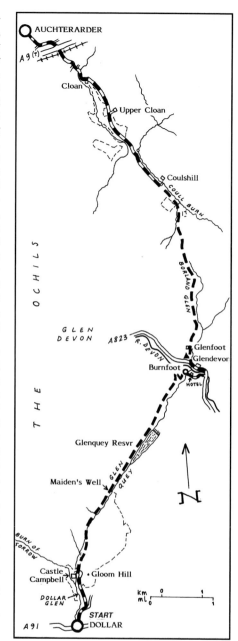

than a handshake.

Many dealers came from England to buy beasts and some of the drovers continued southward to fairs at Carlisle or Norwich, the roast beef of old England on its way south from Scotland.

The Highlanders accompanying the herds could expect to be away from home for weeks as the cattle only did a steady 9 miles (14½km) a day so as to keep them in good condition. The rest stances, many of which are nowadays in private ownership as part of estate land or covered with conifer forestry, were once mainly common land. The drovers swapped stories and news, sang songs, worked hard and enjoyed themselves. They were good stockmen, hardy, sleeping outside in all weathers, wrapping themselves in their pure wool plaids, and with dogs and sentries on guard against predators or raiders.

At night they sometimes cut a thick circular bed of heather and lay in a circle, their feet to the middle, their heads outermost. At that time, the heather had not been burned and 'managed' as it is now to aid grouse shooting, but was long and thick. The old phrase for a fugitive was that he was 'in the heather'—the drovers lay down, warmly wrapped in their plaids, bonnets pulled down tightly over their heads (scrugged, is the Scots phrase) and their leader wove a roof of tightly knit heather over them and left a place open for himself. Then he, too, slipped into his place and pulled a prepared bundle of heather into the gap. Some men soaked their plaids in water and wrung them out to generate a steamy heat. It was not uncommon to find such a mound snow-covered in the morning and the men warmly asleep inside.

The drovers ate oatmeal, mainly as porridge or brose, sometimes adding butter or milk to the hot food, a nourishing and energy-giving diet. Onions and lemons were often carried, blood drawn from cattle was cooked like modern black puddings, and meat on the hoof was available if need be. Sometimes they ate the old campaigning diet of the clans, oatmeal mixed with cold water and a little salt and stirred around, a fare called *drammach*. Even in modern times farm workers will throw a handful of oatmeal into a can of cold water, stir it, and drink it.

In their religion, nature beliefs often existed alongside Christianity, and trees had good or bad spirits attached to them; their landscape was peppered with sites linked to the heroes and heroines of Celtic and Gaelic mythology or supernatural beings.

St Bridget was the patron saint of cattle. One of the most famous saints of Ireland, Bridget of Kildare (*c*.452–*c*.524) was believed in the Highlands to be foster-mother to Christ, perhaps with links to a pre-Christian Celtic goddess.

'St Bridget to keep them, to watch them, and to tend, on the ben, in the glen and in the plain.'
'From the rocks, from the drifts, from the stream's rushing flow, from crooked passes, from the pits where beasts die.
From the slender ban-shee and the shafts of her bow, from envy's heart and from the evil eye.'

The drovers often longed for home and a poem by the Sutherland poet, Rob Donn MacAoidh (Mackay), who lived from 1714 to 1778, captures how many felt:

'Easy is my bed—it is easy,
But it is not to sleep I incline,
The wind whistles northwards, northwards,
And my thoughts move with it.
How pleasant were it be with thee
In the little glen of calves
Than to be counting of droves
in the enclosures of Crieff.'

Once the drovers had concluded their deals, they understandably whooped it up for some days before returning home. Their dogs were sent on ahead alone and that, too, is a lovely Ochils memory, the dogs trotting home, sometimes for hundreds of miles, a remarkable example of the homing instincts of animals.

Their home way of life was environmentally friendly, as we would say nowadays. The people in springtime left their homes in the townships in the glens and straths and headed for the upper moors where they lived in makeshift dwellings called shielings. They fattened their cattle, made cheese and cream, and hugely enjoyed themselves. They returned to their homes at the end of summer (see Walk 7).

The Ochils passes were well used when the southward commercial emphasis moved from Crieff, on the north of the Ochils, to the fairs at Redding Muir and Whitesiderig Muir, near Falkirk after 1770. In 1772 the Falkirk market moved to nearby Rough Castle and in 1785 to Stenhousemuir.

Part of the route of this walk follows a pass through Glen Quey which the drovers used to avoid tolls, which were gathered to build turnpike roads, and which were a source of great irritation. Perthshire and Stirlingshire were considered to be particularly bad. That great engineer, Thomas Telford (1757–1834), suggested that a general drove route exempt from tolls be specifically constructed, but he was too late.

Cattle and sheep were frequently shod, like horses, to help them cope with stony stretches.

When the days of the great droves ended many of the drovers migrated to North America, some willingly, some forcibly removed from their ancestral lands by the Clearances, when people were expelled by nineteenth-century landowners to make way for sheep which produced higher profits or to clear the land for big, sporting estates. These Gaels and their descendants left their mark on the great cattle drives of the American west, in its vocabulary with such phrases as 'the real MacCoy (Mackay)', meaning the real thing or true value, and on the maps with such names as the old Chisholm Trail from Texas to Kansas.

When the land to the south of the Ochils was once bog and marsh instead of today's modern, drained farmland, little villages and towns sprang up on the higher ground at the southern foot of the hills, which later used the water of the tumbling hill burns to turn the mill wheels in a weaving boom which once made this area famous for shawls, plaids and other tartan and woollen clothing.

These villages, Menstrie, Alva, Tillicoultry and Dollar, are known as the Hillfoots and modern Dollar is now a popular residential town. The name Dollar probably derives from *dal-aird,* a high, fertile place or meadow, although *dolour* has been suggested in view of the fact that Castle Campbell was once called Castle Gloume. The famous school, Dollar Academy, was founded in 1818 by John McNabb, a local herd boy in 1732, who became a wealthy London shipowner. His school was originally intended for the local poor, but became a prestigious academic institution and its Grecian design by Scottish architect William Playfair is greatly admired.

Walk up Burnside on the west side and cross a humped bridge in the oldest section of the town. Immediately over this bridge a signposted gap in the wall leads into Dollar Glen. A clear path crosses an open, grassy piece of ground beside the burn known as Mill Green, where Dollar womenfolk once spread linen to bleach and dry. It is now an adventure course and play area, with the golf course on the other bank. The path leads into trees and then into the deep gorge of Dollar Glen.

The paths run below large cliffs and alongside deep pools with bridge-walk ways and railings in awkward spots. The pools and waterfalls can be awesome and impressive particularly when the burn is in spate.

The glen is in the care of the National Trust for Scotland and the paths divide at the foot of the Castle Knoll. Either branch will take you up to the castle. The castle can also almost be reached by road from the town. Just to the east of the gap in the wall at the head of Burnside a road junction, off Hillfoots Road, called Castle Road, runs uphill and is signposted for the castle. This was the line the drovers took, but walkers should not miss the attractions of the glen gorge. This road goes steeply uphill and changes to a much rougher surface. There is a car park at the start in the trees, but cars can also be taken to a higher car park just below the castle level.

The steep-walled castle on its prominent mound is also owned by the National Trust for Scotland and is in the care of the Ancient Monuments Directorate of the Scottish Development Department (the old Ministry of Works). It is open all year.

Neighbouring Gloom Hill and the dark ravine may have caused the burns to be called Care and Sorrow, but these names are relatively modern, romantic inventions.

The castle originally belonged to the Stewarts of Lorne and Innerneath and came to the Campbells in marriage. It has known many distinguished men and women including Colin Campbell, first Earl of Argyll and Chancellor of Scotland in 1489, who enlarged it and changed its name by act of Parliament from Castle Gloume to Castle Campbell. It gave the Lords of the Congregation a refuge in 1560 during the Reformation struggles and the reformer John Knox is reputed to have preached here.

A number of books say it was burned by the royalist army of James Graham, Marquis of Montrose, and Alasdair MacColla, the war leader of Clan Donald, during the seventeenth-century Scottish Wars of the Covenant (see Walk 6), but this is incorrect. The royal army by-passed it on their way to a crushing victory at Kilsyth in 1646, but the MacLean contingents in the army fired the houses of Dollar and the local villages as part of their policy of making life hard for the hated Campbells who led the forces of the Convenant against Montrose. The castle was actually burned later in the time of General Monk, Cromwell's hatchetman in Scotland.

Walk from the castle close to where a cottage can be seen on a knoll to the east and a branch track curves uphill and into the mouth of Glen Quey, a name which may derive from *quaich*, cup- or bowl-shaped. This area is now planted with trees, but a muddy track leads on to the north side of the glen and a clear path then runs eastwards past Glen Quey reservoir. Look out for a small, clear pool just to the right of the path soon after getting properly into the line of the glen. It is known as the Maiden's Well and may have given the glen its name. A local tradition has it that if you fall asleep beside it you will be enticed away by faeries and never wake up.

Just past the reservoir the path runs downhill to Burnfoot and the scattered houses of Glen Devon where the River Devon is crossed by a bridge, a charming corner with little holiday cabins lining the river banks of a type which would never get permission nowadays.

The name Devon derives from *dubh abhain*, black river, and its lower sections were greatly admired by the poet Robert Burns who, also inspired by dalliance, wrote two poem/songs about it and his lady friends. There was a rest stance for cattle here and the hotel, the Tormaukin Inn, was once the site of a hostelry for drovers. Glen Devon curves round westwards into the hills but links with Glen Eagles before doing so and the modern road follows this clean cut of the two glens through the hills.

In the time of James VI this area was the

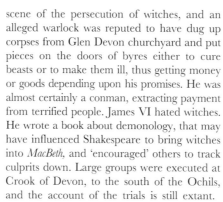

Top **Maiden's Well in Glen Quey.**

Bottom **Glen Devon.**
(Photos Rennie McOwan).

scene of the persecution of witches, and an alleged warlock was reputed to have dug up corpses from Glen Devon churchyard and put pieces on the doors of byres either to cure beasts or to make them ill, thus getting money or goods depending upon his promises. He was almost certainly a conman, extracting payment from terrified people. James VI hated witches. He wrote a book about demonology, that may have influenced Shakespeare to bring witches into *MacBeth*, and 'encouraged' others to track culprits down. Large groups were executed at Crook of Devon, to the south of the Ochils, and the account of the trials is still extant.

Cross the A823 road (take care, as it is busy

in season with hidden bends) to where the wooden youth hostel stands. Follow the burn northwards into the hills, past the farm of Glenfoot and into the Borland Glen where there is a broad, grassy track.

On the higher ground there is a section of lush, green turf and one can easily imagine the drovers and their herds coming this way. A path is marked on the map, but it is sometimes indistinct. Cross the high hill ground between two knolls and descend to the Coull Burn above Coulshill Farm. You then pick up a broad track which turns into a narrow, metalled road.

A little cairn on a knoll to the west of the farm is in memory of two Boys' Brigade officers who took boys camping here. There are magnificent views over Strathearn and this must have been an evocative place for the returning drovers because they would see the Highland hills and the passes to the north and feel they were really on their way home.

This metalled road leads down past Upper Cloan Farm and Cloan mansion, all Haldane territory. As well as A.R.B. Haldane, the historian of the days of the drovers, the family also produced the writer Naomi Mitchison who now lives in Carradale, Kintyre, and Viscount Richard Burdon Haldane, founder of the Territorial Army, advocate, a Liberal MP and later Labour Party activist, Secretary for War in 1905 and twice Lord Chancellor. Viscount Haldane was also an enthusiastic hill tramper.

Metalled roads lead on past the modern railway, the new dual carriageway road and into Auchterarder where there are shops, cafes and public houses. Auchterarder's siting on higher ground, looking across to the Ochils probably gave it its name *Aachdar-ard-thir*, upper highland. Like other villages and towns on the north side of the Ochils, it has a long pedigree but a modern look. The Earl of Mar ('Bobbing John'), the indecisive military leader of the retreating Jacobites during the 1715 Rising, gave orders for these villages to be burned, a deed which harmed the Jacobite cause for years.

James VI used the example of Auchterarder to score a point against some of his English subjects when he became King of Scotland and England at the Union of the Crowns in 1602. A noble had been boasting about a walled town which had many drawbridges. The King said he could take them to a modest Scottish burgh which had at least 50 drawbridges. He omitted to mention that they were small, removable planks which were used to bridge the open burn and gutters that once ran down the middle of the street in Auchterarder.

Auchterarder was once the site of small cattle fairs, preparatory bargaining and planning get-togethers before the herds set out over the Ochils on the last leg of their journey to Falkirk, some eastwards along the north side of the Ochils and via Greenloaning and Sheriffmuir, some by Glen Eagles and Glen Devon and some by Cloan, the Borland Glen and—to avoid tolls— by Glen Quey to Dollar.

Cloan mansion near Auchterader, home of the renowned historian A. R. B. Haldane.
(Photo Rennie McOwan).

WALK 9: *JURA—Mermaids, Saints and a 'Whirlpool' by Rennie McOwan*

An expedition to one of Scotland's natural wonders on a wild and remote island. **Start/Finish:** Car park at Inverlussa at the road-end on Jura, Argyll. **Distance:** 22 miles (35km)—allow one or more full hill days. **Location/Access:** Jura is reached by Western Ferries car and passenger ferry from Port Askaig, on the western, neighbouring island of Islay (pronounced 'ile-ah'), and the visitor lands at Feolin Ferry in the south-west of Jura and across the Sound of Islay. (There is a reduced service on Sunday.) A minor road runs round the southern tip of Jura and up the east side to Ardlussa, three-quarters of the way up the island. There are no roads, other than estate tracks, on the west of the island north of Feolin Ferry, nor in the middle or northern sections. Islay is served by the Caledonian MacBrayne car ferry from Kennacraig, on the Kintyre peninsula, or by Loganair flights from Glasgow. **Map:** OS Landranger Sheet 61.

From Inverlussa to the north of Jura, where the famous 'whirlpool' is sited at the Gulf of Corryvreckan and back is 22 miles (35km). Some groups hire boats and land in the area of Kinuachdrach, a farm in the north-east corner of the island and 9½ miles (15km) from Inverlussa. The Gulf of Corryvreckan is 2½ miles (4km) from Kinuachdrach. A track which is possible (just) for wheeled vehicles, but not recommended for modern cars, runs from a point just north of Inverlussa (where the public road makes a prominent southward loop from

Ardlussa across the Lussa river to Inverlussa) up the east coast to Kinuachdrach. Some visitors take their cars to Lealt, 3 miles (5km) north of Inverlussa, and walk to the Gulf of Corryvreckan from there, and some persevere by car beyond that, but the track is very tough and it is not fair to local farm traffic to take cars beyond Inverlussa.

There is a broad and stony track to near Kinuachdrach, then rough, moorland walking to the north-west and north of the island, and coastal wandering over ground sprinkled with

raised beaches, fissures, rock arches and caves. Go prepared for a full hill day, or a series of days, and make provision for bad weather. Jura is 30 miles (48km) long, sparsely populated and hill trampers and walkers can be many miles from a house and road. Expeditions on Jura will particularly suit people who like wild places and who find enjoyment in sleeping out in caves or sheltered nooks. Care is needed over hidden fissures in some coastal places, their lips masked by long heather. The stag-shooting season starts on 1 July and ends on 20

October. The key period is mid-August to mid-October—if you are walking during that period it is *essential* to make local inquiries as to desired routes. Sensitivity *must* be exercised during the deer stalking season.

Jura has a hotel in Craighouse village, in the south-east of the island and other holiday accommodation including guest houses and bed-and-breakfasts, is available. The Mountain Bothies Association has an open bothy at Glengarrisdale, in the lonely north-west of the island. Islay has several hotels, guest houses and other accommodation. Because of deer-stalking and farming considerations, it is wise to consult locally about camping. Hill trampers planning to sleep in caves should remember that many have dead deer or goats inside.

When George Orwell wanted to write *1984*, his novel of a terrifyingly impersonal and authoritarian future, he took himself off to Jura, that lonely, wild and beautiful island. He knew what he was about even though he was terminally ill. He wanted peace to reflect and think amid near-timeless things and in some ways it is a strange book to have been produced among such magnificent surroundings.

His book is, of course, a masterpiece and still has the power to shock and disturb, although the notorious date of the title has come and gone. George Orwell nearly died during his Jura sojourn—his boat was almost sunk in the wild seas of the Gulf of Corrievreckan and its fringes.

The Corrievreckan 'whirlpool' is one of the great natural wonders of Scotland, although you should time a visit to coincide with the tides being in flood: some visitors have been very disappointed. The Gulf is at its most spectacular in winter and Jura then is no place for the summer-only plodder. The Gulf channel is about 2 miles (3km) long and 1 mile (1½km) wide, running east–west between Jura and the neighbouring northern island of Scarba.

Strictly speaking, it is not a whirlpool at all because the seas swamp boats rather than suck them down. When the film *I Know Where I'm Going* was being made, a life-size dummy boat and figures were launched into the Gulf, only to be spewed out on Scarba.

In past centuries it was regarded as a fearsome place, the haunt of mermaids, the place where the Celtic storm goddesses washed their linen in the cauldron.

The eye of the 'whirlpool' was known as the cauldron of the Cailleach, or the hag, a reference to the Cailleach Bheithir, (pronounced yeir), the best known of the ancient Celtic storm goddesses. Mermaids were also said to sing here and a friend of Sir Walter Scott's Dr John Leyden, wrote a poem called 'The Mermaid of the Coire-Bhreacain'.

When the famous hills of the Paps of Jura, over 15 miles (24km) to the south, had a covering of snow, the old legends said that it was the goddesses' or witches' linen being spread out to dry. It is a magnificent place and Sir Walter Scott, who knew the western seaboard well, wrote in his epic poem, 'Lord of the Isles', 'And Scarba's Isle whose tortured shore, still rings to Corrievreckan's roar.'

When the Corrievreckan was in flood in the winter gales it sounded like the noise of 1000 chariots and nowadays when it is heard over 20 miles (30km) away people liken it to the sound of far-off trains. Waves can reach over 30ft (9m) high and the tidal speed over nine knots, and several boats have been lost here.

It is a place to make people rejoice in the spectacular beauty of the scenery. Lady Hilda Murray of Elibank, when staying with the Marchioness of Breadalbane at Armaddy Castle, near Oban, in 1924, wrote:

*'Let me face the breezes blowing
Fresh along the mountainside!
Let me see the purple heather,
Let me hear the thundering tide,
Be it hoarse as Corrievreckan
Spouting where the storm is high—
Give me but one hour of Scotland,
Let me see it ere I die.'*

Corryvreckan greatly excited travellers in past times. The factor to the laird of the Macleods, Martin Martin, in *A Description of the Western Islands of Scotland*, published in 1716 wrote:

'It yields an impetuous current, not to be matched anywhere about the Isle of Britain. The sea begins to boil and ferment with the Tide of Flood, and resembles the boiling of a Pot.'

The *Old Statistical Account* said, 'The conflux is dreadful and spurns all descriptions. Even the genius of Milton could not paint the horrors of the scene.'

Sir Donald Monro, Archdeacon of the Isles before the Reformation and one of the leading churchmen of the Reformed Scottish Church, in 1549 wrote the first known description of the Western Isles from personal observation and said of Corryvreckan, 'Betwixt this twa iyles ther runnes ane streame, above the power of all sailing and rowing, with infinite dangers, callit Corybrekan.'

It is astonishing to look at the Gulf, or to sail through it, even when calm, and to realise that deer swim between Jura and Scarba.

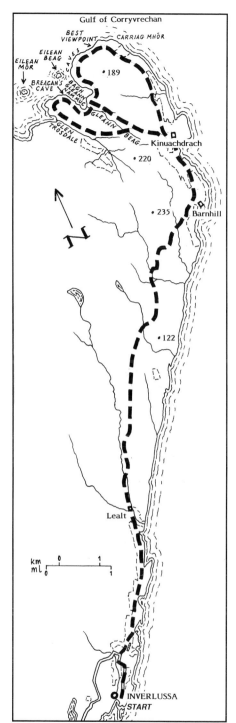

What causes this huge, angry strait? Tremendous tides from the Irish Channel run daily into the narrow basin formed by Islay, Jura, Scarba and Luing on one side and by Kintyre, Knapdale and Craignish on the other. This basin is so confined that the mass of water forces its way through the narrows of Corryvreckan, and submerged rocks, cliffs, shelves and pyramids throw it in different directions.

Unlikely tradition has it that there is a great hole down below through which the sea bores again and again.

Mountaineer and yachtsman W.H. Murray, whose works include an entertaining novel called *Maelstrom,* with background about the behaviour of these seas, wrote that following his own books about the western seaboard he had corresponded with a company director, Mr Kenneth Mackiggan of Bearsden, Glasgow, who had made a two-year study of the Gulf of Corryvreckan. Mr Mackiggan's findings were now incorporated in the Clyde Cruising Club's sailing directions, 'Mull of Kintyre to Ardnamurchan'.

Mr Mackiggan timed the tides and found that the remains of a deep cleft in the Scarba cliffs had been deposited into the Gulf. This formed a high, flat shelf, over which the tidal flow passes. The overfalls are heavier on the flood tide because the rise to the shelf from the eastern end, from where the flood comes, is steeper.

The southern half of the Gulf is free from underwater obstructions and in calm conditions the water is quiet if fast. The flood, impeded by the shelf, is released in a mighty plunge which the water ahead cannot absorb. It was, he found, like a waterfall which creates a standing wave held stationary by opposing forces. This is compounded by an opposing westerly, and especially south-westerly, swell when the overfalls drop to the bottom of deep, angled troughs.

The whirlpool effect is caused by a sudden upsurge of bottom water, the rounded edge of which does not rotate. An overfall is created from within, but it pushes up, rather than sucking down. It is not, after all, a whirlpool in the strict sense. Mr Mackiggan pays tribute to a friend, the late Dr Andrew Tindal, who shortly after World War II, filmed the Gulf and proved this to be so.

But it is difficult for the layman not to use the word whirlpool when the whole Gulf is on the move because sections have that appearance: water falls from one level to another or suddenly foams up as if a hidden skerry had been struck and there is constant, swirling movement. The visitor can see minor versions at the Falls of Lora, Connel Bridge, near Oban.

Experienced sailors can go through the Gulf with ease but in calm times it is like a sleeping tiger with the lines of unexpected waves rippling across otherwise relatively calm water and then subsiding and looking very much like a white-fanged snarl. It is no place for the amateur or the careless.

The name Corrievreckan may derive from the Gaelic *corrie,* a kettle (but cauldron- or saucer-shaped) and *breacan,* the Gaelic word for tartan. Looking at the Jura cliffs from Scarba, or clambering among them, the pattern of rocks and small burns tumbling over and into the sea is not unlike the striped pattern of tartan.

Another theory is the ancient legend of Prince Breacan, from Lochlann (the old name for Norway), who wanted to marry a princess of Lorn. Her father asked him to anchor his vessel in the Gulf to demonstrate his prowess and he had to use three anchor cables, one of flax, one of horse-hair and one of what is delicately called the hair of spotless maidens.

The Corrievreckan 'whirlpool' boils into life—one of Scotland's great natural wonders.
(Photo Rennie McOwan).

On the first night the flax cable broke. On the second the horse-hair cable snapped. Some of the maidens couldn't have been as spotless as all that because that cable also broke and Prince Breacan and his hound were drowned and are reputedly buried in Breacan's Cave at the north of the island. When I went there with some friends on one occasion, one of our party was late at the pick-up point for our departure boat. When we asked him for an explanation he said he had been in Oban looking for spotless maidens. It had taken him *ages,* he said! The Prince Breacan legend might well be true—a stone coffin and a lady's shoe were found in the cave in past times.

Some walkers plan to sleep inside Breacan's Cave or the other caves with which the western and northern sections of the island and dotted, but most have dead goats or deer inside who have sought shelter when ill. Large caves like Breacan's Cave sometimes have protective walls built up at the entrance and were used by fishermen earlier this century. Some were known as *corpachs,* caves where bodies were rested *en route* to the sacred islands of Oronsay and Iona, and the Celtic saints knew this coastline well.

St Columba may have sailed in these waters, but his biographer Adamnan's description, may also apply to seas between Northern Ireland and Rathlin island. Adamnan certainly used the name Charybdis Brecan, Breacan's Cauldron, but most historians set the scene of Prince Breacan's death in the Gulf of Corryvreckan and not off the coast of Antrim.

The name Jura derives from the Norse *dyr,* deer-isle, and even in the later days of the clans, the MacLeans, MacDonalds, MacPhees, and expansionist Campbells, it was mainly an island used for hunting. Sir James Turner, adjutant to the skilled General Leslie in the seventeenth-century Scottish Wars of the Covenant, said it was 'a horrid isle fit only for deer and wild beasts', but he was somewhat soured from chasing the remnants of the royal army of the Marquis of Montrose and the war leader of Clan Donald, Alasdair MacColla.

Jura was a special place to Clan Donald and a small island off the south-west corner in the Sound of Islay, called Eilean Fraoch, the heathery isle, had a special significance for them as a symbol of their land holdings, and particularly in the great days of the Lords of the Isles. The small island gave Clan Donald its war slogan and its badge of heather, partly used for clan identification and partly as a talisman or charm.

The modern visitor can expect to see many deer and goats, and probably eagles and otters, and in sheltered corners in summer midges can be a nuisance.

The southern tip and much of the eastern side of the 30-mile (48km) island now has farms, forestry and a distillery, but many people were forcibly evicted in the last century to make way for sheep and the big sporting estates. The population, once over 1000, is now down to about 200. The cattle drovers of the late eighteenth and nineteenth centuries swam their beasts from the fertile island of Islay across the Sound of Islay to Feolin, on the same line as the modern ferry from Port Askaig, no mean feat considering the force of the tidal currents.

From there they plodded up the eastern side of Jura from where they swam or crossed by boat to the mainland and then onwards to the great fairs or trysts at Falkirk, Stenhousemuir or Crieff. (see Walk 8).

The much-respected mountaineer and writer W.H. Murray said that one had to climb these fine hills, the Paps of Jura, to get them out of one's system. The word pap means a breast and such is their siting in the south of the island that these stony, rough, cone-shaped mountains are seen from many parts of the Scottish mainland. A lovely Gaelic song talks of 'Long Looking to Jura' and many mainland hill trampers do indeed do that. But there are actually three Paps and a traverse of all three is a full day's expedition of 5000ft (1520m), with much awkward and rough going, including picking one's way up or down boulder fields. The three Paps are: Beinn a' Chaolais, mountain of the sound (of Islay), 2407ft (734m) Beinn an Oir, mountain of the boundary (sometimes given as mountain of gold), 2571ft (784m); and Beinn Shiantaidh, sacred or consecrated mountain, 2477ft (755m). The views can be immense, ranging from most of the main inland mountains to the coast of Northern Ireland from where the Celtic saints came in their tiny boats. They waited until the tides were right and were then carried across to the mouth of long Loch Indaal, on Islay, sailed to its head, crossed Islay to where modern Port Askaig now stands, crossed the Sound of Islay to Jura, walked or rode up the eastern shore and then crossed over to the mainland where they journeyed far inland and brought Christianity to the turbulent kingdoms. The island of Scarba was a favourite retiring place for monks and abbots from the sacred island of Iona.

But Jura is ideally suited to more gentle walks as well, providing fascinating coast wandering with raised beaches, rock arches, caves, much bird life, and the standing stones and forts of the vanished races of pre-history. Loch Tarbert, which almost splits the island in two, is a favourite haunt of yachtsmen. There are some wildly beautiful bays and beaches. Port

Askaig, the departure point from Islay, is a charming place, a little sheltered harbour with the Paps of Jura just across the Sound, and it figures in that hilarious film *The Maggie,* the tale of a west coast puffer (a small coastal steamer). A rollicking pipe tune is often played called 'Leaving Port Askaig'.

Follow the track from the car park at Inverlussa on to Kinuachdrach Farm. You pass through an attractive wooded section and then on to the farm at Lealt and the road then rises over high moorland and turns inland for a time before descending to the coast and Kinauchdrach. Keep an eye out for Barnhill Farm about a mile south of Kinuachdrach, and between the road and the sea: it was there George Orwell wrote *1984*.

At Kinauchdrach follow an old track up behind the farmhouse, keeping above the woods, and either angle round the eastern coast or go north-west down Gleann Beag (The Little Glen) to the bay called Bagh Gleann nam Muc, bay of the pig or boar (although sea-pig, dolphin, has also been suggested). Breacan's Cave is on the north-west side of the bay just before it curves westwards (map reference 685006). A knoll above Carraig Mhor, at the northern tip of Jura, is an excellent viewpoint for the Gulf and the 'whirlpool' and also for views of neighbouring Scarba, an island which derives its name from the Gaelic word *sgairbh,* a cormorant, and its hill Cruach (meaning heaped up).

Some walkers continue along the coast westwards round the headland and then walk back south-westwards up Glentrosdale, following the northern arm of the burn, and descend again into Gleann Beag and then return to Kinuachdrach.

This northern section is rich in legend and story. Kinuachdrach was once famous as a resting place for bodies being taken to the island of Colonsay for burial and cattle were also rested here before being taken to the mainland for sale.

It was also the site of an armed camp when one of the MacDonalds of Islay got annoyed when his daughter, Una, eloped with a MacEarchern from Craignish, on the mainland. He sent armed men to bring her back, but bad weather forced them to camp at Kinuachdrach. The cunning Craignish men lit large fires at night and this enabled Una's sympathetic stepmother to persuade her husband that anyone who could command so many armed men must be a worthy person. She suggested discussions instead of war and the couple were eventually married.

Some misguided people say Jura is an empty and dull island. In fact, its riches and pleasures cannot be exhausted by anyone in a lifetime.

WALK 10: *DUMFRIES & GALLOWAY*
Covenanters and Killing Times
by Rennie McOwan

A hill walk in the Moffat Hills section of the Southern Uplands in an area which is partly 'wild' hills and partly tree plantations. It typifies the kind of terrain used by the Covenanters who in the seventeenth century worshipped in secret places in the hills to avoid persecution. **Start/Finish:** Car park, Grey Mare's Tail waterfall. **Distance:** 7 miles (11km)—allow 5 to 6 hours. **Location/Access:** The start is 5 miles (8km) south-west of St Mary's Loch on the A708 Moffat–Selkirk road, and 8½ miles (13½km) north-east of Moffat. Check locally for bus services. **Map:** OS Landranger Sheet 79.

Initially a well-laid path rises sharply above a glen gorge and then you are hill tramping on rough moorland, grass and heather. The walk includes an ascent of White Coomb (2695ft/821m), the highest peak in the Moffat Hills range. Great care must be taken not to deviate from the path at the waterfall—there have been several accidents as a result of people trying to climb the steep, grassy slopes, including four deaths. Dogs should be kept tightly under control.

The Covenanting period in Scottish history is highly complex. If one uses the word covenant nowadays it is thought to be solely a method of paying tax so that charities will benefit. But once it was a word which instantly suggested harried bands of worshippers secretly gathering together in hidden hollows in the hills, while sentries kept watch, a mixture of a grim adherence to religious freedom and healthy Scottish cussedness in the face of arrogant authority.

This walk should be read in conjunction with the famous winter hills march to Inverlochy in 1645, undertaken by the royal army of James Graham, Marquis of Montrose, and his renowned second in command, Alasdair MacColla, war leader of Clan Donald (Walk 6). The events are connected.

Covenanter is the name applied to Scottish Presbyterians who signed two major religious and political declarations, the National Covenant of 1638 and the Solemn League and

Covenant of 1643, and to their successors who during the reigns of Charles II and James VII (II of England) resisted the Episcopal (i.e. Anglican) system of church structure and worship forced upon Scotland.

The National Covenant was a manifesto first signed in Greyfriars Church, Edinburgh, at the end of February 1638, to consolidate Scottish opposition to Charles I's innovations in worship and in protest at interference with Scottish church authority structures. It is a document strong in the Scottish pysche and the concept of 'covenant' was revived in modern times by Scottish nationalists, who in 1930 pledged themselves to restore independent, national status to Scotland. In 1949 many signatories from all parties pledged their support for a Scottish parliament within the framework of the United Kingdom.

The Solemn League and Covenant was an agreement whereby Scottish Covenanters agreed to assist the English Parliament against Charles I on condition that England would, in effect, adopt a Presbyterian church system. It was drawn up in August 1643 and accepted, with some modifications, by the English in September.

These declarations are often confused with one another by some writers, which is a pity because they helped shape the modern political, religious and emotional face of Scotland, and the distinction between them should be understood.

The resistance which began when Charles I tried to impose the new liturgy on the Scots, and which continued with the alliance between Scots Covenanters and the English Parliament, ended with the defeat and execution of the King.

The Covenanters did not want the King killed, but they did compel the young Charles II to assent to both covenants in order to obtain the Scottish crown.

Such strains inevitably brought trouble when, after the eight-year interlude of the Commonwealth and the Protectorate, the Stuart dynasty was restored to the British throne.

Presbyterianism was then outlawed and replaced by Episcopacy, the Covenants were denounced as illegal and a period of savage persecution began. Seeing the issue as obedience to God or to King, many Covenanters became outlaws. Many resorted to field preaching and were hunted, jailed, killed or banished overseas.

It has to be said that many Covenanters were themselves not averse to swinging a sword in the name of the Prince of Peace and that political allegiances and religious adherence often went hand in hand.

In the many historical strands of our hills, the memory of ordinary people singing hymns and psalms in secret hollows while sentries kept watch for dragoons and other soldiers is a strong and evocative one, and can be appreciated even by those whose sympathies or personal beliefs are linked to the Episcopal or the Roman Catholic churches and who, understandably, see these events from a different viewpoint.

The hill country around Moffat and Selkirk and in other parts of the Borders, Galloway and Ayrshire are dotted with Covenanting sites and memorials. They hid at Dobb's Linn, just under a mile up the A708 from the Grey Mare's Tail. John Graham of Claverhouse, Viscount Dundee, persecuted them with relish. Nicknamed 'Bloody Clavers', he is reputed to have ridden his black charger across the side of Bran Law, the hill above the Grey Mare's Tail, a spot which Sir Walter Scott said was so precipitous that no earthly horse or mortal rider could do it. Claverhouse was said to have devilish powers, but it depends on where your sympathies lie. To others he is Bonnie Dundee, dying a martyr's death in the moment of victory at the battle of Killiecrankie in 1689, which launched the Jacobite movement—those who supported the House of Stuart when James VII went into exile (see Walk 5).

The National Trust for Scotland purchased this property of 2383 acres, extending it to Loch Skeen and White Coomb in 1962 by using money from the Trust's Mountainous Country Fund, formed by the late Mr Percy Unna, the Trust's mountains benefactor who passionately believed that hill country should be kept 'natural' and who outlined his wishes or 'Unna Rules' for the management of such properties. A further 128 acres at Dobb's Linn were purchased in 1972 with a grant from the Countryside Commission for Scotland. The area is part of a much larger region of the Moffat Hills designated by the Nature Conservancy Council for special conservation.

The Trust car park at the falls is relatively free from some of the unwise development which has marred other hill properties. Information boards are discreetly hidden inside an old sheep fank or stell (pen).

To the northbound traveller on the Carlisle–Glasgow road the group of hills lying to the north of Moffat form the first marked area of high ground to be seen in Scotland. The stretch of road between the Grey Mare's Tail and the Birkhill Pass to the north is one of the most impressive in the Southern Uplands because of the steepness of the hills on both sides which is maintained as the valley of the Moffat Water narrows.

It has the classic U-shape of a glaciated

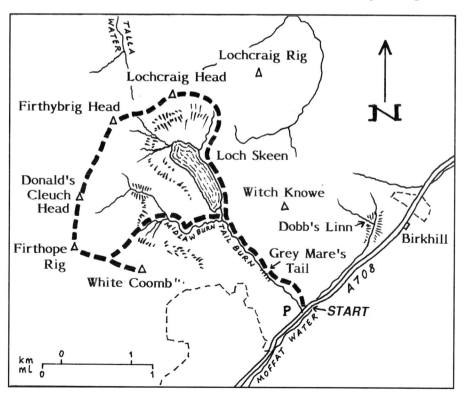

***Approaching the Grey Mare's Tail
waterfall.*** *(Photo Rennie McOwan).*

valley and is situated on a geological fault. This accounts for its straightness as the weakness of the rock along this fault made it easier for the ice to cut its way down the valley. On either side are a number of hanging valleys that held tributaries of the main glacier.

About a mile from the car park is Birkhill Cottage, once a summer inn which catered for drovers, where the Galashiels school teacher Charles Lapworth (1842–1920), stayed while studying the geology of Dobb's Linn. Lapworth found many graptolite fossils in the black shales in the main cliff near the linn. These were 'colobial' organisms that lived in the sea some 400 million years ago and the fossils enabled Lapworth to date the rocks. He published his findings and became Professor of Geology and Mineralogy at what is now Birmingham University. Geologists still visit Dobb's Linn.

Two paths are clearly seen from the car park. One leads to the base of the falls and is blocked by a fence, a viewpoint used by most tourist visitors. The other runs diagonally uphill to the north and leads to the lovely Loch Skeen.

In the pecking order of falls, the Grey Mare's Tail is the biggest in the Borders and probably the sixth in Scotland. It is one of ten or so which have that name, a tribute to the effect of Robert Burns's epic poem. 'Tam o'

Shanter' in which the drunken Tam gatecrashes the witches' party and just manages to escape, leaving the tail of his grey mare in the hands of his pursuers. The burn is called the Tail Burn. During the last Ice Age, when the area was covered with glaciers, the larger and faster glacier in the Moffat Water gouged out a deeper valley than the glacier in the Tail Burn where Loch Skeen lies. This created this classic hanging valley. The Tail Burn falls 200ft (60m) to the Moffat Water. It is what waterfall connoisseurs call an unsupported fall and is in three sections. In spate, it is a striking sight. It has been climbed more than once when frozen in winter by parties experienced in ice-climbing techniques.

Sir Walter Scott brought the falls into his poem, 'Marmion':

*'Where deep deep down, and far within
Toils with the rocks the roaring linn;
Then, issuing forth one foamy wave,
And wheeling round the Giant's Grave
White as the snowy charger's tail
Drives down the pass of Moffatdale.'*

James Hogg, the Ettrick Shepherd, who is enjoying a new popularity as a writer, is reputed to have lost money in the area of the falls and Loch Skeen and then found it again many months later. Among Hogg's many works is a song, 'The Covenanter's Tomb'. Sir Walter Scott, like Hogg, liked waterfalls, despite the fact that he and his horse went into a bog hole nearby and were hard put to get out. The area is rich in wild flowers, particularly around the falls. The varied flora cover of the lime-rich rocks contrasts with extensive areas of grass and heathland developed on acid peat. Some sheep hang around the car park at the foot of the falls hoping for titbits from tourists. This is all very much sheep country: wool from here was exported to Europe through Berwick-upon-Tweed as early as the thirteenth century.

The path to Lock Skeen beside the Tail Burn is attractive and so is the loch, cradled by green and brown hills. Keep a look out for feral goats.

Loch Skeen is still sometimes spelled Skene, the older form, and at the beginning of the last century the white-tailed sea eagle, a bird now being re-introduced from Norway to the western seaboard of Scotland, was said to breed here. It is colonised by black-headed gulls and has brown trout.

Loch Skeen is $\frac{3}{4}$ mile (1km) long and enclosed by the steep face of Lochcraig Head and broken-up ridge which runs eastwards from the hill called Firthybrig Head towards the foot of the loch. A flat and featureless moor stretches eastwards towards St Mary's Loch. Many visitors just visit the loch and go back but to sense the feel of the area as it might

have been in Covenanting times it is necessary to go into the hills to look out from the highest tops.

From the south end of Loch Skeen turn left over a small ford and angle back slightly in a southerly direction until the line of the Midlaw Burn is picked up. Follow that burn until a junction, take the burn running from the south-west and then head for the upper ground between Firthhope Rig and White Coomb, turning eastwards to strike the broad top of the range's highest hill. If the weather is fine, spend some time there, absorbing the feel of the area. Tramp westwards to Firthhope Rig again and then work your way north and north-east over Donald's Cleuch Head until you strike Firthybrig Head hill, just to the north-west of the loch. Descend eastwards into the dip known as Talla Nick from close to where the Talla Water runs northwards and then up again to the plateau of Lochcraig Head, due north of Loch Skeen. There are lovely views down the length of the loch. Curve round eastwards and again south (you pick up a fence) and pick a way among peat hags on the lower ground around the loch's shore. Keep following the loch's shores until an intermittent track is picked up which takes you back to the main Tail Burn path upon which you descend to the car park again.

It's still beautiful hill country nowadays and the Killing Times have gone, but particularly in storms and mist the atmosphere of the days of the Covenanters can still be sensed.

Facing page **The bailey and keep at Warkworth Castle, set on a hill above the River Coquet.**

WALK 11: *NORTHUMBRIA—Coastal Castles*

A bracing hike along Northumbria's wild, beautiful coastline linking border fortifications and fishing harbours. Wide sandy beaches, rocky foreshore, dunes and a little road walking, with few appreciable gradients. **Start:** Warkworth Castle. **Finish:** Bamburgh. **Distance:** 26 miles (42km)—2 days suggested. **Location/Access:** Warkworth lies east of the A1 between Morpeth and Alnwick; nearest railway station—Alnmouth. Bamburgh is reached on the B1342 east of the A1, not far south of Holy Island; nearest railway station—Chathill. **Maps:** OS Landranger Sheets 81 and 75.

The Northumbrian coast—on a scale somehow more expansive than one expects in Britain—spreads its vast sandy bays and rocky foreshore from Tyneside to the Scottish border. Harbour villages, exposed for centuries to the merciless North Sea, squat defiantly against the waves, wind and salt spray. It is an elemental coastline, glimpsed tantalisingly here and there from the A1 or from trains on the main line from Berwick to Newcastle. Its full, stern beauty, however, is reserved for the walker able to experience at first hand the succession of pale, dune-backed sands, rocky promontories, low grassy clifftops and coastal settlements.

Northumbria's many castles (not to mention the relative proximity of Hadrian's Wall) point up another dimension to be found here—the area's embroilment in historical conflicts between south and north. Indeed, near this walk alone a dozen castles and towers bear witness to the strategic importance of this region in the border wars.

And so it is that we have a walk of unique character, combining natural grandeur with significant insights into some of Northumbria's military fortifications through several layers of history. In a predominantly low-lying coastscape, the castles themselves become points of visual focus, accentuated by outcroppings of the Whin Sill, a resistant basalt intrusion running across northern England.

I had hoped to extend the walk north to Lindisfarne—that quintessentially romantic coastal castle—but the difficulties of following the shoreline round Budle Bay, Ross Back Sands and Fenham Flats proved almost insuperable. Dangerous mud and quicksands, treacherous tides, a lack of rights-of-way and a resolution to resist large stretches of road walking, all conspired against a satisfactory pedestrian route beyond Bamburgh. Visit Lindisfarne on a separate occasion and enjoy this walk for its uncomplicated splendour and interest.

Most will consider the route too long for one day, so overnight accommodation will be required around Craster/Embleton/Newton-by-the-Sea. Alternatively it makes two fine day walks but in either case transport arrangements will need to be made as the walk is not circular. In all but the most benign summer weather, you should go prepared for chill winds. In the holiday season there are plenty of refreshment places along the way but a winter expedition is less favoured.

It all begins at Warkworth Castle, built originally as a motte and bailey on a hill above the River Coquet. It emerges into the light of history in AD 737 when Ceowulf, King of Northumbria, bestowed it on the monastic community of Lindisfarne. Little is known

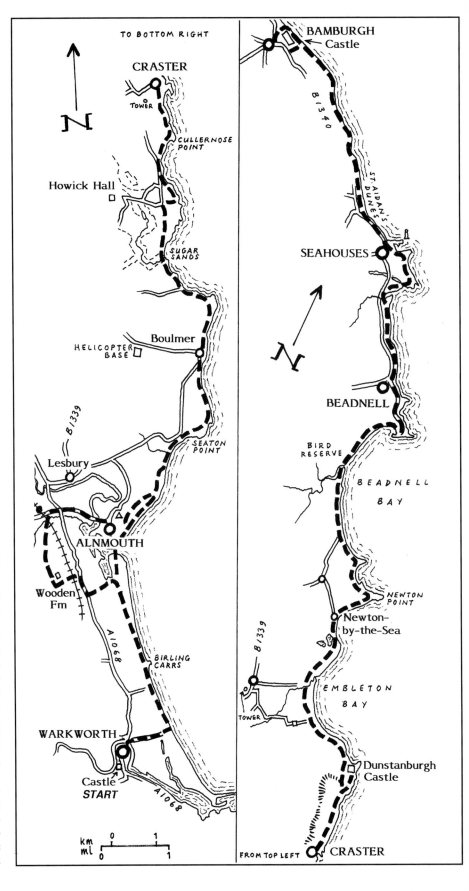

about the ninth century, other than raids by the Danes who burned and plundered the monasteries, laying much of the country waste.

During the twelfth century a stone curtain wall was constructed and the stronghold passed to Roger FitzRichard whose descendants held it for nearly 200 years, defending it against the Scots. In 1332 the great Percy family took over. It was the third Percy, Lord of Warkworth and a central figure in the general history of England at that time, along with his son Harry Hotspur—hero of the battles of Otterburn and Homildon Hill—who conspired against Henry IV whom they had previously helped gain the throne. The conspiracy led to the death of Hotspur at Shrewsbury in 1403 and to the King besieging Warkworth Castle in 1405, battering it into submission with cannon fire. Three scenes from Shakespeare's *Henry IV, Part 1* take place here at Warkworth, 'this worm-eaten hold of ragged stone where Hotspur's father, old Northumberland, lies crafty-sick'.

In Tudor times, through the changing fortunes of the Percy family, the castle remained in good repair, but by the late 1500s it had succumbed to systematic plundering by Sir John Forster, Warden of the Middle Marches, and was semi-ruinous. More damage was suffered throughout the seventeenth century, the building's fabric being robbed for lead and timber and abandoned to the elements; it was even used as a fold for farm livestock. Around the mid-1800s the fourth Duke of Northumberland had the keep repaired and made partially habitable and in 1922 the eighth Duke passed the castle to the Commissioners of HM Works. English Heritage have managed the ruin since 1984.

Standing atop the ancient motte, the hugely impressive keep dominates all. It dates from the early 1400s and is designed on the pattern of a Greek cross, though later altered and restored. Much of the ruin seems surprisingly intact, so that when you enter its interior spaces there is an immediate transition from daylight to shadows and shafts of light thrown into the stone-cool darkness by small windows; outside are fragmentary views to Amble and across the lawned bailey, or courtyard.

Once entered across a drawbridge and defended by timber balconies, the gatehouse is a magnificent example of Early English military architecture. On three sides of the bailey, ruined buildings (originally two or more storeys high) cling to the curtain wall. Other features include a chapel, the solar (private chamber), Carrickfergus Tower, the Great Hall, a buttery, pantry and kitchen, Lion Tower, Grey Mair's Tower and the superb keep itself. To accompany your tour of the castle, I recommend purchasing a copy of English Heritage's guide booklet.

Day 1—Warkworth to Craster (13 miles / 21km)

You set off from the castle by walking down Warkworth's main street—the distractingly busy A1068—beside which stand various shops, pubs, tea rooms and bed-and-breakfast establishments. The village sits in a loop of the River Coquet and until the fairly recent addition of a modern road bridge, all traffic had to pass through the fourteenth-century fortified bridge tower—one of very few in the entire country.

Across the river you take a rising lane on the right, 50 yards along the A1068, which heads directly past a caravan park and through dunes to the seashore of golden sand. Progress north is now straightforward, your actual line past Birling Carrs depending on the state of the tide. Ahead, the River Aln's mouth is fordable $1\frac{1}{2}$ hours either side of low water in normal conditions: forget this option in rough seas or after heavy rain! From the National Trust's Buston Links, the inland route cuts left up a lane past the old harbour—once an important grain port before a severe storm in 1806 separated Church Hill from the rest of Alnmouth and destroyed the church. At the main coast road you walk right for 550 yards (500m) then left over a railway crossing to Wooden Farm. A field path takes you downhill, under the railway, over a stream and up to houses near Alnmouth Station.

A circuitous but scenic riverside path loops north through Lesbury, but many walkers opt for half a mile or so along the B1338 to Alnmouth. Here, as at Warkworth, you will find hotels, refreshment places and a few shops. Down at the duny foreshore you can either continue north-east along the beach and over Marden Rocks, or climb the brackeny ridge for superb coastal views. Warkworth Castle and Amble are both in sight, with Coquet Island looking for all the world like a supertanker, its lighthouse the bridge!

Round Seaton Point you are walking over sandstone slabs or channels of sand then crunching in across a bouldery, shell-littered beach to the grassy back-shore at Boulmer. Don't be surprised by the clatter of helicopters: Boulmer, a mile ($1\frac{1}{2}$km) inland, is an RAF Rescue Base. Rock-girt Boulmer Haven is backed by a straggle of buildings, among them the Fishing Boat pub, a diminutive post office and the erstwhile lifeboat station (closed in 1968 and now used by a volunteer service). As befits a remote, exposed settlement, Boulmer has a long tradition of smuggling and lifesaving.

A succession of bays and rock pavements on this wild, flat edge of land bring you past a lane-end car park to Sugar Sands at the mouth of Howick Burn. If the tide is high you can take the path along low cliffs and there is a delightful woodland walk inland to Howick Hall. It was built in 1782 on the site of the medieval Howick Tower, first mentioned in 1415 when owned by an Emeric Hering and described as 'a little pile a mile from the shore'. The present hall was rebuilt in 1926 following a serious fire.

Erosion has undermined the onward cliff path, necessitating a detour inland, but if you can walk the beach you will pass a large aperture in the rocks called Rumbling Kern. Just beyond stands a Victorian bathing house, built by the Grey family above a rectangular pool. Over Cullernose Point the path passes Black Hole, ducks round Hole o' the Dyke and enters Craster by a children's play area. This final mile or so is a geologist's dream—complex exposures of the earth's skeleton in the form of yellow sandstones, contorted grey limestone and hard, columnar dolerite are all spectacular at low tide.

Heughs—low hills to the north and south—afford some protection for Craster's dark-stoned cottages. A natural anchorage here, created by a geological fault, was reinforced in 1906 by two substantial jetties from which locally quarried whinstone was exported for road-building—specifically as kerbstones for London streets. Craster's oak-smoked kippers enjoy a wide reputation but nowadays local catches are supplemented by imports from western Scotland. Cobles still fish for lobster and the pots form picturesque stacks on the quayside.

Half a mile ($\frac{3}{4}$km) west of the village stands Craster Tower, now part of a private residence. It is first mentioned in a list of fortifications compiled in 1415 and its masonry has withstood the passage of time well. Rectangular in shape, two storeys high and with a vaulted basement, its crowning battlements are a modern addition.

Day 2—Craster to Bamburgh (13 miles / 21km)

There are no complications in the northward leg from Craster. A well-trodden path over close-cropped turf leads pleasantly for just over a mile ($1\frac{1}{2}$km) to Dunstanburgh Castle. 'Surpassing all other Northumbrian castles in the grandeur of its site, it alone abides as a castle should abide in all the majesty of a shattered ruin,' wrote Freeman. Being remote from population centres (and a mile even from the nearest modern road) there is indeed a sense in which Dunstanburgh Castle remained aloof from the mainstream of historical conflicts in Northumbria and has since escaped the distracting presence of neighbouring buildings.

The site—the largest in the county—occupies 10 acres. Its history begins in 1313 when Thomas, Earl of Lancaster ordered a castle to be built on this prominent knoll of basalt—part of the same Whin Sill along whose outcroppings further west Emperor Hadrian built his great defensive wall almost 1200 years earlier. Following the Battle of Boroughbridge in 1322, the Earl was executed for treason and custody of the castle changed several times as an English stronghold against the Scots. A tower and gatehouse were added by John de Lilburn and John o' Gaunt respectively and at that time a small port existed in a natural inlet to the south, now a marshy depression crossed by the path.

During the Wars of the Roses, the castle changed hands twice but eventually lost any strategic importance it might have had and by 1550 had deteriorated 'in wonderful great decaye' (Sir Robert Bowes). Despite its exposed position and over five centuries of neglect, the ruin is astonishingly imposing. Much of the keep and outer walls are standing, while outlying towers mark the fortress's original perimeter. Its profile, defiantly romantic against an often frowning Northumbrian sky and immortalised in water colours by none other than J.M.W. Turner in the mid-nineteenth century, is still capable of stirring the imagination.

A path leads up to the entrance (English Heritage), or you can skirt behind the castle promontory beneath John o' Gaunt's gateway and Lilburn Tower to the north side where sheer cliffs of black, guano-smeared volcanic rock form an unassailable natural defence.

Wide sands or a dune path via golf links round Embleton Bay pass by Embleton Tower, situated a mile (1½km) inland. A typical 'vicar's peel tower', it was erected in 1395 following a particularly destructive Scottish raid on Embleton.

The way crosses Embleton Burn (perhaps by the Skaith footbridge), passes chalets and Newton Pool Bird Reserve and reaches Newton-by-the-Sea. Its pretty grass square flanked by a pub, cafe and low-built fishermen's cottages is set above tilted beds of dark limestone, from which a field path takes you out round Newton Point. Atop its columnar cliffs there are dramatic views back to the brooding, ragged silhouette of Dunstanburgh Castle, 2 miles (3km) away across Embleton Bay.

Secluded sands and planes of pungent, weed-covered rock stretch out from Football Hole bay and suddenly you are past Snook

Point at the threshold of Beadnell Bay. Should the tide prevent beach walking, there is a dune path right along to Beadnell Bay Caravan Park and Beadnell Harbour. Sandstone boulders form intriguing rock pools seaward of the massive masonry piers enclosing Beadnell's tiny anchorage and the bay is popular with watersports enthusiasts. What at first appears as a towered and arched fortress backing the harbour is in fact a cluster of eighteenth-century limekilns, impeccably preserved by the National Trust.

Beadnell village, a shade farther north, contains the remnants of a sixteenth-century, three-storey peel tower now incorporated in the Craster Arms pub. The original vaulted basement is used as a beer-cellar while the restored eighteenth-century exterior bears the Craster family coat of arms.

Two miles (3km) north of Beadnell, you skirt the cliff edge at Braidcarr Point to approach Seahouses' harbour basin with its quayside fish boxes, crab pots, floats and ropes, its net-mending, the coming and going of craft and its colourful ticket stalls for trips to the Farne Islands. Offshore the Whin Sill affirms its resistance to marine erosion by forming a group of low islands some 7½sq. miles (19km²) in extent. Sea birds and grey seals breed prolifically there, attracting trippers by the thousand during the summer season. Landing is allowed on Inner Farne (or Farne Island) upon which was built another border peel tower, with associated chapel and well dedicated to St Cuthbert. The tower held a coal-fired beacon, kindled nightly for many years to warn shipping off the islands.

Once more the route forward lies along apparently limitless sands or through St Aidan's dunes past Greenhill Rocks. Bamburgh Castle looms—a veritable fortress city when seen from seaward. Its position on the Whin

Sill is virtually impregnable and is thought to date back to Roman times.

Ida, King of Northumberland, constructed a timber stronghold here in AD 547, the complex taking its name from Bebba, wife of his grandson Ethelfrith—hence 'Bebban burgh'. Raided and plundered twice by the Danes in the tenth century, the fortress slid into decline until eventually rebuilt by Henry I who added a stone keep. It played an active role in the border wars but was never as strategically vital as nearby Alnwick Castle. In the seventeenth century it passed from James I to the Forster family who were obliged to sell their assets after a period of reckless extravagance ending in bankruptcy. In 1704, Bamburgh Castle was purchased by Lord Crewe, Bishop of Durham, who established a trust so that restoration work begun by him could continue after his death.

In the late nineteenth century, objections were raised at the castle's use as a girls' school. Drainpipes, smoke cowls and fake battlements, it was argued, detracted from the building's historical dignity. It was soon acquired by the Tyneside inventor Lord Armstrong and restored at great cost, though because of his personal whims much architectural authenticity was lost. Today it is divided into apartments but is open to the public and contains much of interest, including an old 150ft (46m) well and the original keep walls up to 11ft (3½m) thick.

So imposing is the castle, so completely does it monopolise the skyline, that you might be forgiven for overlooking Bamburgh village. However, this delightful community of eighteenth-century cottages, tasteful shops, a few hotels and refreshment places is well worth exploring. Not to be missed is the little Grace Darling Museum and, opposite, her memorial in the thirteenth-century St Aidan's churchyard.

Bamburgh Castle—a city fortress when viewed from seaward.

Facing page **Housesteads Fort. These granary floor supports are just part of an intensely evocative and well preserved site.**

WALK 12: *NORTHUMBRIA—Hadrian's Wall*

Exploring the most spectacular central section of Britain's most famous Roman monument. The path is clear throughout but contains numerous gradients, some steep, and the open Northumbrian landscape is exposed to wind and weather. **Start:** Housesteads car park and information centre. **Finish:** Greenhead. **Distance:** 10½ miles (17km)—allow at least 5 hours. **Location/Access:** Both Housesteads and Greenhead are connected by the B6318 which runs north of the A69 Newcastle-upon-Tyne to Carlisle road. Nearest railway stations—Bardon Mill and Haltwhistle. **Map:** OS Landranger Sheet 86.

In AD43, Emperor Claudius initiated the long-expected invasion of Britain and a succession of military governors consolidated the conquest which was to leave an indelible mark on the country's history. The Roman army, consisting of some 50,000 men organised in 25–30 legions, was the largest, as well as the first, long-service professional army in the world. Iron Age Britons, resourceful and skilful though they were—in the south at least—proved no match for the disciplined Roman forces who advanced north and west.

Despite steady progress and the systematic building of straight roads to London, it was not until AD78 or thereabouts that the army had destroyed the independent power of the tribes of northern England and Wales. Julius Agricola reached the Tyne–Solway line before AD80, pushing forward to the Forth–Clyde and further still into the mountains where he eventually defeated the Caledonian tribes at a place called Mons Graupius (corrupted by a sixteenth-century scholar to Grampian and thereafter applied to the whole range of Scottish Highland mountains).

The imperial government regarded the Highlands as difficult and unprofitable and no attempt was made to exploit the region. Instead, troops were withdrawn, military expansion abandoned and the northern boundary of the empire was controlled by a fortified road—the Stanegate—between Carlisle and Corbridge.

In AD122, already Emperor for five years, Hadrian visited Britain with his friend Platorius Nepos. Anxious to establish a clear border in this far-flung outpost, he ordered a great defensive wall to be built against the still troublesome northern tribes. It would run 76 miles (122km) from Wallsend on the Tyne to Bowness-on-Solway and would be constructed by professional legionary craftsmen of the II Augusta, VI Victrix and XX Valeria Victrix legions under the governorship of Nepos. Guard posts (milecastles) and watch towers (turrets) were to be incorporated and a signalling system established, with defences, for 40 miles (64km) down the Cumbrian coast. During construction, Nepos decided to add forts at regular intervals to facilitate the deployment of troops, and a second ditch—the *Vallum*—was dug behind and parallel to the Wall to define and secure a military zone.

By about AD130 the Wall had been finished, though it was much later before turf sections in the west were replaced with stone. In accordance with the policy of the new Emperor Antonius Pius, a second push was made into Scotland and in AD142 the turf-built Antonine Wall was completed 85 miles (137km) further north. A few decades later,

however, this northern line was permanently abandoned in the face of continuing hostility and Hadrian's Wall remained the official frontier of Roman Britain for the next 200 years.

Ultimately, of course, the Roman way of life disintegrated when Saxons, Scots and Picts launched concerted attacks on Britain during the second half of the fourth century. A long period of peace thus ended in terror and uncertainty, and although repairs to the by-then damaged Wall were effected, Roman troops were gradually withdrawn from the country and pleas for help by Romano-British townships fell on deaf ears. In AD410, the Goths took Rome and Britain effectively ceased to be part of the Roman Empire, even though it remained Roman in culture, economy and sympathy.

Although its entire course can still be traced, much of the Wall has been lost beneath the streets of Newcastle and the eighteenth-century military road, and its stone has been stolen for farm building. By far the most rewarding section for walkers lies either side of the approximate halfway point within the Northumberland National Park. Sites along the remainder of the Wall can readily be explored by car or by separate outings on foot. Public transport is not helpful in providing a return to the start of this linear route, but you are never far from the B6318 and there are several intermediate vehicle access points in addition to the start and finish car parks. The Wall runs across wild, open countryside, so go equipped for hill walking and be prepared for numerous ups and downs and rugged underfoot conditions.

Housesteads (Vercovicium) is one of the most visited sites on the Roman Wall. The hilltop fort—laid out to the customary rectangular plan with rounded corners—is reached from the National Trust car park/museum/information centre by half a mile (¾km) of stony track. The approach slopes would have been built over by the *vicus*, a dense cluster of dwellings, shops, storehouses, inns and workshops in which the families of Roman soldiers lived, along with local tradespeople and passing visitors. Tickets are purchased at the Visitor Centre which also contains models and archaeological finds. You enter the fort through the South Gate, though the main entrance was originally the east gateway of dressed stone, closed by double wooden doors turning in still-visible pivot holes. All the Wall forts were built to a standard pattern, but each has particular features of interest today. Housestead's gateways flanked by guardrooms, its granary floor supports and its well-preserved latrine system are all easily recognisable

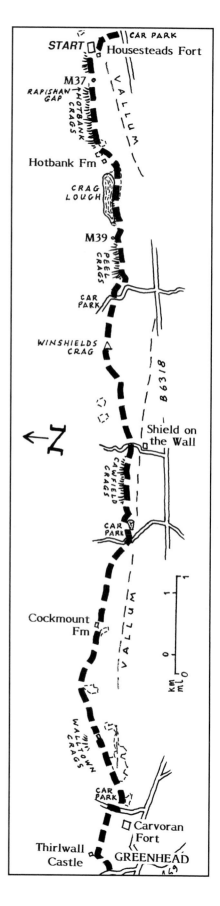

provided you know what to look for: a guide booklet is well worth purchasing and will greatly enrich your visit by filling in detail more comprehensively than this book is able to.

I found Housesteads immensely impressive despite the presence of many visitors and the incongruous tarmac pathways. Sufficient masonry remains for one's imagination to be nudged into visualising how the fort would once have looked, while the sweeping infinities of the Northumbrian landscape readily evoke images of raids by barbaric tribesmen, repulsed by the ordered military efficiency of Roman legionaries during the Wall's operational years.

You leave through the West Gate and climb on to the much-trodden Wall top (probably a mere third of its original height) at the north-west corner. Housesteads Wood leads easily to Milecastle 37 and many non-walking visitors return from here via the Military Way through fields. Dropping then climbing—a process that becomes second nature on this walk!—you next traverse Cuddy's Crags and are treated to a definitive view of the Wall switchbacking east over the crest of the Whin Sill. This ridge of hard, volcanic rock outcrops right across northern England and gave Hadrian more than a head start in his defensive plan. Even without the Wall, the Whin Sill scarp would be considered a dramatic landscape feature. Its stone was too hard for the Roman builders to work, the Wall itself being formed from sandstone or limestone blocks.

Before long you reach Rapishaw Gap where the Pennine Way strikes off north into the border forests after having followed the Wall east from Greenhead. About 400 yards (350m) to the south stands an old limekiln magnificently restored by the National Trust. Going steeply upwards, the path takes you over Hotbank Crags (1074/327m), with wide views in

all directions taking in nearby lakes, or 'loughs'. As you drop south-west with the fall of the slope, another classic view unfolds. Beyond Hotbank Farm near the site of Milecastle 38, Crag Lough appears, frowned upon by sheer rock faces. Like some vast breaking wave, the distant crest of Winshields peaks against the sky.

Throughout much of the walk, the Roman Wall, still shoulder-high, snakes beside you over natural undulations in the ground. Today, erosion threatens its fabric just as the careless removal of stone for sundry building purposes did in earlier centuries, and we are often requested to use the flanking path rather than the walltop itself.

There is a good stretch of *Vallum* visible nearby. In addition to a sizeable ditch north of the Wall (an added defensive obstacle), this ditch to the south defined the edge of army territory. There were crossings at intervals to monitor civilian access, and between it and the Wall ran a Military Way along which troops and supplies were moved.

From Milking Gap you climb through mixed woods above the steely waters of Crag Lough. These stretches of open water are remnants of glacial meltwater from after the last Ice Age some 12,000 years ago. Plant growth is slowly encroaching and it seems likely that the loughs will one day become mere marshy depressions. Crag Lough supports waterfowl and trout, while farther along, Highshield Crags are well known among rock-climbers. Indeed, the exposed edge provides walkers with vertiginous glimpses down as formidable a natural barrier as could be imagined.

Through the abrupt descent to Sycamore Gap, excavations reveal the Wall's broad, original foundations, foundations that in fact were never used. The next gap contains the recently excavated Milecastle 39, known as Castle Nick,

then a sharp pull-up leads to Peel Crags where a fine stretch of wall, restored in 1910, accompanies temporarily easier walking. Repetitive descents through gaps such as these demonstrate graphically how ice and meltwater found weaknesses in the otherwise resistant Whin Sill basalt during 2 million years of the Ice Age. Softer limestones and sandstones were eroded away in the process, leaving the pronounced scarp we see today.

From Peel Crags an exceptionally steep path, provided with steps, gives way to Peel Gap where the Wall was being rebuilt at my last visit. Here you veer up right to the National Trust's Steel Rigg car park, cross the road, and tackle a gentle gradient towards Winshields Crag. As you climb beside the Wall, the mind can ponder just how labour-intensive the careful dressing of all those stone blocks must have been!

At 1132ft (345m) above sea level, Winshields Crag, the highest summit on the Roman Wall, is in view for several miles in both directions. From its OS pillar on heather-clad ground, views are wonderfully extensive: on a clear day you can see from Cross Fell to the Cheviots, from the Solway Firth to the North Sea. Hardy black Galloway cattle and Blackface or Swaledale sheep dot a landscape of hilly pasture, field patterns and dark edges of forestry plantations—it is a spectacular, if breezy, place at which to savour the essence of walking Hadrian's Wall. A conspicuous sign directs walkers south to Winshields for bed and breakfast or camping and it is not much further to the Once Brewed youth hostel and the Vindolanda Museum.

Hadrian reincarnate . . . ?!

After the next gap, Wall and path descend to cross a minor road near Shield on the Wall Farm, then surmount the rugged Cawfields Crags and drop past Milecastle 42 to the old quarry lake at Cawfields car park and picnic site. Conveniently close to the B6318 and Haltwhistle railway station, this would be a sensible place to call a halt if a further 4½ miles (7km) seems too much. A refreshment van is usually present during holiday periods.

Beyond the road, you pass the fragmentary remains of Aesica fort. The path itself is on the Military Way to Cockmount Farm. For a time the wall is an English one but built mainly of Roman stones. Once uphill past Milecastle 44 you are atop Walltown Crags (also known as the Nine Nicks of Thirlwall) and are nearing Walltown where a turning on the right brings you to the recently opened Roman Army Museum on the site of Carvoran fort. Various audio-visual displays interpret the Roman invasion and daily life for the legionaries. There are a car park, toilets and refreshments.

By pursuing the lane westwards to Walltown, you will encounter one of the finest stretches of the Wall—up to 12 courses high in places, though Greenhead Quarry has destroyed its continuation. Keeping to the route of the Pennine Way, you now lose height beside the well-defined ditch to reach the romantically crumbling ruin of Thirlwall Castle, a fourteenth-century peel tower built using Roman stones on a little green hill overlooking the tree-fringed Tipalt Burn. Alas, the Wall itself has vanished almost without trace here, its valuable ready-fashioned blocks plundered mercilessly over the intervening centuries.

You have reached the boundary of the Northumberland National Park, as well as the busy A69 trunk road between Carlisle and Newcastle. An hourly bus service might be of interest—otherwise the Greenhead Hotel will provide a welcome drink or meal after a surprisingly strenuous outing!

Facing page **A retrospective panorama from near Thornthwaite Crag. To the right of the humpy Yoke-Ill Bell-Froswick ridge lie the Troutbeck valley and distant Windermere; to the left, Kentmere.**

Recently excavated Milecastle 39, at Castle Nick, occupies one of several gaps in the Whin Sill formed during the Ice Age.

WALK 13: *CUMBRIA—The High Street Roman Road*

A long, high-level fell walk in the steps of Roman legions. Considerable ups and downs and exposed to wind and weather, though the way is clear on the ground. **Start:** Troutbeck. **Finish:** Pooley Bridge. **Distance:** 16 miles (26km)—allow a full day. **Location/Access:** Troutbeck lies approximately 3 miles (5km) north of Windermere; nearest railway station—Windermere. Pooley Bridge stands at the northern end of Ullswater just east of the A592; nearest railway station—Penrith. **Map:** OS Landranger Sheet 90.

Following their invasion of northern England around AD78–9, the Romans reinforced the Cumbrian coast with a line of forts, constituting a logical extension to Hadrian's Wall. Ravenglass (Glannoventa), built about AD130 and the most important coastal fortification, might well have been intended as a naval base from which an invasion of Ireland could be mounted. Only the Bath House has been excavated (in 1831), but the site is clearly impressive, with walls still standing some 12ft (3½m) high. There is ample evidence that the garrison enjoyed sophisticated standards of sanitation and comfort.

Rome's interest in Cumbria was an almost exclusively military one and their establishment of forts connected by road through difficult country demonstrates extraordinary levels of surveying and engineering skill. From Ravenglass they drove a troop and supply line right through the heart of the Lake District via their fort at Hardknott Pass to Wrynose Pass and the fort at Ambleside (Galava). Undaunted by the fells that lay between there and the fort at Brougham (Brocavum), the road was taken up to and along the High Street ridge, maintaining a height of 2000ft (610m) or thereabouts for 12 miles (19km) and reaching 2700ft

(823m) at its loftiest point.

Here and there the original roadway construction—a raised central section flanked by ditches—is still evident. By walking in the footsteps of the Roman legions, you do begin to grasp the scale of this civil engineering feat, which spanned a total of 25 miles (40km) of mixed terrain with a firm, durable surface.

In many places the old road has disappeared beneath modern development and there is some speculation as to the precise line it takes at either end of the High Street ridge. It seems likely that it left Ambleside via Jenkin Crag and High Skelghyll to Troutbeck, crossing the beck

57

at Ing Bridge and rising beside Hagg Gill to Scot Rake and Thornthwaite Crag. However, it might equally have crossed Trout Beck just south of the present squat old church and ascended the slopes of Sour Howes towards the Garburn Pass, here swinging north along the Yoke–Ill Bell–Froswick ridge to Thornthwaite Crag. Characteristically, both lines seem more intent on northward progress than visiting summits *en route*, all of which are by-passed.

Because it makes an infinitely more exhilarating hike in the early stages, I have opted to follow the higher line. Some claim that views are superior when walking north–south, but one usually stops to take in the scenery; the wind is more likely to be at your back when walking north. A good circular route could be made by visiting High Street summit along one path and returning by the other.

The described route is linear, so unless you are backpacking or have arranged accommodation at either end you will need the co-operation of a non-participating driver to set you down and pick you up. There is little shelter from the weather so choose a fine day for this magnificent tramp: in mist much of its charm is lost and you may need to navigate carefully over the middle section.

A short way south of the river bridge at Troutbeck (map reference 413027), a lane leaves the A592, climbing past The Howe then doubling back as a stony, walled track northeast up the fellside above the big Limefitt Park caravan and camping site. The Ill Bell ridge beckons invitingly ahead.

Where the ground eases you swing off left up to the ridge line which sharpens as you approach Yoke, the first summit. The way stays west of the highest point, continuing as a down-and-up to Ill Bell. There are sweeping views into the wild upper recesses of Kentmere with its diminutive reservoir.

West of Froswick the path drops again then begins to converge with the track up Scot Rake and before long you have reached Thornthwaite Crag, one of the premier viewpoints on the entire walk and crowned by a splendid beacon cairn. Behind you to the south, the humpy ridge just ascended falls gently to the Troutbeck valley and distant Windermere, more precipitously east to Kentmere. Renowned since the early days of hill walking, the panorama takes in almost all the major Lakeland fells, from Black Combe to Saddleback, both Harter Fells, Scafell and the Pikes to name but a few.

Roman roads are not noted for their elevation, but the beeline a shade east of north offered by the High Street ridge must have seemed irresistible to those early engineers who

so liked to get from A to B in as straight a line as possible.

There is a gentle climb now, shadowing a wall but traversing below High Street summit which is marked by an OS pillar at 2717ft (828m) above sea level. The top is actually a smooth, nearly flat plateau known as Racecourse Hill upon which, in the old days, shepherds would assemble each year to exchange lost sheep. Such occasions drew in other dales folk too who would engage in wrestling contests, feasting, drinking and dancing, and horse-racing—welcome relief no doubt after winters confined to the low ground. Such annual fair days and shepherds' meets eventually transferred to pubs in neighbouring dales and the High Street venue was abandoned in 1835.

Straight and true, the Roman road takes you north downhill towards the Straights of Riggindale, a dramatic constriction in the ridge which allows you to gaze into corrie depths at the implacable faces of Haweswater and Hayeswater. The surroundings could hardly be wilder or lonelier and one wonders how Roman legionaries felt on their marches across a bleak upland landscape so markedly different from their balmy Mediterranean homeland.

Forking right up over Rampsgill Head (the left fork descends via Angle Tarn to Patterdale) and west of High Raise, the latter only 85ft (26m) lower than High Street itself, a profound sense prevails of walking on a high-level promenade fringed by shattered crags and plummeting drops. Soon, however, height is lost with gathering consistency, interrupted by a short rise to Wether Hill (skirted to the west as all the tops have been) and a descent to a broad saddle. Along this stretch, the road's central 'agger' *(raised section)* is clearly visible.

Two possible Roman road lines diverge from Loadpot Hill, one heading north-east towards Askham, the other—favoured by tradition and by Alfred Wainwright—leading west of the fell and out over Moor Divock. We take the latter, accompanied by superb views of Ullswater, down the long flank of Barton Fell to the head of Elder Beck. Here again the side-ditched roadway is well seen.

The abundance of tumuli, ancient cairns and stone circles on Moor Divock bear witness to a civilisation considerably pre-dating the Roman occupation. There is one such stone circle (the Cockpit) just right of the path beyond Elder Beck, its sarsens tilted or half buried in turf. The whole area, almost flat and confusing in mist, is worth exploring at your leisure on another occasion.

Ahead, High Street continues as a public right-of-way as far as Celleron, then onwards

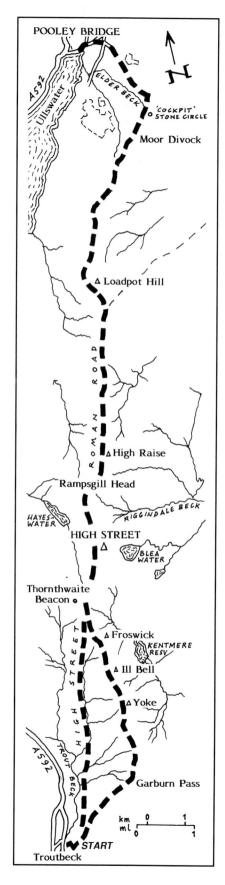

to Tirril but there the certainty ends. Medieval Brougham Castle, near the site of Brocavum fort, stands less than 3 miles (5km) north-east across the M6. It commanded the bridge over the River Eamont and controlled the junction of the principal Roman road from York to Carlisle with the secondary road—that just walked along—to Ambleside, Hard Knott and Ravenglass. The name Brougham is thought to be a corruption of *brokaven*—Celtic for home of the badgers.

Five hundred yards (450m) north from the Cockpit, you meet a stony track and follow it left. Lower down, signs of civilisation—the first since leaving Troutbeck—increase as campsite and road give way to the fleshpots of Pooley Bridge at the northern extremity of Ullswater.

Brougham Castle, near the site of Brocavum Fort—a strategic stronghold in Roman times.

WALK 14: *YORKSHIRE DALES—A Lead Mining Trail*

Rugged paths and tracks over the moors past numerous relics of the lead-mining industry. Few navigational difficulties but rough underfoot. **Start/Finish:** Gunnerside. **Distance:** Short route—4½ miles (7km); longer route—9 miles (14½km). Allow 3 and 6 hours respectively. **Location/Access:** Gunnerside lies on the B6270 moor road between Richmond and Kirkby Stephen. Nearest railway station—Settle. **Map:** OS Landranger Sheet 92.

Facing page **Exploring the Sir Francis (Denys) Mine. The open wound of North Hush still disfigures the moorland slopes opposite.**

Below **Walkers at the ruins of Blakethwaite Smelt Mill, set in a high fold of the hills.**

Lead is well known for its uses in roofing and pipes, in coffins and pigments. Evidence in the form of 30 or so ingots (or pigs) suggests that lead was mined as far back as Roman times, though the earliest dated workings—small hand-hewn tunnels—belong to the seventeenth century. Until 'black powder' (gunpowder) and other new techniques were developed from the eighteenth century onwards, mining methods had remained unchanged for centuries.

During the eighteenth and nineteenth centuries, Britain was the world's main producer, with new uses emerging alongside traditional ones: crystal glass manufacture, lead pottery glazes, metal enamelling, paints, pastes and waterproofing—even, horrifyingly, the whitening of bread! Cheaper imports from Spain and later Australia, along with the exhaustion of the best veins, caused a collapse of the British industry and few mines survived into the twentieth century.

Lead is a difficult ore to deal with. Lacking the regularity of coal seams, its extraction was always considered an 'adventure'. Deposits are found in all the upland regions of Britain. Most were formed between 230 and 180 million years ago and are particularly common in limestone, whose fault-line fissures filled with solutions containing minerals and heavy metals which crystallised to form mineral ores.

Since these intrusions are linked with older, mountain-building rocks, they usually occur in faults or joints where the rock has been folded and cracked. Veins are thus typically near-vertical, extending to a great depth but perhaps only a few hundred metres long with a width measured in inches—so-called 'ribbon' deposits. Concentrations of lead varied dramatically and a vein could as easily shrink suddenly to a negligible size as 'belly out' into a large mass. Prospecting and working the valuable ore was the most unpredictable of occupations: lives were spent in unhealthy discomfort anticipating the discovery of a rich vein.

The exact origins, formation and deposition

of ores is a complex subject which demands further specialist reading. Relics of the lead-mining industry itself, however, are far more accessible. There are ruined buildings and installations, heaps of spoil, adits, 'hushes' and dams, and a plethora of tracks and pathways along which miners once tramped from home or lodging to the mine site. Armed with a little knowledge and properly equipped for a hike in the hills, a walker can piece together a remarkably vivid picture—at least of the surface workings and processes if not of conditions underground.

Important lead deposits have been found in the Mendips, the Peak and Lake districts, the northern Pennines and Devon and Cornwall. Scotland, too, had lead mines, as did many parts of Wales, while significant extraction also took place on the Isle of Man. Of all these areas, the Pennines offer some of the most extensive mining remains combined with superlative upland scenery. The mining field (a collective term for a mass of veins) around Swaledale and Arkengarthdale in the Yorkshire Dales is particularly rewarding for the walker-cum-industrial archaeologist and the following route takes in some of its most fascinating sights.

Gunnerside nestles to the south of sheltering hillsides in one of Swaledale's most picturesque reaches. It is not a pretty place in the sense that a Cotswold or Devon village often is, but its huddled cottages and its valley meadows held within a matrix of drystone walls and barns possess a functional beauty of their own.

As lead miners won increasing quantities of ore from the neighbouring fells, Gunnerside prospered. The London Lead Company, remembered for its benevolence, granted small-holdings to its miners and helped build cottages on the edge of the moor. With a cow, a pig, sheep-grazing rights and a few acres of land to tend, life contained some healthy outdoor activity to offset the strain of work underground. Cottages and large tracts of intake land still characterise the moorscape north of the village. By the end of the nineteenth century, the industry's fortunes had waned and Gunnerside's population shrank to a modest farming community. In recent years the area has enjoyed something of a revival as visitors flock to Swaledale for its magnificent walking and scenic drives.

For those with limited time or walking range, a short route returns from Blakethwaite Smelt Mill back along the west side of Gunnerside Gill—a total distance of some $4\frac{1}{2}$ miles (7km). The longer route (9 miles/$14\frac{1}{2}$km) strikes off east over the moors and down past the famous Old Gang ruins to Surrender

Bridge, thence by field paths and lanes round the southern flanks of Brownsey Moor back to Gunnerside.

You begin by taking a path along the east bank of Gunnerside Gill and turning right up steps at some cottages. The paved pathway leads pleasantly alongside a bouldery curve in the gill to a bifurcation: straight ahead weaves on through woods, while up to the right a parallel trod takes a higher line through fields and past barns. Either way you soon arrive at a widening of the valley adjacent to old spoil heaps and ruined ore bunkers—a mere foretaste of what is to come.

From a stile, the path rises as a delightful grassy track above the intake wall. Views open out at last and the wild moorland scene ahead clearly shows the scars of its industrial rape. Directly opposite, pale orange rivers of spoil flow down from fellside workings. Before long you reach extensive ruins on a terrace well above the beck.

Known as the Sir Francis (Denys) Level, this was one of many trial levels driven to explore new ground or to tap existing veins at a greater depth. It began operations in 1864 and represented an historic breakthrough in mining technology. Compressed-air drills were used to force the shaft through hard rock down to about 800 fathoms, or 4800ft (1463m), and an hydraulic engine of 50 horsepower driven by water channelled from the Sun Hush dam worked pumps and a hoist. The Arkengarthdale and Darwent Company (A.D. Co. for

short) constructed a dressing floor here, employing large crushing mills powered by water-wheel. Material extracted from mines by pick, hammer, drill and later gunpowder, was a mixture of galena (lead sulphide), rock and spar called bouse. The incidental minerals—or gangue—included barytes, fluorspar, witherite, zinc, quartz and an ore of iron. At the dressing floor, bouse was first crushed to a suitable size then the galena was separated off by hammer and water-flow to produce a concentrate ready for the smelt mill. Across the beck, the Old Gang Company also had a large dressing plant. By 1880, £32,000 worth of ore had been drawn from this mine, but following a slump in 1882 the levels below Sir Francis were permanently flooded.

The upper path provides a grandstand view of the extent to which lead-mining transformed the upper reaches of Gunnerside Gill. Opposite now, the moor is riven by the vast open wound of North Hush. Surface veins were sometimes exploited by damming water high on the fell then suddenly releasing it in a torrent that ripped away the weathered rock and vegetation. Being denser than the other material, galena washed from the vein was easily collected. This process—hushing—required steep ground and a good supply of water, but the vein could be worked without recourse to underground tunnelling; it was, however, environmentally brutal and the results will never disappear.

Not far ahead the path traverses a grassy

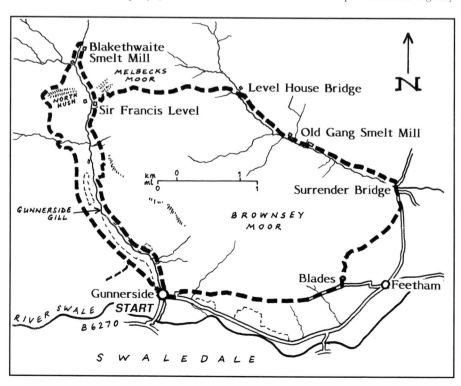

terrace above Blakethwaite Smelt Mill. You could dodge steeply downhill from here, but a more pleasant approach continues to a ruined building, turns left to cross the gill above a waterfall and doubles back south past a well-preserved kiln. Blakethwaite Smelt Mill ruin, set deep in the junction with a ravine-like tributary valley, speaks fluently of the remote and inhospitable locations in which lead miners were obliged to work.

Smelting went through several developmental stages, beginning with small hearths operated by foot bellows in Roman times. Up to the sixteenth century the blast was provided by wind on the shoulders of adjacent hills—bloomeries, or 'baile-hills' in Yorkshire. In principle, concentrated lead ore was subjected to roasting and reducing, the first to burn off sulphur, the second to bring the material into contact with high-temperature charcoal which yielded the liquid metal itself. Later, small vertical furnaces with water-wheel driven bellows were introduced and by the end of the seventeenth century larger reverbatory furnaces—the last major refinement—were running continuously, smelting the ore from a whole group of mines. Masonry-lined flues carried the highly toxic sulphur dioxide gas to hilltop chimneys and sufficient lead, as vapour, condensed within the system for its periodic recovery (fume) to be profitable. Flues induced a strong updraught for the furnaces, as well as protecting the fellsides, with their complement of sheep and cattle, from lead poisoning.

Despite being well visited these days, there is a gaunt, rather melancholy air at Blakethwaite Smelt Mill. Little imagination is required to evoke images of its heyday in the early nineteenth century when this damp fold in the hills echoed to the shouts of workers, the clatter of pack-ponies and the muffled roar of the smelting hearth.

A massive stone slab spans Gunnerside Gill and this is now crossed by those following the shorter option who simply take a rising grassy trackway along the west bank. This soon encounters at close quarters the dramatic gash of North Hush before leading into a jeep track which sweeps straightforwardly south. There are bird's-eye views across to a ravaged landscape of spoil, hushes, ruins and innumerable pathways—a landscape almost entirely despoiled by man's industrious quest for lead a century or more ago. Where the track veers downhill to the right, you strike off left over rough pasture, picking up a path lower down that enters Gunnerside opposite the little car park.

The longer route—for a while on Alfred Wainwright's Coast to Coast Walk—backtracks to about 100 yards before the Sir Francis Mine then slants half-left up over stony wastes. Ascending steadily to the farthest hush, you reach open slopes above and meet a track coming up from Gunnerside. Melbecks Moor presents a sorry sight! Natural grasses and heather have been displaced by an arid desert of gravel and spoil and this stony waste continues to suffer the attentions of heavy machinery as material is reclaimed. The only consolation is a motorable track down which speedy progress on foot is possible. Beyond Level House Bridge over Hard Level Gill, you

Passing old spoil heaps and ruined ore bunkers by Gunnerside Gill.

reach Old Gang Smelt Mill, one of the walk's major highlights.

A good deal of fallen masonry confronts you, but the old chimney still stands, as do the walls of numerous buildings. A vast network of inter-connecting underground levels enabled bouse from many mine workings to be brought out at Old Gang for dressing and smelting—witness the huge tips of debris. A new mill built around 1804 and with greatly increased capacity was fuelled by peat and coal, the latter brought from William Pit on Tan Hill. The ruins are being restored—or at least consolidated—so that their eventual destruction by the elements can be avoided. What a pity it would be if future generations were deprived of these fascinating glimpses into an industrial era gone forever.

In less than a mile of easy walking you arrive at Surrender Bridge, a popular picnic spot in summer on the moor road from Arkengarth-dale to Swaledale. The remains of another large mill which served the Surrender mines can be seen ahead, but our route now turns right up the Feetham road.

After about 500 yards (450m) you can fork off right over pasture and down into Blades hamlet, then take the lane west. Climbing gently across a little stream valley, watch for a track to the right just before the lane drops towards Smarber. Making a beeline for Gun-nerside over Low Row Pasture, the way loses height and enters a lane at Lodge Green, returning you to the start.

It would be wrong to leave this exploratory walk with any romantic illusions about the lives of lead miners and their families. Despite the sense of adventure, mining work was hard and tedious. To reach the levels often involved hundreds of feet of descent on ladders (stemples) and until the advent of explosives after 1700, pick and wedge advanced the cramped workings by mere inches a day. Sur-face workers were little better off. Smelters often developed lead poisoning from fumes, while women and children customarily wound up and dressed the ore—heavy work exposed to the prevalent cold, wet weather for 12 or 13 hours at a time.

Despite the occasional lucky strike by the independent miner whose efforts were almost completely speculative, few fortunes were made until mining became organised and large com-panies began systematic prospecting and mine development. The introduction of horse, water and steam power in the 1800s greatly enhanced production but did little to alleviate the hardships endured by workers. Wages were low and a family's smallholding was often a lifeline when the price of lead dropped.

How starkly such existence compares with our own leisured appraisal of the mining sites!

NOTE: Old mine levels and buildings are potential hazards. It is extremely dangerous to enter the workings and care should be taken near unstable masonry.

Below **Old Gang Smelt Mill.**

Facing page **Twentieth century nostalgia on George Stephenson's 19th century railway line between Pickering and Whitby.**

WALK 15: *NORTH YORK MOORS*
The Grosmont Historical Railway Trail

An easy walk along the disused trackbed of the old Whitby–Pickering railway, returning on field and woodland paths. The North York Moors Railway runs nearby throughout the walk, offering superb views of steam-hauled trains during operating periods. **Start/Finish:** Grosmont station. **Distance:** 6½ miles (10½km)—allow 3–4 hours. **Location/Access:** Grosmont is situated in the North York Moors National Park approximately 6 miles (9½km) south-west of Whitby, and has a station on British Rail's Esk Valley line. **Map:** OS Landranger Sheet 94.

As history goes, our railway system is comparatively 'modern'. Despite roots way back in the early sixteenth century when coal-mining wagons were run along parallel timber planks, the railway age did not really begin until George Stephenson had pioneered steam traction with his locomotive 'Rocket'. The famous Stockton and Darlington Railway of 1825—the world's first public steam railway—was followed by the introduction of timetabled services, a double-track route and rudimentary signalling on the Liverpool and Manchester line which became a huge success in the early 1830s. By the end of that decade, 1500 miles (2414km) of line linked London and the major industrial centres of the Midlands and the North-West. Britain became gripped by 'railway mania'—not dissimilar to the 'canal mania' half a century or so earlier—and the 1840s saw a tripling of track mileage. The railways provided a vital catalyst allowing all the burgeoning energy and enterprise of the Industrial Revolution to reach fruition.

Since those early days, huge advances in railway technology have speeded travel and rendered it safer. However, many amongst us rue the axing of branch lines by Dr Beeching in 1964 and the phasing out of steam: diesel and electric power somehow lack that elemental magic that transforms a machine into a living, breathing presence.

There is also a sense in which the significance of our railways has been displaced by the ubiquitous, convenient, endlessly adaptable internal combustion engine. Understandably, traffic jams, exhaust pollution and the current high cost of rail travel do tempt us to glance back at the days when personal mobility depended more upon the railways and when a train ride was something special. Perhaps this explains the nationwide proliferation of private steam trusts whose mission is to resurrect disused branch lines and rolling stock for the enjoyment of a public apparently hungry for nostalgic experiences of this kind.

Many such lines now operate and walks in their vicinity will usually yield rewarding views of trains in action. One of the best from every point of view is the North York Moors Railway which recommenced passenger services between Grosmont and Pickering in 1973. Not only may walkers alight at stations *en route* to enjoy the adjacent moors, dales and forest, but a special Historical Railway Trail has been established between Grosmont and Goathland. It follows the original trackbed parallel to the improved line, providing vivid insights into the problems of railway construction, as well as magnificent close-up views of steam trains during the seasonal operating periods.

There is a little gentle climbing here and

there, and field paths on the return leg may be muddy in wet weather, but the walk is not a demanding one and you can set any pace you wish. Easiest of all would be to catch a train back to Grosmont from Goathland.

Grosmont's humble origins as the little industrial village of Tunnel date back to around 1836 though ironstone had been worked in the area since medieval times. When navvies tunnelling George Stephenson's Whitby–Pickering line through Lease Rigg in the early 1830s discovered unusually rich deposits of iron ore, Grosmont became a boom town. Early photographic records depict a scene of intense industrial activity and by the 1870s the population had risen to over 1500—five times its present level. Ultimately, cheaper imported iron sounded the industry's death knell and the blast furnaces finally shut down in 1891. Thanks to the railway's proximity, roadstone from the volcanic Whinstone Ridge (or Cleveland Dyke) continued to be quarried until 1950.

Someone had suggested building a canal over the moors between Whitby and Pickering—not such a daft idea as it sounds considering the well-developed state of canal transport and the embryonic nature of railway technology at the time. However, the idea was abandoned in favour of a railway and work began in 1833 under George Stephenson's supervision. Watercourses had to be diverted, valleys bridged and rock blasted away by a veritable army of navvies (the word is derived from the canal 'navigators'), but on 26 May 1836 the 24-mile (39km) track was officially opened. Carriages then were little more than stage-coaches mounted on bogies and for the first 11 years freight and passengers alike were pulled along by horses. Only when George Hudson of York—the so-called 'Railway King'—acquired the line to expand his York and North Midland Railway were steam locomotives introduced.

Steam enthusiasts will happily while away a day watching trains come and go at Grosmont. A museum, engine sheds and rolling stock, and the sights and sounds of steam, all conspire to hold you back from walking! However, you head off from a 'Footpath to Goathland' sign, over the Murk Esk footbridge and up past a schoolroom and St Matthew's Church. Down to your right is the smaller tunnel through which horse-drawn coaches passed and at its far end visitors can view the engine shed from a spectator's gallery. Crossing the railway bridge, you soon reach a superb vantage point back over Grosmont before a left turn leads downhill and alongside the modern track where a miscellany of ageing diesels and trucks are parked, slightly forlorn.

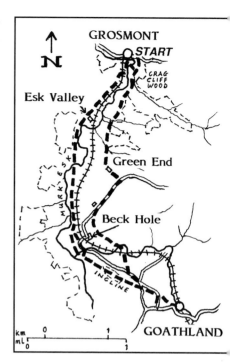

Ahead, the working line diverges left to cross the Murk Esk, leaving the original track to pedestrians who now pass the one-time ironstone miners' hamlet of Esk Valley. Coal and provisions were still brought in on a fortnightly train until 1951 when the old track finally became unusable and local funds were raised to build a motor road.

Farther along the cinder trackbed, meanders in the river are spanned by a steel footbridge, then a path takes you up through Blue Ber Wood—a diversion necessitated by floods in 1930 which swept away a bridge. Back on the trackbed, you cross Eller Beck on giant stepping stones—the residual foundations of yet another bridge—and continue past Beck Hole hamlet.

Beyond Incline Cottage, the 1 in 10 gradient to Goathland proved a persistent headache for the early railway operators. Too steep for horses to deal with, coaches and wagons had to be hauled up by rope (later metal cable) and accidents inevitably occurred. Following a fatality in 1865, a 'deviation line' was blasted and bridged along the steep-sided Eller Beck valley at the then considerable cost of £50,000. In July the first steam train passed through and Beck Hole Incline was abandoned. Today you would scarcely recognise that it ever belonged to a railway, so densely have trees and vegetation colonised the hillside.

After ¾ mile (1.2km) you reach a road not far from Goathland village. In fact, the Historical Railway Trail continues to Goathland Station, built to the standard North East Railway design of the 1860s and little changed since then. Goathland's pleasant moorland ambience and its little refreshment places are likely to draw you into pausing here before starting the walk's return leg.

Turning right on the road at the Incline's summit, you keep left at the nearby crossroads then watch for a stile on the right leading into a narrow, hedged lane. Once through the ensuing field, steps descend towards Eller Beck, but if a train is imminent there is no better viewpoint than the bank to the right of the path. At 1 in 49, the gradient up to Goathland remains one of the steepest in Britain and steam locomotives labouring up the slope present a stirring sight.

Over the beck you rise to another viewpoint, trend left above Lins Farm and turn right uphill opposite Hill Farm. A narrowing trod shadows a wall through bracken and over boggy ground to reach the country lane by Hollin Garth. Five hundred yards (450m)

north-east along the road you turn left to Green End then right along a farm track. This rather agricultural section of the route concludes by crossing Crag Dikes footbridge and entering Crag Cliff Wood.

The broad-leaved woodland is a delight at all seasons of the year and you soon pick up a fine stretch of paved causeway—a fitting finale for a walk through history! Causeways like this occur widely in the North York Moors region (and in other parts of Britain too), pre-dating roads and railways and constituting the main thoroughfares along which people and goods travelled from one community to the next, principally on horseback. Their presence is due partly to the availability of sandstone which could be readily cut into blocks, and partly to the soft moorland terrain which was unsuitable for wheeled transport.

Emerging from the trees, more paved causeway extends forward to a country lane. Having

passed through a gate on the left there are exciting glimpses over a low bank to the tree-shrouded Murk Esk flowing below an almost vertical drop.

Grosmont can be reached directly across the footbridge ahead, round by the church and back alongside the railway line. Alternatively you could strike off right on a woodland path which ends opposite Park Villa some 200 yards up the steep road from Grosmont Station.

Grosmont station—northern terminus of the popular North York Moors Railway.

WALK 16: *YORKSHIRE DALES—Mastiles Lane and the Monks Road*

An ancient drove road and monastic trackway across exposed limestone uplands in the Yorkshire Dales. **Start/Finish**: Kilnsey. **Distance**: 15 miles (24km)—allow 6 to 7 hours. **Location/access**: Kilnsey is on the B6160 10 miles (16km) north of Skipton. **Map**: OS Landranger Sheet 98.

In the years following the Norman Conquest, the Pennines were considered a wasteland and distributed among a handful of northern barons. Cistercian monks from Clairvaulx in France first arrived hereabouts in the twelfth century, keen to settle in wild country where they could pursue an ascetic existence. Rievaulx Abbey was established in 1131 and other monasteries followed, notably Fountains on the River Skell 3 miles (5km) south-west of Ripon.

Clairvaulx's Cistercian Order was well versed in the production of iron and the management of sheep for wool production and these skills, especially the latter, were to prove as profitable here in northern England as they had been in France. Attaching little value to their vast holdings of unsuitable moorland, landlords such as the Romilles and the Percys made generous grants of land to the monastic communities: it is estimated that Fountains Abbey alone eventually owned a million acres of fellside and moor in the Craven area around Malham and Kilnsey. During the first half of the thirteenth century, prodigious quantities of wool were being produced and substantial sales to Italian merchants financed ambitious extensions to Fountains Abbey whose noble ruins receive so much admiration from present-day visitors.

Though geographically separated from each other, Fountains Abbey and Fountains Fell are, indeed, connected. As the monastic estates developed, outlying granges were set up to

administer arable and stock farming and to supervise local labour. One such was at Kilnsey, 22 miles (35km) distant but close to an ancient trackway which also ran near the Abbey. This was improved for use by carts, wagons, packhorses, stock and, of course, the passage of humans both on foot and horseback. The road extended onto Malham Moor and its line continues west via Fountains Fell to Abbey estates in the Lake District.

Now known as Mastiles Lane (originally Strete Gate, a common name for ancient trackways), the section from Kilnsey to the tarmac road north of Malham at an intersection called Street Gate represents one of the finest examples in Britain of an old drove road. It also makes a splendid hike and links up with the Monks Road down to Arncliffe, of which more later.

During the four centuries or so of monastic activity before the Dissolution in 1539, this upland landscape was largely bereft of stone walls. Village and field boundaries were defined by hedges or hurdles and even dwellings were mainly timber on stone foundations. Few tracks crossed the moors. Mastiles Lane would have been an exception—it was already well used by carts and wagons—but it, too, was unwalled. Its course was delineated by the strategic positioning of wayside crosses, some of whose bases and socket stones can still be traced.

The walk begins up a tarmac lane from near the Tennant Arms at Kilnsey. Kilnsey was the site of an important grange of Fountains Abbey, its hall being a prominent feature amidst a cluster of small thatched cottages. A later version of the hall, built in 1648, stands by the lane and is used as a farm store. Its external stone staircase and part of the original grange gatehouse lend an authentic air of antiquity.

Beyond Coolsar Quarry the way climbs out on to Kilnsey Moor and its surface changes to uneven stone and gravel, though parts of the steeper gradients still bear patchy tarmac (this initial stretch is an unclassified country road). As you gain height, an increasingly wild, moorland ambience prevails; drystone walls march slowly over the swells and troughs of a grassy ocean flecked here and there with 'white horses' of limestone.

A stiff pull up brings you to a crest of high ground at 1385ft (422m) above sea level. Impressions of walking this green lane will depend largely upon the weather—even a strong wind can slow your progress, while in heavy rain or snow the outing can take on quite a serious complexion, for there is little in the way of shelter.

So it is that thoughts may wander back to times when this was a main artery along which people travelled routinely on business between Fountains Abbey, its Yorkshire farms and its far-flung estates around Derwentwater and in Borrowdale. Generation upon generation of tenant farmers and monastic officials negotiated this exposed moorland track in all conditions, those of importance on horseback, servants on foot. Raw materials, foodstuffs and commodities of all kinds in wheeled vehicles added to the already considerable passage of sheep flocks, cattle herds and trains of laden packponies. Wool merchants from Venice or Florence, bedecked in finery and accompanied by an entourage of servants, would periodically visit the grange farms in order to gauge the quality and availability of fleeces, particularly during the thirteenth century when wool production burgeoned. With so much traffic, it is little wonder that the old road is etched deeply into the surface of the land!

As you make progress westwards, limestone cobbles give way for a time to deep and often waterlogged ruts, but further on the lane, now held between walls, lies over firm pasture. Weathering takes its toll of any high-level track, but it is the multiple ruts caused by centuries of wheels, hooves and boots that have left an indelible mark. Any stone base will deteriorate with heavy use and lack of regular maintenance. Modern-day travellers add to the erosion process—not only tractors, Land Rovers and motor cycles, but in a gradual, cumulative way, walkers, cyclists and horse-riders as well. Yet such a magnificent moortop thoroughfare can never be protected from use by a population with ever increasing leisure time at its disposal. My own view is that wheeled motor traffic should be restricted, though even that measure would cause inconvenience to farmers whose land abuts the lane.

Double walls snake ahead over gently swelling tracts of close-cropped turf towards high ground, culminating to the north-west in the sprawling summit of Fountains Fell. Over the next lip of land, Mastiles Lane crosses the large, rather indeterminate rectangle of a Roman camp—a scheduled ancient monument in some danger, it seems, of being seriously damaged by vehicle wheelings. Thereafter you descend over Gordale Beck, spanned by an old clapper bridge, and soon reach the crossroads at Street Gate.

Monks Road connected Malham and Arncliffe. It remains a public bridleway and will take you over to Littondale where a return route to Kilnsey is picked up alongside the River Skirfare. To join this ancient hill track, you turn right up the tarmac lane from a National Trust 'No Cars' sign and, parallel to a wall, walk over to Great Close Mire. In monastic times it was an undrained swamp—the vestiges of a glacial lake once frequented by hunters and fishermen from the Middle Stone Age. Even today, the stony hollow is muddy and filled with water, home to a number of interesting bird and plant species.

Two hundred years after the Dissolution of the Monasteries in 1539, the appearance of the dales landscape was transformed by the construction of the great enclosure walls. Pasture land was divided up to facilitate the feeding of cattle when Great Close became the scene of one of the area's major cattle fairs. Each summer, as many as 10,000 beasts were driven here from the Scottish Highlands and Islands, resting in the walled enclosures and guarded by drovers and their dogs. After being bought up by butchers, the cattle would be dispersed all over Craven to fatten up on the succulent pastures.

Over to the west through a gap near Great Close Plantation, you will catch a glimpse of Malham Tarn (a footpath below Great Close Scar will take you closer if there is time to spare). The tarn's small dam at its exit was constructed in the late 1700s, so during the monastic era the water level would have been somewhat lower, held back by the original moraine of glacial debris. Its stocks of trout, a valuable addition to the diet, were tended and harvested by monks from Fountains Abbey.

From Great Close Mire, the surfaced track continues north over a broad sweep of green upland punctuated by outcrops and boulders of white limestone. In all but the dimmest weather these expansive landscapes are full of dramatic contrast and in blustery conditions cloud shadows animate the surrounding fells with their fleeting interplay of light and dark.

Some distance short of Middle House Farm, you fork up left past a complex of ancient stone walls and crofts to the site of a much older Middle House. Here, during the heyday of Fountains Abbey's prosperity, an Abbey tenant, accompanied by two or three shepherds and boys, would tend the flocks, living out in rough shelters on the fellsides and returning to the stone-walled crofts around the main buildings for lambing and shearing. Oxen-drawn wagons loaded with wool would trundle along the green lanes from these upland farmsteads to the fulling mill at Kilnsey grange where a proportion of the wool would be spun and woven into cloth.

There is a new wildness to the track which now undulates over the rugged terrain of Out Pasture at around 1500ft (450m). Swinging gradually north-east, it passes the head of a stream valley, threads a course through rocky outcrops, crosses a wall stile and follows cairns downhill to a knobbly, grassy ledge high above Cowside Beck. Fountains Fell lurks back over your shoulder to the west, but eyes will doubtless be drawn to the precipitous drop on your left at Yew Cogar Scar. High on the opposite valley side, above walls that cling to a seemingly impossible gradient, a minor road rises from Littondale on its way over to Malham.

Eventually the Monks Road, now no more than a sketchy footpath, descends through a lip of small crags towards the stone cottages of Arncliffe and angles down to a wall gate and into a farm lane. The views up tree-patched, wall-lined Littondale are magnificent—a symphony of greens and greys. You pass a fine old house and emerge via a farm into Arncliffe's village square near the Falcon Inn; in season

there is a tea-room along the street to the left.

Arncliffe is not quite at the road's end (a precarious ribbon of tarmac does continue west across the fells to Stainforth) but it feels as if it should be! The largest of Littondale's four settlements, it is lyrically situated on a gravel delta above the River Skirfare's flood plain and is flanked by steep, limestone-strewn hillsides. The village seems to face inwards to its broad green and there are numerous old buildings worthy of inspection.

The final leg of this route differs radically in character from the moderately strenuous and exposed walking undertaken thus far. It is all gently downhill—Kilnsey is some 165ft (50m) lower and 6 miles (6½km) distant—and you have a choice of three parallel ways

shadowing the Skirfare. A footpath strikes off over meadows from south of St Oswald's church, crosses a tributary stream after a mile (1½km) and joins a by-road about a quarter of a mile (400m) short of Hawkswick Bridge. From here you are best keeping to the minor road on the river's north bank. Alternatively, simply walk from Arncliffe along the northern of the two dale roads, past Hawkswick Wood and Hawkswick hamlet, with its tastefully converted barns, to reach the B6160 at Skirfare Bridge. A third option takes the southern dale road via Hawkswick Cote to Skirfare Bridge, but this is inclined to be busier during the main tourist season.

The last mile along the B6160 passes beneath Kilnsey Crag, a spectacular, overhang-

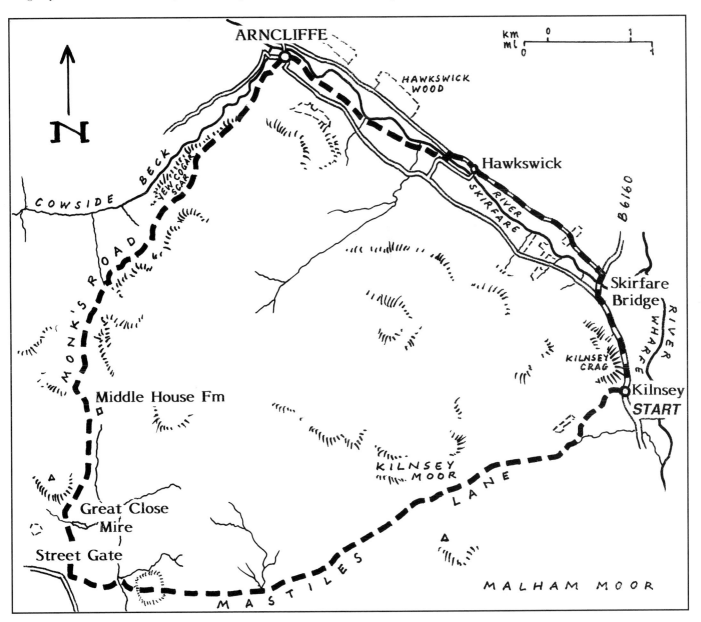

ing prow of Great Scar Limestone jutting 170ft (52m) above the road. Frequented by rock climbers, it is best viewed by passers-by on foot, for endless frustration is caused by thoughtless motorists slowing down to ogle and holding up the traffic!

Kilnsey itself has a fine Riverlife Aquarium and a Visitor Centre geared mainly to fishing and wildlife in the Dales. It is all a far cry from the historic trail you have just completed and will underscore the vast changes our society has undergone over the past 800 years.

Facing page **From behind the Deanery, views of York Minster grow increasingly majestic.**

Cowside Beck and Littondale, from the Monks Road as it approaches Arncliffe.

WALK 17: *YORK—A Tour of the City Walls*

A short but fascinating stroll along ancient city walls. Several flights of steps and a few natural gaps interrupt the actual walltop. **Start/Finish:** York railway station. **Distance:** 2½ miles (4km)—allow at least 3 hours to include detours to adjacent sites of historical interest. **Location/access:** York stands at the hub of a road network north-west of the Humber and has a main-line railway station. **Map:** Street plan required—available locally.

York is a veritable treasure-house of history and you would need more than a single day to do it justice. In addition to the incomparable Minster, the famous Jorvik Viking Centre in Coppergate and the National Railway Museum, the old city exudes charm and historical interest at every turn. Set astride the rivers Ouse and Foss, it is, too, a colourful, bustling sort of place, well endowed with amenities to serve the many thousands of visitors who flock here from all corners of Britain and from overseas.

As you would expect in such a tourist mecca, your enjoyment will inevitably be shared with others—except, perhaps, on a rainy winter's day! Although a busy commercial and industrial centre, York's driving force is tourism. At the season's height the processing of visitors takes precedence over all else. Buses roar round on 50-minute sightseeing tours, with ponies and traps or riverboat trips offering less frenetic alternatives. The theatre, art gallery and museums, often thronged with people eager for cultural experience, nonetheless provide some respite from city-centre traffic which can get oppressively fumy.

Only the city walls offer escape from this seething cauldron of human activity. The 2½-mile (4km) circular walk will not remove you entirely from the hustle and bustle of city streets—you are returned to it at each break in the wall—yet for surprisingly long sections you are suspended in relative peace and tranquillity at rooftop level as the walls swing in a wide arc around the central fulcrum of York Minster.

Of course, the walking itself is of the simplest kind—no call for boots and rucksack here! Nevertheless, those who suffer from vertigo might find the inner, unguarded drop up to 20ft (6m) uncomfortable here and there where the wall narrows. Everyone will benefit from wearing comfortable shoes and clothing. Steps lead down to street level at gateways—or bars—where historically important roads radiate from the city centre and it is at such points that short detours can be made to visit nearby buildings or take refreshment. I advocate a leisurely approach to the walk in order to maximise your appreciation of York's ancient origins and to savour the unique visual perspectives obtained from the walltop. You could scoot round in less than an hour but you would miss a very great deal!

Information panels are posted at strategic places, though I recommend carrying one of the detailed guidebooks available at local newsagents. The wall gates, embellished with York City crest, are locked at dusk and dogs are not allowed on the walls at any time. Before describing the walk, a little background

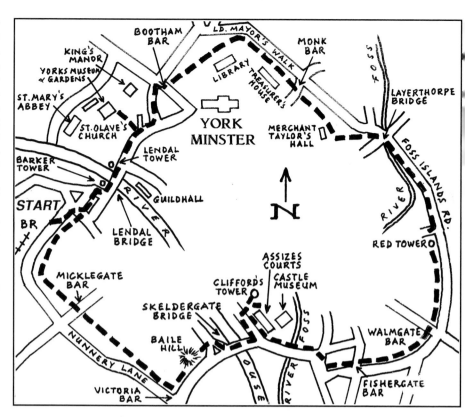

can be sketched in to set the scene.

There is some evidence that a tribal settlement known as Caer Ebruc existed here before the Roman Governor of England, Quintus Petilus Cerealis, established a fortress on the north-east side of the River Ouse around AD71. The ancient earth rampart was enlarged by Hadrian (how different a proposition it must have been to his great border fortification further north) and was later flanked by a stone wall built by Severus. Within this grew up the city of Eboracum whose importance increased with the development of the Roman road network. The original Roman walls formed a square, though little remains of their fabric today.

When the Romans finally departed, anarchy prevailed and periodic attacks took place, first by Saxons then by land-hungry Vikings who eventually colonised this part of England and renamed the town Jorvik. Only recently, following the Coppergate excavations upon which Jorvik Viking Centre is based, has the true commercial significance of this early settlement been fully appreciated.

Throughout the subsequent period, York's defensive walls were strengthened and extended. From the first timber-palisaded earth banks of Eboracum they grew to the impressive structure we see today, dating largely from the thirteenth century and built of stone quarried near Tadcaster.

It is possible to start the walltop walk at any point (and in either direction), but in deference to York's illustrious role in railway history the station seems entirely appropriate. At first you must cross busy Station Road to climb steps on to the wall south of Lendal Bridge, from which the anti-clockwise circuit begins.

This initial stretch is rather artificial, having had to accommodate Leeman and Station roads and, further south, an arch which took George Hudson's York and North Midlands Railway to the city's heart. The first train left on 29 May 1839 amid much celebration and heralded the birth of one of York's main industries. There is a grand view back over flowery gardens to the towers of the Minster.

Rounding the corner ahead you reach Micklegate Bar, the royal gate straddling the London road and the original terminus of Via Pretoria. It is a gateway which has seen more pageantry than any other. Here on numerous occasions royalty has been met by the Lord Mayor and led in colourful procession to the city centre. Of Norman design, the gate has two stout timber doors giving access to the barbican defences (now, unfortunately, removed). In less peaceful times the heads of traitors would be spiked atop the Bar—a gruesome fate which also befell the Duke of York after the Battle of Wakefield in December 1460. There are shops and cafés below, reached down steps, but the walk continues above, parallel to gaily

painted houses along Nunnery Lane.

A small gateway—Victoria Bar, dating from 1830—interrupts this quiet section of wall which makes a 90 degree turn to the north-east, passing the tree-crowned grassy mound of Baile Hill. No hard proof exists that one of William the Conqueror's stone castles stood here, but the site is clearly a twin of Clifford's Tower mound ahead on the opposite bank of the Ouse, which **was** built by William.

Leaving the wall, railings channel you left after you have crossed the Ouse on Skelder-gate Bridge which replaced an earlier ferry service. For centuries, York was a busy inland port and the bridge was made to lift, allowing tall-masted ships access to large warehouses: York's equivalent to the Pool of London. In their day, the Romans connected the rivers Trent and Ouse with a canal called the Foss Dyke so that cargoes of spices, glassware, pottery and other commodities could be shipped

in from Lincoln on the east coast.

Facing you now are the Assize Courts and the fascinating Castle Museum. Impressive Clifford's Tower on its man-made hill to the left is all that remains of a castle built by William the Conqueror, Clifford having been one of its governors. An exploding powder magazine shattered the rest of the castle in 1684 during the Civil War. A climb to the circular keep's interior parapet provides wide city views.

By keeping right, you cross the River Foss on Castle Mills Bridge and rejoin the walls at Fishergate Postern. To the right from Fisher-gate Bar stands St George's Church in whose cemetery lies the legendary John Palmer, alias Dick Turpin, executed on 7 April 1739 for horse-thieving and highway robbery.

Walmgate Bar is next, the principal eastern gateway. Its barbican tower, unlike all the others in York, stands intact, the fifteenth-

At the walk's start there is a grand prospect back over flowery gardens to the famous Minster complex.

century oak gates and portcullis ready to close off Walmgate from attackers. Enemy forces would have had to pass the barbican's narrow neck and risk bombardment from rocks, arrows and other missiles. Until weapon innovation eroded the advantages of wall defences, archery—and, later, cannon fire—performed a vital role in combat. As you stroll along the walltop, the raised outward-facing edge often bears castellations and narrow apertures of use to the defenders. A timber-framed Elizabethan house (now a bookshop) built on Walmgate's city side adds architectural richness to this historic city gate.

Walking on past modern flats and above the

busy Foss Islands inner ring road, one must sometimes make a mental effort to blot out the less appealing aspects of twentieth-century life! You soon reach the Red Tower, originally a defensive structure dating from the sixteenth century and situated at the edge of King's Fishpool, an artifical lake created by William the Conqueror by damming the River Foss; it was subsequently stocked with fish. This natural gap in wall walking temporarily diminishes the

route's quality, apart from willows fringing the River Foss. A derelict footbridge is quickly followed, however, by Layerthorpe Bridge where, with the Minster already in sight, you regain the walls.

Beyond the fifteenth-century Merchant Taylor's Hall you are treading the original outer defences of Eboracum—the Roman eastern corner built by the 10th Legion. Excavated foundations below can be explored from Monk Bar. Down to the right stands an early nineteenth-century ice house, built to store winter ice for domestic use in summer.

Monk Bar is the most heavily defended of all the gates—and the tallest to boot. It is probably named after a nearby monastery. Inwards lies Goodramgate, containing some of Europe's oldest buildings. You can either walk through the bar on payment of a small fee, or descend to street level and climb dark steps through an arch in the tower's base.

Above the road called Lord Mayor's Walk lies one of the most interesting and picturesque sections of wall, flanked on the city side by the Treasurer's House, a scheduled monument owned by the National Trust. Originally built to accommodate the Treasurer in whose care the assets and maintenance of the Minster were entrusted, the house has long associations with the entertainment of royalty and contains many valuable works of art and pieces of antique furniture.

Delightful lawns, shrubs and flower beds behind the Deanery lead on past the backs of yet more historic buildings. In medieval times a moat lapped the foot of the grassy bank which now sweeps down to a row of trees. Views of the Minster, previously obtained over jumbled rooftops, are now excitingly close-range and increasingly majestic. In the charming foreground of the Deanery garden stands the Minster Library, once the chapel of the old Archbishop's Palace, while superimposed against the Minster soars the Chapter

House—reputedly the tallest in England. You will have turned left and entered deep shade—in summer at least, when trees are in full foliage.

Before reaching Bootham Bar, the Minster's origins can be contemplated. Many pages could be devoted exclusively to this architectural gem, yet even without the benefit of such knowledge its presence stirs the spirit. The very first church here—a timber structure—was built in AD 627 following Northumbrian King Edwin's baptism into the Christian faith. Repeatedly burned and pillaged by the Vikings and again by the Normans, it rose each time from the ashes. During the reign of Henry VIII, Archbishop Walter-de-Grey supervised the beginnings of the present Minster—the Cathedral Church of St Peter. Added to over the intervening span of generations by the work of hundreds of masons and labourers, the magnificent edifice bears witness to both the enduring force of Christianity and to the building skills of man.

Like the dome of St Paul's in London, York Minster stood intact when all around was bombed in April 1942: symbols of faith rising above the smoke and flames. In more recent years, drastic measures have been required to reinforce the central tower's foundations and to repair damage caused by air pollution and lightning strike. Viewing the Minster's interior is almost *de rigeur* for visitors to York—there is so much of beauty to see, not least the marvellous stained glass.

And so to Bootham Bar, the last gateway of the tour, of Norman construction but standing on Roman foundations. Its façade of weathered stone crowned by three figures evokes for me all the defiance and clamour of those early armies marching out to defend their city. You can still peer out through arrow slits down to the narrow confines of High Petergate, built over the Roman Via Principalis.

Although there is no wall to follow as such, St Leonard's Place and Museum Gardens contain some notable sights. Immediately facing you is the City Art Gallery with its prominent statue of William Etty, RA, a local painter of renown. To the left stands historic King's Manor, now part of the University of York.

Other relics of York's ancient past revealed in Museum Gardens include St Mary's Abbey ruins (the setting for York's triennial Mystery Plays), St Olave's Church and the medieval hospital. Most imposing of all, however, is the Multangular Tower, acknowledged as one of Britain's finest Roman buildings.

Lendal Bridge, constructed in 1863, represents the final jewel in this historical necklace. For many years Lendal Tower on its north side housed various machines for pumping the city's water supply. A chain used to be hung from here to Barker Tower, a lookout post across the Ouse, to control the paying of tolls by craft using this important waterway. Beyond Barker Tower it is but a stone's throw past floral gardens to Station Road where the walk began.

Below **Barker Tower.**

Facing page **Heptonstall's old graveyard—insufficient space for centuries of burials.**

WALK 18: *WEST YORKSHIRE—Todmorden to Hebden Bridge on the Calderdale Way*

Along paved causeways, field and woodland tracks and country lanes above a well-known Pennine valley. Between two bustling towns, the walk explores landscapes and buildings associated for centuries with the textile industry. **Start**: Centre Vale Park, Todmorden. **Finish**: Hebden Bridge. **Distance**: 12½ miles (20km)—allow a full day to include town trails. **Location/access**: Both Todmorden and Hebden Bridge lie on the A646 Burnley to Halifax road and both have railway stations. **Map**: OS Landranger Sheet 103.

I have always found the Pennines compelling for their sombre beauty overlaid with a detailed map, so to speak, of man's occupation and his need for mobility. Everywhere are signs of endeavour and pragmatism—from the channelling of streams for water power to the laying of paved packhorse ways over the wet moors; from sternly functional yet sometimes flamboyant nineteenth-century architecture to the improvement of marginal land for grazing or cultivation.

Visiting Calderdale, an archetypical Pennine valley, you feel today the crush of a dense population and can sense its ancestry stretching back to the seeds of the Industrial Revolution. Here, from the late fifteenth century onwards, there developed an industry which was to shape the lives of generations and leave its mark permanently upon the landscape. That industry was cloth.

Until the late 1200s, most people hereabouts were engaged in farming and lived in small communities set on natural terraces above the flood-prone and heavily vegetated Calder valley. A precarious living was eked out between the inhospitable moortops and equally uninviting lower ground. Recovering from plagues in the fourteenth century, the population began looking for ways to reduce their vulnerability to the vicissitudes of farming and

pland weather.

Calderdale's abundant soft water, running off the moors with force enough to drive machinery, was exploited by resourceful villagers who helped create an alliance between subsistence farming and the production of woollen textiles—a kind of dual economy. The manufacture of worsted—a smooth, close-textured fabric with no nap—began around 1700. Out-workers were widely employed to card, spin and weave, while the moorland

Facing page **From Eaves Rocks there are magnificent views over Mytholm and the Calder Valley.**

Right **Stoodley Pike Monument—an insistent landmark throughout much of the walk.**

Below **The original 'Hebden Bridge' dates from 1510, replacing an earlier timber structure.**

streams drove fulling mills built along their banks.

At this time, Calderdale was relatively isolated, its principal trade and communication routes contouring along mid-height terraces on the hillsides and dipping in steep gradients through side valleys. Unsuitable for wheeled vehicles, these ancient trackways—often paved for use by packhorse trains and known as causeys—were by far the most prevalent mode of transport. However, by the mid-1700s radical changes were afoot. A new road was pushed through the Calder Valley from Halifax to Tormorden and on to Burnley and Rochdale. With greater prosperity came canals—notably the Calder–Hebble Navigation and the Rochdale Canal—and by 1841 the first trans-Pennine railway was operating.

Though by no means overnight, mechanisation of the textile industry did begin to spread, steam power replacing water and large mills displacing hand processes. Industrial development in the valley-bottom towns drew in its workforce from the surrounding hillsides which, as a result, were rapidly depopulated. Thus, with their pre-Industrial Revolution character largely untouched, old-established villages such as Heptonstall and Mankinholes saw no further growth, becoming in effect, fossilised.

In October 1978, a 50-mile (80km) footpath, the Calderdale Way, was opened to provide a circular walk exploring layers of history and landscape around this fascinating valley. Along the way it passes wild gritstone moorland, old mills and paved causeys, ancient halls, laithe houses and weaving hamlets, hill farms and bustling towns. It was tempting to include the whole itinerary as a Classic Walk, but that would have meant sacrificing detail and comment in order to cover all the ground. In my view, the following section captures the true flavour of Calderdale and represents a stimulating day's hike. There are several link paths short-cutting to the valley, and it is easy to return from Hebden Bridge to Todmorden using public transport.

With the background now sketched in, the walk can begin and features can be brought into focus as they are encountered. Todmorden's town centre south of the viaduct contains scarcely a single twentieth-century building. Classical Greek and Italian-style Renaissance architecture in the Town Hall reflect the level of civic pride in the 1870s. Yet sharp contrasts can be drawn between it and other buildings such as the Unitarian Church, the stately elegance of Tormorden Hall, or the ranks of renovated back-to-back terraces and turn-of-the-century shopfronts. Unlike most of its Yorkshire counterparts, Tormorden's suc-

cess was based on cotton. Comprehensive detail lies outside the scope of this book, but if time allows follow the Tormorden town trail with the help of the official booklet issued at local tourist offices.

Walking begins from Centre Vale Park, an 88-acre amenity estate flanking the A646 Burnley road north-west of Todmorden centre. There is car parking in the vicinity. Towards the far end of some playing fields you turn right into Stony Royd Lane which soon deteriorates to a track beneath a railway arch and climbs past Stannally Farm. Zig-zags continue as the walled track grows steeper, its ancient surface overlaid by a mosaic of modern materials. It is a tree-shaded ascent in places and whisks you surprisingly quickly from the traffic-laden valley corridor into glorious open country.

At the moor gate there are good views left over to Stannally Stones. You veer right with the wall and by-pass Rake Hey Farm, climbing to reach a junction where you bear right again into an old packhorse road. It soon levels off below the tor-crowned escarpment of Whirlaw Stones, while Todmorden is just visible over a rim of fields held between dark gritstone walls.

On Whirlaw Common, a superb section of paved causey takes you over wet moor and gently downhill past East Whirlaw farmstead. This packhorse way—almost as even as a city pavement—graphically demonstrates how a train of pack-ponies could traverse terrain completely out of bounds to wheeled carts or waggons.

At Hole Bottom you turn right down the lane then branch off left over a small step-stile, following the path over three more stiles adjacent to Todmorden Golf Club. At the metalled Hey Head Lane, take a left turn, passing East Hey Head Farm and cutting straight across Law Hill.

In common with most walks, the route is invariably more complex over farmland, so watch carefully for waymarks—a yellow symbolic tree motif, composed of the letters C and W but looking more like a cluster of three circles. Threading past Killup and Higher Birks farms, you reach a country road leading to Great Rock. If visibility is favourable, there is a fine view south-east to the Stoodley Pike monument from this defiant gritstone outcrop on the moor edge.

Turning left at Great Rock sets you on a course in a walled track over Staups Moor, ending in a heathery path down to Hippins Bridge. Bearing right then left between farm buildings, the path links more farms to arrive at Blackshaw Head (pub), at the intersection of two ancient packhorse ways, one from

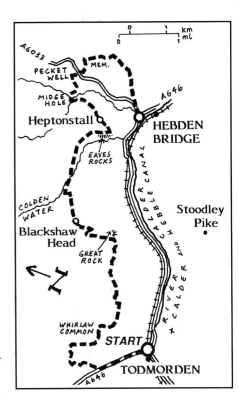

Halifax and Hebden Bridge, the other via Long Causeway to Burnley. Over the road, you cross a step-stile and follow a paved field path past old huts. Gates and fields continue, well waymarked, to Shaw Bottom just down from Jack Bridge (another pub!).

Already there are tempting glimpses ahead of Heptonstall, the principal mid-walk highlight, and soon you join the Pennine Way down steps to the picturesque Hebble Hole Bridge. Your sojourn on the Pennine Way is a very short one! Leaving it for a splendid stretch of paved path, you rise above Fostor Wood and cross fields to a lane above Lumb Bank House, once the home of poet Ted Hughes and now a centre for creative writing. Once up Lumb Bank, a high-level path takes you through Eaves Wood in a big loop round the valley of Colden Water, ending in a scramble up left on to the crest of Eaves Rocks.

This, one of many marvellous viewpoints over the Calder valley, deserves an extra star in its rating! Below your gritstone stance, the land falls away to the tree-shrouded mills of Mytholm and on over swelling hillsides to the still-prominent monument on Stoodley Pike. Erected in 1815 to commemorate the Peace of Ghent (which ultimately led to the abdication of Napoleon), it collapsed in 1854 but was rebuilt and has become a landmark of major significance. 120ft (37m) high, it is much bigger close to than it appears from a distance.

Joining a stepped path rising from the right,

you turn left through an extensive new housing development and enter the hill village of Heptonstall. Its cobbled street and square-cut terraces of blackened gritstone, with none of the valley greenery to soften their edges, hold echoes of an austere post-eighteenth-century economic past. The community did enjoy considerable prosperity before then through a combination of hand-loom weaving and farming and for a time the population reached 4000—twice its current size. But the textile industry's mechanisation in Calderdale, based on Hebden Bridge just down the hill, rapidly deprived Heptonstall of its usefulness and it was left in a kind of suspended animation.

First to command attention will be the two churches, sharing a common graveyard in a site where space is at a premium. The Old Church—a gaunt ruin now—is largely the fifteenth-century extension of an original Chapel of Ease built between 1256 and 1260 and dedicated to Thomas à Becket. Over the years, parts were repaired as necessary, including the porch, but in 1847 a severe storm ripped away the west face of the tower and although services continued to be held for a further seven years, the church closed in 1854 when neighbouring St Thomas's Church was completed. The latter's interior is disappointingly modern.

Said to contain the remains of 100,000 souls, the graveyard is a fascinating place! Space was so tight until the New Graveyard was started in 1915 that tombstones were laid like paving slabs, many bearing epitaphs on both sides. Two are very old but perhaps the most colourful is the grave of a David Hartley, hanged in 1770 for leading a gang of counterfeiters at nearby Cragg Vale—the so-called 'Cragg Coiners'. Gold clipped from the edges of coins was melted and recast in forged dies by the gang. Their fraud was on a such a serious scale that the Government was forced to make urgent plans for their arrest; in the ensuing hunt, an official was murdered.

Adjacent to the Old Church stands the Grammar School which now houses a museum. Heptonstall is so compact that a complete tour takes only half an hour. Among features to look for are the old Cloth Hall, weavers' cottages and the village pump at 'Top oth Town', Weavers Square, the Methodist Chapel, the White Lion and The Cross pubs, and a wealth of vernacular buildings. A guide map is situated at the lower crossroad.

You leave the village along Northgate and Northwell Lane, dropping through woods to Hebden Water and past the weir to Midgehole. Over Horse Bridge, you ascend past the entrance to Hardcastle Crags (there are miles of delightful walks west and north from here in National Trust woodland) and on up quite sharply to Raegate. Through beech woods, the path is signed 'Pecket Well' and leads over a stream at Kitling Bridge where you join a paved way up to the Hebden Bridge–Keighley Road near Pecket Well. Above rears the Pecket Memorial, a visual clone of the Stoodley Pike monument but dedicated to the dead of two world wars.

Turning right along the top road, the way branches left past Shaw Croft Hill and on along the moor edge. A short distance ahead this walk takes its leave of the Calderdale Way, following a link path below Bog Eggs Edge, down through Old Town and Nut Clough to the centre of Hebden Bridge.

The town developed as a river crossing—initially just a ford—on the old way between Burnley and Halifax. The original timber bridge was superseded in 1510 by a stone structure around which several inns, a smithy and a mill were built. Increasing trade, based on a happy combination of geology, climate and human resourcefulness which greatly favoured the manufacture of textiles, ultimately led to the need for better roads. The old bridge, too steep and narrow, bowed out in 1772 to a new one at West End.

Water-powered mill machinery required the proximity of fast-running streams, but the advent of steam power removed many previous constraints on a mill's location. Hebden Bridge grew apace as an industrial centre, mills on the flat valley floor, housing stacked along the steep hillsides.

The boom could not last forever. New reservoirs in the Pennines channelled the good, soft water to other areas and gradually Hebden Bridge lost its vital advantage. Following a period of serious decline which lasted all of 60 years, the town has adapted to change. In its new role it not only accommodates modern small-scale industries but has become something of an historical showpiece, a centre for Pennine arts and crafts and a holiday destination in its own right, flanked as it is by so much marvellous walking country.

The Old Bridge is as good a place as any to head for. From there, a self-guided trail (booklet available, as with Todmorden, from tourist information offices) will reveal no end of historical detail, though the full tour takes $1\frac{1}{2}$–2 hours.

A superb example of paved packhorse 'causey' leads you over wet moorland on Whirlaw Common.

WALK 19: *DERBYSHIRE—The Roystone Grange Archaeological Trail*

A walk along a Peak District railway trackbed and old drovers' ways, taking in the site of an excavated medieval grange, Roman period cultivation terraces and a nineteenth-century pump house. Easy walking but muddy in places. **Start/Finish:** Minninglow car park and picnic area. **Distance:** 5½ miles (9km)—allow 3 to 4 hours. **Location/access:** Minninglow car park lies ½ mile (¾km) south of Pikehall on the A5012 between Cromford and Newhaven. Nearest railway station—Matlock. **Map:** OS Landranger Sheet 119.

So often in crowded lowland Britain layers of evidence substantiating what we believe to be historical fact are lost to the plough or buried beneath new building development. Sometimes in hilly regions, however, where past settlement reached its upper limit and where modern man finds it too costly or inconvenient to exploit the land, signs of our ancestry remain intact.

One such location lies in the heart of the Derbyshire Peak District—well off the tourist track but an historical treasure-house for the observant and interested walker.

Two factors distinguish this itinerary: first, the concurrence within a remarkably compact area of remains from fourth-century Romano-British occupation, a monastic grange, drove roads from the medieval period and the more conspicuous manifestations of nineteenth-century industrial activity; and secondly, the fact that this historical feast is set upon a table of outstanding landscape quality. Here are brought together all the distinctive features for which Derbyshire's limestone country is renowned: fields bounded by a matrix of old drystone walls; rounded, tree-crowned hills often bearing a prehistoric tumulus; woods and coppices adding texture to every view; and long

horizons extending north towards the gritstone moors of the High Peak.

Minninglow car park is one of several established by the National Park authorities at strategic points along both the High Peak Trail and the other two disused trackbeds in the Peak District, the Tissington and Monsal trails. Equipped as picnic areas too, they represent ideal bases for walks as well as resting places for cyclists who, along with horse riders, also use the trails. With no refreshment places in prospect on this walk, it is as well to come prepared with your own food and drink; the nearest pub is at Parwich, some distance away by road.

Running north-west–south-east through nearby Pikehall, the course of the King Street Roman road is poorly defined on the ground, despite the promise of better things on the

1-inch OS map. There is no public right-of-way access and only the alignment of field walls and the occasional tree belt provide clues to its existence.

You set off east over a minor road and along the cinder trackbed of the former Cromford and Highpeak Railway. Originally conceived as a waterway to connect the Cromford Canal with the Peak Forest Canal at Whaley Bridge (hence stations called wharves), for technical and economic reasons it began life in 1830 as a railway line—one of the earliest operations in Britain.

At first, passengers and freight were hauled by horses, while stationary steam engines driving a cable system winched wagons up the steeper inclines. Later, locomotives were used. Over the years the fortunes of trackside quarries declined and the line's usefulness waned. In 1967 the final working section from Friden to Parsley Hay was closed down and four years later 17½ miles (28km) of track running within the National Park was adapted as a trail for use by the general public. Many trackside features and relics remain *in situ,* and throughout its length the trail penetrates to the very heart of the finest White Peak scenery.

Immediately there are marvellous views south-east to the skyline hump of Minninglow. Not evident until you can look back from beyond a curve in the trackbed is the high, stone-built embankment wall atop which you are walking and which takes on the massive appearance of a dam.

Reaching a quarry cutting, you come across the rusting hulk of an old Smiths Rodley crane once used to load cut stone on to railway wagons. Here the trackbed swings south and crosses another substantial masonry embankment, passing the collapsed beehive shape of a limekiln to arrive at the intersection with Minninglow Lane.

Just off to the right, half obscured by overgrown grass and rubble, stands the ruined base of a nineteenth-century brick kiln. Deposits of silica sand down near Minninglow Grange were used in the production of high-firing refractory bricks, mainly for furnace linings in the steel industry. Other sites for this process were located at Friden Grange, about 4 miles (6½km) to the north-west, and at Harborough, a similar distance to the south-east, though the Minninglow kiln was first to become operational.

You now leave the High Peak Trail through gates on the left and enter Gallowlow Lane, waymarked with black Rs (for Roystone Archaeological Trail) over the customary yellow arrows. This ancient walled drove road whose name chillingly means 'hill surmounted by gallows', crosses the White Peak plateau

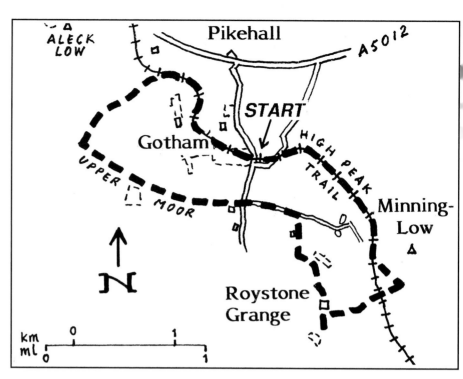

from Wirksworth to Hartington—remarkably intact for long stretches though named differently here and there. Minninglow itself, a compelling landmark for so much of the walk, is now close at hand, its Neolithic chambered burial mound sprouting a stand of wind-bullied beeches at 1220ft (372m) above sea level. The slopes are stone-scattered and grazed by sheep but there is no public access.

Gallowlow Lane dips and rises, where a stile on the right in a very old wall leads you downhill past a mere (one of countless clay-lined ponds on this limestone tableland where water is scarce) and through an arch in the railway embankment. The upper valley into which you are heading typifies White Peak dale scenery: invisible from the plateau, deeply incised and steep sided, yet lacking a watercourse. Formed by glacial meltwater towards the end of the last Ice Age, the dales drain underground through hollows, cracks and fissures in the limestone—at least in their higher reaches—only carrying streams and rivers lower down.

Stiles link onwards downhill over pasture. Large base stones in the wall you accompany on the descent may well have been positioned during Roman times and subsequently built upon to define field boundaries as they developed. Crossing a paddock at the bottom of the slope, you will reach a handgate giving out to the valley track just below Roystone Grange Farm.

A short detour downdale is now necessary, first to the chapel-like building standing alone beside sheep pens. It was constructed at the

turn of this century to house a pump, cooled by water from a nearby spring, which conveyed air to the rudimentary pneumatic drills used in the adjacent hilltop quarries.

Of more significance are the excavated outlines of a medieval grange on the terrace below the dew pond before you. During the reign of Henry II, the Cistercian Abbey of Garendon in Leicestershire was given 'pasture, beasts and appurtenances in the vill of Revenstones' (Roystone) by a local lord, Adam de Herthill. Poor grazing and rough moorland in the northern parts of Britain were little valued by the land-owning gentry and were often donated to Abbey foundations who established outlying grange farms manned largely by lay brothers. Among other activities, sheep-rearing for wool figured prominently: certainly Roystone Grange kept large flocks over the best part of two centuries, selling fleeces to Flemish merchants.

Excavations have shown the original grange sited directly below a spring and consisting of a hall some 50ft (15m) long. This was replaced around the thirteenth and fourteenth centuries by a larger aisled hall at the centre of the terrace. It contained a kitchen at the south end, a hall and a byre, and measured approximately 66ft (20m) long by 39ft (12m) wide; its low drystone walls and a steep-pitched, thatched roof were supported by internal wooden posts.

In addition to the buildings themselves, many artefacts have been unearthed, including fragments of locally made jugs and a variety of metal ware such as knives and sheep-shears. Animal bone remains reveal the lay brothers' liking for mutton—not surprising when you consider their ready supply of sheep!

Archaeological work on this fascinating project, undertaken by Martin Wildgoose of Closes Farm, Kniveton, and Richard Hodges of Sheffield University, has been carried out with the enthusiastic encouragement of the present Roystone Grange farmer, Mr David Twigg. At the time of writing (Easter 1990), a good deal of the work is unfinished; the dairy annexe is clear to see, but it is hoped that when completed all the buildings will have been conserved and the various rooms signposted on the ground.

A quarter of a mile (400m) further down the dale track, a series of low banks runs up the hillside on your left. It is thought that these small terraces formed allotments in Roman times, their boundaries probably reinforced with thorn hedges. Hardy crops such as oats would have been grown here by farmers living higher up the valley—a possible indication of hard times during the later stages of Romano-British settlement when pressure to increase self-sufficiency resulted in the cultivation of otherwise unpromising land. That the ancient, if by now indistinct, terraces exist at all is due to this steep hillside having been untouched since the fourth century.

A little lower down still are signs of Saxon strip lynchets, but to venture further is to encounter the ugly face of twentieth-century quarrying at Ballidon. The continuing encroachment of the workings close to significant sites of antiquity is a cause for great concern and surely flies in the face of National Park policy to preserve all that is characteristic of this special environment.

Retracing your steps up the dale, you pass through the farmyard of the present Roystone Grange, a solid eighteenth-century farmstead which at my last visit was animated by an extraordinary menagerie of livestock, from geese, sheep, chickens and dogs to peacocks and bullocks! An old brick cowshed on the left stands near the foundations of the main Roman farmhouse—the hub of a small community farming this valley and rearing stock between the second and fourth centuries AD.

At Roystone Cottages the often muddy track improves to tarmac, leading you uphill to Minninglow Lane—a section of old drovers' way adopted as an unclassified road but little used. You turn left and follow it to the junction with Parwich Lane (glancing back now and again, for there are magnificent views back to Minninglow), where two options present themselves. For a speedy short cut back to the start simply turn right alongside Cobblersnook Plantation. I recommend the onward route as described below, however; it gives countryside walking of great character and culminates in what I consider to be the most enjoyable stretch of the High Peak Trail.

Walled Cobblersnook Lane undulates invitingly ahead—a rural thoroughfare unchanged in centuries. Beyond Nook Cottage the way rises gently on to Upper Moor; at a fork you keep right, continuing straight along an open field boundary to re-enter the old lane at a gate and stile. Soon after you arrive at the junction with Green Lane. Level initially, with views left to Aleck Low, this dips gradually downhill and sets you on to the High Peak Trail once again, heading right on the walk's final leg.

Swinging round south above Pikehall, there is an almost limitless vista to the north in clear weather, extending to where the White Peak merges with the sterner High Peak moors. The trackbed is narrow and you will undoubtedly be passed by the occasional cyclist, but otherwise the going is delightfully straightforward. Between Upper and Lower Gotham granges, the track makes an astonishing 80 degree turn: in fact, the Gotham Curve is the tightest on any British line and during its operational period only locomotives and rolling stock with a short wheelbase could negotiate such an acute bend; even then a speed limit of 5mph (8kph) was necessary.

One of the great charms of the High Peak Trail, from a walker's standpoint, is its twisting course furnished with frequent cuttings and embankments as it weaves across undulating limestone countryside. Perspectives are constantly changing and there is a pastoral intimacy about the line not normally associated with a railway enterprise. Chapel Plantation, through which you conclude the walk, is a case in point—a woodland grove filtering sunlight and leading you pleasantly back to Minninglow car park.

The famous Gotham Curve called for special rolling stock with a short wheelbase, and a 5 mph speed restriction.

WALK 20: *THE MIDLANDS—Along the Staffordshire and Worcestershire Canal*

Exploring one of Britain's oldest canals, past old locks, bridges, pubs and narrow boats. Lots to see along the way and easy walking throughout.
Start: Stourton Junction. **Finish:** Cookley. **Distance:** 5 miles (8km)—2–3 hours plus stops. **Location/access:** Stourton Junction lies beside the A458 Birmingham to Bridgnorth road west of Stourbridge. Nearest railway station—Stourbridge. **Map:** OS Landranger Sheet 139.

Crucial to the development of Britain's economic growth during the Industrial Revolution was the ability to transport bulky raw materials—especially coal—cheaply and in large quantities. Boats were the traditional method and at first the length of navigable waterways was extended by improving rivers. By 1725, the industrial north had been linked to a nationwide network of some 1160 miles (1866km) and many inland towns, thus inter- connected via the coasting trade, enjoyed considerable advantages over their land-locked European neighbours.

The Canal Age dawned during the second half of the eighteenth century, reaching its zenith in a veritable 'canal mania' during the 1790s when no less than 81 acts were authorised by Parliament for canal construction and the setting up of canal companies. Before the advent of railway transport, canals provided the best means to shift heavy industrial materials such as the clay, lime and coal used in pottery making. A cost per ton-mile as low as 1d was achieved, compared to 6d overland.

Although large capital outlays were involved in construction, long-term returns on investment ultimately proved quite favourable. The first 'dead water' canal (ie. one not incorporating an existing watercourse) was sponsored by the Duke of Bridgewater who became known as the 'Canal Duke'. From his coal mines at Worsley it ran to the Manchester turnpike road at Stretford and had been designed by a poorly educated but brilliantly practical millwright called James Brindley. Born in 1716, Brindley masterminded many canal projects from Salisbury in the south to Glasgow in the north. His vision was to form a 'Grand Trunk' linking the Trent and Mersey, the Severn and Thames, but he died before this was fully realised in 1783.

By the time the railways came in 1830 with the opening of the Liverpool and Manchester line, Britain had approximately 4000 miles (6400km) of navigable waterways and for years afterwards canals continued to fulfil specific transport needs. Designed and built by a generation trained in new engineering technology and working methods, the canal system undoubtedly made a vital contribution to Britain's industrialising economy.

As methods of transportation—for people as well as for goods—grew ever more sophisti-

cated and the pace of industrial output quickened, the ultimate fate of canals was sealed. Today there is a growing interest in reinstating old, neglected waterways—part of society's new awareness of its heritage—but even so it is estimated that over 1000 miles (1600km) of river and canal towpath have been lost. Indeed, nearly 100 canals have virtually disappeared altogether from modern maps—some engulfed by urban development or farmland improvements, others abandoned, derelict and often waterless. A dozen or so canals remain commercially active.

There can be little doubt that the country's remaining rivers and canals represent a valuable leisure amenity. Some 200,000 people per year take holidays on them in hire boats or private pleasure craft. There are hotel boats, floating restaurants and trip launches, not to mention canoes, a quarter of a million anglers and innumerable strollers and walkers who utilise the towpaths.

Enormous potential exists for devising walks of all lengths along river and canal towpaths. Of course, the nature of the terrain is highly specialised and unlikely to appeal to devotees of hill country! However, canals were the arterial trunk roads of our predecessors and at the water's edge grew up an infrastructure of services catering for the needs of man, horse and cargo. Some stretches of the 2000-odd miles (3200km) of canal pathways open to walkers provide a unique window on to life two centuries ago. Locks, weirs, wharves, bridges and associated buildings, represent the state-of-the-art transport technology of the 1700s. With a little prior knowledge, canals can even be dated by the course they take in relation to land forms and how the engineer has attempted to solve construction problems. Occasional single locks, modest cuttings and embankments, along with narrow tunnels, for example, suggest a pre-1790 origin. On the other hand, ambitious flights of locks and long, elevated embankments or deep cuttings indicate later—perhaps nineteenth-century—engineering. Towpaths were built for walking along: freed from any need to haul a barge, today's walker is well placed to contemplate the detail of a now antiquated system.

Selecting a canal walk for this book proved no easy task. Worthy contenders abound, each with its own historical associations and walking qualities. However, I was guided by three self-imposed criteria. The walking itself should be enjoyable—not obstructed or rendered disagreeable by city pollution; it should be modest in length—towpaths are not, in my opinion, intrinsically varied enough to sustain long-distance hiking; and the canal, I decided, should represent the earliest phase of the sys-

tem's development, which began around 1760.

And so it was that I chose a 5-mile (8km) section of the Staffordshire and Worcestershire Canal, completed in 1772 and perhaps the most typical of its age. It retained its independence until the inland waterways were nationalised in 1948 and many of its original redbrick bridges, some circular weirs and interesting locks are well preserved.

Approaching 46 miles (74km) in total length, the Staffordshire and Worcestershire connects the River Severn at Stourport with the Trent and Mersey Canal at Great Haywood. It parallels, and is never far from, the River Stour which, long before the canal was built, had been widened to take barges serving riverside iron-smelting works early on in the Industrial Revolution. Almost its entire length is now protected from unplanned development by its classification as a conservation area.

The walking starts at Stewponey Lock, just across from a parking lay-by on the A458 a short distance west of where it crosses the A449. Before heading off south, I recommend a 275-yard (250m) detour to the north. Here you will find Stourton Junction where the Stourbridge canal comes in from Birmingham through a smartly painted black and white lock. Opened seven years after the Staffordshire and Worcestershire, it forged an important link with the Black Country industries. The junction, an area the size of a small lake, is an oasis of rural tranquillity today but would once have been bustling with noise and movement as boats were manoeuvred across the intersection.

From the towpath bridge there are good views to Stourton Castle whose grounds contained one of many ironworks in the valley, all long since disappeared. Further afield to the south-west rises the wooded Kinver Ridge. An old signpost points north to Wolverhampton and south to Stourport, the line of our walk.

Back at Stewponey Wharf there is a good deal to take in. The canal had a long working life and even in the early 1930s as many as 800 vessels registered at the toll-house in a six-month period—an average of five per day. Behind the toll-house, buildings include the one-time lock keeper's cottage and stables, with the Stewponey and Foley Arms a little way beyond. Stewponey, a most curious name, is reputed to derive from Estepona, the birthplace of a Spanish bride brought back to England by one of Wellington's soldiers following the Peninsular War. He subsequently opened an inn and named it—approximately!— after her home town.

The lock's weed-green gates lead you via an unusual towpath underpass beneath Old Stewponey Bridge No. 32, then the modern A458

road bridge. Throughout the first three decades of this century, a trestle bridge here carried the Kinver Light Railway on its course between the Black Country and Kinver village. Road transport eventually killed off its business and it closed in 1930, but we shall encounter its trackbed later in the walk.

Despite the rumble of traffic initially, the towpath almost immediately resumes a pastoral ambience, channelled between the tree-lined canal and the little River Stour's meanderings. Canals provide a variety of habitats for birds, small mammals, insects, flowers, plants of marsh and woodland and, of course, fish. But a delicate balance has to be maintained between neglect and over-use if species are to thrive: too few boats and the waterway becomes choked with reeds and undergrowth; too many craft going too fast and banks are eroded and waterline plants destroyed.

The Southern Oxford Canal and the Leicester arm of the Grand Union are particularly noted for their wildlife, but the Staffordshire and Worcestershire is a close rival. Look out for rosebay willow herb and vetch, for foxgloves, balsam, thistles and parsley, also elderberry, hawthorn and the ubiquitous weeping willow. Overall, impressions on the walk are dominated by the punctuation marks of bridges, locks and buildings, but perhaps the most persistent single motif is one of waterside trees reflected in the canal's mirror-like water.

Curving right, you pass through the 23ft (7m) Dunsley Tunnel (not over the top as would have been more usual). The New Red Sandstone through which it is hewn is laden with pebbles from an exposure of the Bunter Pebble Beds laid down over 200 million years

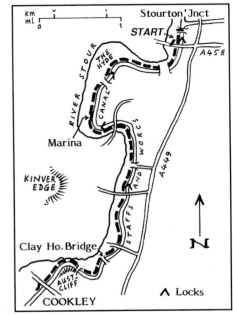

90

ago. Grooves inside the narrow, unlined tunnel were worn by ropes from the hauling horses.

Next comes The Hyde, a more heavily wooded area and site of the largest ironworks in this valley. Towards the end of the nineteenth century it had 20 puddling furnaces in which pig iron was converted to wrought iron by heating it with ferric oxide to oxidise the carbon. Numerous associated mills and forges were all served by nearly 400ft (122m) of canal frontage and a private side wharf. Already operating before the canal was cut, Hyde Ironworks expanded significantly once the new waterway connection with the Black Country was established. There is nothing to see of the complex today other than a few undulations in the ground where buildings and slag heaps once stood (the latter removed for ballast). A short way along a path on the right, the light railway trackbed can be seen.

Beyond Hyde lock and bridge, you pass a semi-derelict waterside house and approach Kinver Marina, with cruisers and narrow boats lining the towpath. Originally, the dimensions of narrow boats were closely related to those of locks, their shape to the cargoes they carried. Horse-drawn to begin with, boats were later fitted with steam engines and ultimately, of course, became diesel-powered. Their fine decorative paintwork featuring roses and castles, geometric designs and scrollwork, is legendary—an art form akin to that of the fairground—but not one easily matched by present-day practitioners.

Now Kinver Church draws your eye to the wooded ridge of Kinver Edge, while closer at hand rough ground on the opposite bank is grazed by goats. Kinver Pumping Station was built on the railway terminus site.

Ahead stands The Vine, a waterside pub at which you could take refreshment and ponder the fact that in the heyday of canals, six or seven times as many hostelries existed as do now. They would have provided welcome relief from drudgery and the elements for the 100,000 or so men, women and children who worked the boats and for whom the cramped vessels were permanent homes. Far from enjoying a contented, picturesque lifestyle, boat people were often regarded as social outcasts—water gypsies—and education for their children was well nigh impossible to arrange. Many families were forced through economic necessity to live out their entire existence afloat, unable to participate in community life.

If you've time to spare, turn right at the lock for a glimpse of some extraordinary caves carved into the brown-red sandstone and probably once inhabited by boatmen. Further up the hill in a commanding position stands St Peter's Church, of Saxon origin.

Over the road from The Vine, towpath walking resumes past moored craft and along by gardens, mature oaks and horse chestnuts but you are soon out again into open pasture. As its name suggests, Whittington Horse Bridge was built for horses crossing the newly cut canal to a local ironworks, though the construction of nearby wharves soon made it redundant.

To the left on the A449, and reached by a lane between cottages over the bridge, stands the Whittington Inn. An inn for two centuries, it is named after Dick Whittington's grandfather who owned the original manor house on the same site. Yet another pub—the fifteenth-century Anchor, is reached by a footpath to the right.

Past Old Mill Cottage, you arrive at Whittington Lock and Bridge, beyond which, across the road to Kinver, ensues a lush section of path overhung by trees and heavily overgrown in high summer (for that reason, incidentally, not the best season for towpath wandering). Half a mile ($\frac{3}{4}$km) farther on stands Caunsall Bridge carrying the road to Caunsall village. The surrounding countryside is typically middle-England—a gentle patchwork of fields and cattle pasture. The canal saunters on, still shadowing the Stour and accompanied by a fringe of willows.

Very soon you will encounter Clay House Bridge, one of the best surviving examples from the Brindley era and an official ancient monument. Walking south, your appreciation of its weathered brickwork and simple lines may be marred by new building on rising ground ahead; the bridge is best seen looking back.

Following quickly on its heels is Austcliff Bridge and Austcliff itself—a sheer face of cross-bedded sandstone some 25ft ($7\frac{1}{2}$m) high and topped by vegetation. It is an astonishing sight to see the canal forced hard up against the slightly sinister rock by the proximity of the River Stour. Had Brindley tunnelled or built aqueducts—here the only other alternatives—constructions costs would have rocketed.

Narrowing perceptibly, the canal approaches Cookely Tunnel which takes it right underneath a terrace of houses and Cookley's main street! Equipped either end with wharves, it is the oldest tunnel in Britain's waterway system, as well as the longest on the Staffordshire and Worcestershire at 194ft (59m).

As by now you might expect, Cookley's development was based on iron-making and dates back to the seventeenth century. By 1886, however, this industry had declined and a steel stampings works took its place, served by canal transport up to the 1930s. The steel-works is still there, beyond the tunnel, but it signifies the end of this walk and a footpath brings you up to Cookley High Street.

WALK 21: *NORFOLK—The Peddars Way*

A long-distance hike through varied, mainly gentle countryside on the course of an old Roman road, itself built over a track of prehistoric origins. **Start**: Knettishall Heath. **Finish**: Holme-next-the-Sea. **Distance**: 46 miles (75km)—3 days suggested. **Location/Access**: Knettishall is situated just south of the A1066 between Thetford and Lowestoft; nearest railway station—Thetford. Holme lies east of Hunstanton off the A149 coast road; nearest railway station—King's Lynn. **Maps**: OS Landranger Sheets 144 and 132.

Facing page and below **Castle Acre's priory ruins form the high point on a walk of mostly rural horizons.**

A group of prehistoric trackways which ran along the chalk spine of southern England from the Chilterns to the Norfolk coast is followed today by the Icknield Way, a long-distance walkers' route from Ivinghoe Beacon to Knettishall Heath. From there the line continues north as the Peddars Way, one of the finest examples of Roman road in Norfolk.

To understand its development, we must first appreciate that the Icknield Way (and, farther west, the Ridgeway) was already an important trade and communications route during the Neolithic period, though it is unlikely to have been one single trackway.

By the Bronze Age, pastoral communities were becoming established, some of which may well have comprised immigrants from the Low Countries. Collectively known as the Iceni, these tribal groups seem to have been favourably disposed at first towards the Roman invasion. Increasing unrest, however, led to a

bloody revolt in AD61, led by the enigmatic figure of Boudicca (or Boadicea), a woman of formidable appearance and charisma. A vast army of wild and undisciplined tribesmen descended first upon Colchester (Camulodunum), then upon London (Londinium) and St. Albans (Verulamium), but thousands were slaughtered and the Iceni tribe was obliterated.

Immediately following the uprising, Roman military engineers built a road along the Norfolk chalk ridge through the very heart of Iceni territory. Men and materials could thus be moved swiftly if required and there may even have been fortifications at regular intervals. In common with most Roman roads, construction was substantial, utilising 'aggers', or embankments, and causeways of local flints and gravel.

Other Roman thoroughfares in Norfolk vary from mere paths to tracks and lanes, only the Peddars Way being of military proportions. Even so, its usefulness was probably short-lived, for a period of social and economic stability followed on the heels of the Boudiccan revolt. Over ensuing centuries, its durable surface has been trodden by medieval pilgrims, by the hooves of farm animals, run over by wheeled carts and waggons, used as a parish boundary marker and, in places, simply abandoned to

the vagaries of weather and encroaching vegetation. Its curious name is most likely to have derived from 'ped', an eighteenth century semi-circular basket in which local produce was carried.

Side by side with their historical associations, landscapes along the Peddars Way are unique to East Anglia. The walk is a lowland one—though not without small hills—and for most of its first half passes through Breckland. This name applies to open heathland interspersed with flinty fields and pine forest—the legacy of over-grazing by sheep and rabbits in centuries past and by extensive planting of Forestry Commission Scots and Corsican pines since about 1930. Today, Breckland's flora and fauna are of international renown and the area has been designated as Environmentally Sensitive to protect it against exploitation.

The shallow valley of the Little Ouse river, where the walk begins, marks Suffolk's border with Norfolk. From here, in Knettishall Country Park, the Peddars Way sets off north into woodland, crossing the river at Blackwater. Beyond the Thetford to Diss and East Harling roads, the old Roman embankment can be made out and appears again as you approach the river Thet just past Thorpe Woodlands

campsite. In Roman times the roadway would have aligned with a ford. Nearby Brettenham is the site of several Anglo-Saxon and Romano-British settlements.

Soon, having crossed the main A11 and railway line, you are flanking more conifer plantations, with glorious views over Breckland Heath towards Thetford. From the left, the Great Fen Road, or Harling Drove, joins the Peddars Way—another ancient way adopted and improved by the Romans and later used for driving cattle and sheep to market. The dismantled Thetford to Watton railway line once ran on your left and you pass between bridge foundations at Stonebridge.

You may well be tempted, as many walkers are, to call in at the Dog and Partridge pub, but a short distance beyond, the way swings left away from the main road, though still along tarmac owing to its use by present-day military vehicles from the Stanford Battle Area. To the possible accompaniment of gunfire and explosions if an exercise is in progress, walking continues north past the secluded nature reserve surrounding Thompson Water and 'Willie's Clump', a copse of native trees planted in 1983 to the memory of J.F. Wilson. There are many splendid old trees in Lord Walsingham's Merton Estate, whose edge is skirted by the route over Sparrow Hill.

The next section of the Peddars Way, whilst following the ancient line as closely as possible, does of necessity include more road walking than most hikers would like. Some progress is made westwards at first to Little Cressingham and thence past tumuli, over the River Wissey and along an undulating lane through delightful countryside to North Pickenham. Chapel sites in the area—including a hermitage and holy well dedicated to St. Paul—recall the passage of thousands of pilgrims on their way to and from Walsingham during the fifteenth and sixteenth centuries.

Once North Pickenham is behind you, the 1½ mile (2.5km) stretch ahead is known as Procession Way, probably named after the ceremonial beating of the bounds at the conjunction of several parish boundaries hereabouts. The market town of Swaffham lies about 2 miles (3km) to the west.

Over the busy A47, you stay on country lanes past Palgrave Hall near the sites of two deserted medieval villages, before reaching an important intersection of roadways—ancient and modern—on Bartholomew's Hills. Soon, Castle Acre's church and priory ruins are in view and a winding lane leads you beneath the Bailey Gate to Stocks Green.

Rather than Roman as one might expect, Castle Acre's origins are Norman and the flinty village is set around its eleventh century castle's outer baily; the two round towers are thirteenth century. In the summer season you are unlikely to have the place to yourself, for its twin attractions of historical remains and rural tranquillity draw in many visitors. As you might anticipate, there are plenty of places at which to eat and drink, as well as some accommodation.

Twenty miles (33km) now separate you from the coast. The landscape has changed completely from conifers and Breckland to infinities of fields transected by hedges, tree shelter belts and tracks. With small villages set back from the route and therefore entailing detours to reach, a growing sense of remoteness is felt, heightened by treading stony, rutted tracks on which only the occasional farm vehicle is encountered. You may be tempted to ponder the impact and wisdom of modern farming practices that produce high yield crops yet at the same time rob the countryside of human scale and dramatically deplete wildlife habitats.

Beyond the A148 at Harpley Dams, one of the few appreciable gradients on the Peddars Way takes you onto Harpley Common, only about 5 miles (8km) east from Sandringham House. Bronze Age barrows are much in evidence in fields around the Anmer–Harpley road, some topped by trees and bushes. Views tend to be more extensive towards the east, as the great chalk ridge rises parallel to the west.

Bircham windmill stands proud of the skyline as the path levels off and drops amidst profuse vegetation to the old ford at Fring Cross; the Heacham river itself is often dry here. Up over Dovehill Wood, you reach Sedgeford's Magazine Cottage, believed to have been built by Sir Hamon le Strange as an armoury in 1640. Soon you pass Magazine Farm and cross the erstwhile Heacham to Wells railway line, now dismantled.

Ringstead returns you to civilisation—I can recommend the Gin Trap Inn for its fare and an array of fascinating odds and ends on display. To the west, the Icknield Way terminates in a small chalk valley and a branch of the Peddars Way may well have connected with Old Hunstanton on the coast. However, the main routing presses on towards an ever more visible North Sea, to end rather inauspiciously in the dunes at Holme-next-the-Sea.

The North Norfolk coast is rightly celebrated for its salt-marshes, dunes, flats and shingle ridges and the official long-distance path which effectively extends the Peddars Way as far as Cromer is well worth sampling. Though perhaps lacking the rich historical associations of the inland journey, the theme of spaciousness and unique natural beauty persists.

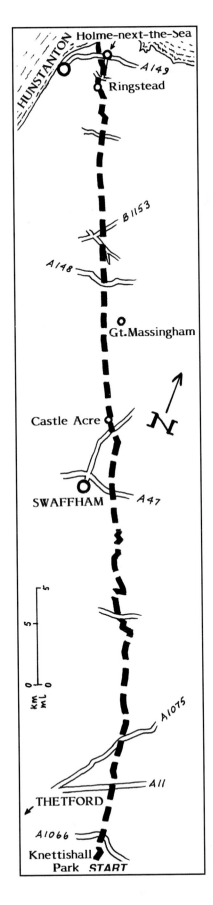

A corner of old Broadway.

WALK 22: THE COTSWOLDS—*Villages, Hailes Abbey and Belas Knap*

Field paths and farm tracks, mostly along the Cotswold Hills escarpment, with several appreciable gradients and muddy underfoot after wet weather. Between villages of Cotswold stone, the walk passes numerous sites of historical interest in pastoral but sometimes dramatic landscape settings. **Start:** Broadway. **Finish:** Cleeve Hill youth hostel or Southam. **Distance:** 19 miles (31km)—a long day's hike, or two shorter days with more chance to explore if staying overnight at Winchcombe. **Location/Access:** Broadway lies on the A44 between Evesham and Chipping Norton about 12 miles (19km) due east of the M5/M50 junction; nearest railway station—Evesham. Southam lies on the B4632 north-east of Cheltenham, with Cleeve Hill youth hostel further up the hill; nearest railway station—Cheltenham. **Maps:** OS Landranger Sheets 150 and 163.

Rather than embracing one aspect of man's past, or manifestations from a single layer of history, this walk passes sites as diverse as thirteenth-century abbey ruins, a Neolithic long barrow and a grand fifteenth-century castle. It is a walk during which you are, so to speak, being constantly nudged by history as the way threads through an ancient countryside. If there is one unifying theme it will be the mellow, rolling Cotswold landscape which bursts into spectacular climax at the route's conclusion on Cleeve Common.

Throughout, you are following part (the best part in my view!) of the Cotswold Way, a 95-mile (153km) long-distance footpath linking Bath with Chipping Campden; because of this, waymarking and footpath clearance should pose no problems. The Cotswold Way itself keeps resolutely to the western scarp of the

Cotswold Hills overlooking the Vale of Berkeley, the River Severn and the Vale of Evesham. In fact, I would suggest that the land here is uncharacteristically wooded and intimate, and more typical Cotswold country—the intensively cultivated, high, open plain of the dip slope further east—is never ventured into. This is, of course, to the walker's advantage for the scarp's little stream-filled valleys, its heady views and its plethora of interesting wayside features offer considerably more than the impersonal infinities of the plateau farmland in which the pedestrian would inevitably feel alienated.

Much of the landscape's appeal derives from Cotswold stone which, as J.B. Priestley observed, renders walls 'faintly warm and luminous, as if they knew the trick of keeping the lost sunlight of centuries glimmering about

them'. Limonite, a rust-coloured mineral, has stained the limestone to varying hues, so that while Painswick's houses are palest of all, those at Stanway appear creamy yellow and Chipping Campden's blush brown.

Sometimes it is difficult to appreciate the Cotswolds showpiece villages without a twinge of regret that they have become either inhumanly neat, or else spoiled by proclaiming their charms too loudly to a public ever hungry, it would seem, for somewhere quaint to visit. Broadway undoubtedly falls into the latter category but it is not a bad place from

Stanton—the archetypal Cotswold hamlet, frozen into a kind of inhuman neatness by the quest for perfection.

which to start a walk—there are plenty of refreshment and accommodation places and you can get there by public transport. However, for much of the year—summertime in particular—there is a sense in which the place falls victim to its own popularity.

I have often wondered whether car parks and amenities in such locations are simply serving the needs of increasing numbers of visitors, or whether—like new roads—they actually generate more traffic. Certainly the majority of tourists arrive at Broadway by road—often nose to tail—and will be occupied in the shops, restaurants and tea rooms for the duration of their visit. Just how many raise their eyes above the village green, the beckoning shop fronts and all those street-level signs to contemplate the dignified, immensely attractive architecture which distinguished this village in the first place, is a matter for conjecture!

Happily the walker can turn his back on all this at a moment's notice and be transported to quieter delights in a matter of minutes. The walk turns right just past the modern parish church along the Snowshill road from The Green. A kissing gate and footbridge lead off across a minor road at West End where height is gained up through the edge of Burhill Wood. Entering a hilltop track, you have passed from Hereford and Worcester into Gloucestershire. Due east stands the folly tower on Broadway Hill which the Cotswold Way visits on its last stage east to Chipping Campden.

At a gate by Buckland Wood, you veer right, though those with time to spare might consider a detour straight on to the fifteenth-century Snowhill Manor, owned by the National Trust and containing a collection of museum objects; you would rejoin the route on Shenberrow Hill, a spine of quarried high land between valleys which onward walkers will now traverse. From the Iron Age hill fort by Shenberrow Buildings, you swing north-west and make a steep descent of the scarp to reach Stanton near its pub at the top end of the village.

It is no ordinary village! In reaching for perfection it has rid itself of all the unsightly appurtenances which twentieth-century life and especially motor traffic seem to generate, so that even parking a car in its timeless street leaves you feeling sheepish and irrationally guilty! Whilst applauding its uncluttered, vernacular beauty and its sleepy, flower-fragrant ambience, some argue that through its very exclusivity it has suffered a kind of fossilisation. Whatever your own conclusions, turn left at the bottom road junction and you will pick up an easy field path running south-west to parkland surrounding Stanway House.

Stanway itself is little more than the sum of house, gatehouse, church and a very large tithe barn. The Jacobean gatehouse, built by the celebrated Inigo Jones, is particularly impressive, its three scallop-shell finials cresting an elaborate three-storeyed façade. Beyond Stanway Church, a road corner is cut and you come out by the Old Bakehouse to cross the B4077 at the foot of its long wooded ascent of the escarpment.

A straight field path leads to Wood Stanway, another cluster of yellowish seventeenth- and eighteenth-century cottages. Here, loins will need girding up for a stiff 500ft (150m) climb via Lower Coscombe to Stumps Cross. (An easier alternative could use the right-of-way heading south-west to a track and the minor road just north of Hailes Abbey.) A stump it is, easily overlooked below a wall near a post box, and all that remains of a wayside cross probably erected by the monks of Hailes Abbey to guide travellers along ancient Campden Lane. You now follow this broad, grass- and tree-lined bridleway as it heads south-west past Upper Coscombe.

You are guided by yellow arrow waymarks and after two changes of direction you will reach the Iron Age earthworks of Beckbury Camp. Here at 882ft (269m) above sea level there are good views west out over the River Isbourne which runs into the Avon at Evesham a dozen miles (20km) to the north. Just beyond Beckbury Camp, to the left of the path in a clump of trees, stands the Cromwell's Seat Monument. From this spot, Thomas Cromwell is reputed to have watched the partial demolition of Hailes Abbey (in some accounts, its burning) during the Dissolution of the Monasteries in 1539, though this is somewhat at odds with actual events of the time.

Below the trees a field path brings you through gates, downhill to a lane into which you turn right for a mile's pleasant stroll, past Hayles Fruit Farm entrance to the ruins of Hailes Abbey. There is a small museum adjoining the entry gate which would prime you well for a tour of the site, which is owned by the National Trust.

Hailes' tiny parish church pre-dates the adjacent abbey ruins by more than a century.

Top **Inigo Jones designed the elaborate gatehouse façade at Stanway House.**

Bottom **The remains of Stumps Cross—probably erected originally as a travellers' waymark by the monks of Hailes Abbey.**

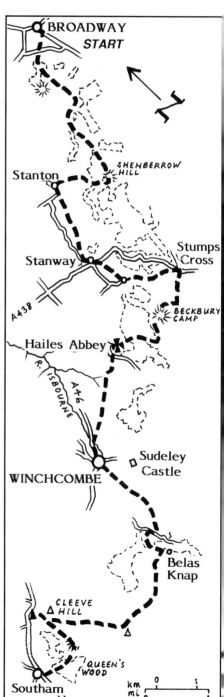

Hailes was (and still is) a tiny settlement nestling beneath the Cotswold scarp in 1245 when Henry III granted his brother, Richard Earl of Cornwall, land here upon which to found a religious house—the result of a solemn pledge made by Richard three years earlier when he was nearly drowned off the Isles of Scilly.

In 1251 the abbey building was dedicated in the company of royalty and no fewer than 13 bishops, but despite this auspicious start the Cistercian monks soon fell into debt. Salvation arrived in 1270 when Edmund, second son of Earl Richard, presented the Abbey with a phial containing the Holy Blood of Christ; this was placed in a specially built shrine of continental pattern and quite rare in English architecture. Pilgrims flocked to see the relic and for a time the community's fortunes seemed to have revived.

Subsequent building repairs, difficulties in collecting revenues from distant parishes, and an uncertain, fluctuating income from wool, all contributed to a period of financial instability after Earl Edmund's death in 1301—instability which lasted for the next 150 years. Only the Abbey's last few decades saw the situation ease, following Abbot Hendley's journey to Rome and the Pope's granting of lavish indulgences to all who worshipped God and the Precious Blood of Hailes. As late as 1533, pilgrims were arriving by the hundred to view this, one of the country's most celebrated shrines.

In 1538, Henry VIII's commission removed the blood to London where it was discredited as being 'honey clarified and coloured with saffron'. On Christmas Eve of the following year the Abbey was closed.

Soon after 1542 the Abbey was sold and its church demolished, though other buildings remained intact and became a domestic residence in the seventeenth century. Finally converted into two farmhouses in 1729, all but the monastic barn had been dismantled by the end of the eighteenth century and a hundred years later had been extensively excavated—a process that is currently being repeated.

Before continuing the walk, be sure to look at the little walled parish church behind the car park opposite. It stands intact despite predating the Abbey by 120 years, and contains a number of interesting features including frescoes.

It is 2 miles (3km) from Hailes Abbey to Winchcombe Church—a walk over low hills on the Pilgrim's Way (though Winchcombe Abbey has long since disappeared) and into Puck Pit Lane, over the River Isbourne and up the motor road which has come south from Broadway on a much more direct course than ours.

Winchcombe is a bustling little centre—altogether more of a town than Broadway and well appointed with amenities for the walker. A visit to the tourist office near The George, an old coaching inn, will yield all the local detail you require. However, should sights be set already on crossing Cleeve Hill before the day is out, there will only be time to take in the 40 or so extraordinary gargoyles on Winchcombe's fifteenth-century church (an entertaining 5-minute detour) before setting off.

Those with a more leisurely schedule could visit Sudeley Castle, regally set amongst trees and cornfields back above the village. Originally built around 1440, it is a magnificent showpiece of golden Cotswold stone and was for a time the home of Katherine Parr following the death of Henry VIII. She died there in 1548.

Our way passes the castle lodge gates then ascends steadily past the elegant Wadfield farmhouse and Humblebee Cottages to the country road between Winchcombe and Charlton Abbots. Here you turn right, then soon left over a stile at a 'Belas Knap' sign. The woodland path is steepish and often muddy but emerges into a field whose boundary is followed uphill by a drystone wall. Wide views begin to open up as you climb, especially back over Winchcombe.

An 'Ancient Monument' sign points the way forward from a kissing gate, along by trees and into the Belas Knap enclosure. Immediate impressions of a grand forecourt and portal embraced by two 'horns' faced with drystone walling are deceptive, for Belas Knap belongs to a type of Severn-Cotswold 'false entrance' long barrow developed to reduce the risks from tomb robbery. Behind the great door is solid stone! The primitive burial chambers themselves, each enclosed by its own small mound, are reached by relatively crude entrances in the barrow's sides and south end.

Built by Neolithic man around 3000BC, Belas Knap's name derives from the Old English *bel* (beacon) and *cnaepp* (hilltop). Nineteenth-century excavations (not noted for their delicacy!) left the site in a poor state, but restoration a few years later by a Mrs Emma Dent of Sudeley complicated the task of archaeologists W.J. Hemp and Sir James Berry during their excavation work in 1928–30. Finds were few, but some may be viewed at Cheltenham Museum.

Now carefully restored, the huge grassy mound—178ft (45m) long by 60ft (18m) wide and 13ft 6in (4m) high—is a compelling object in the landscape; something to wander round, to peer into and contemplate from every angle. The fact that it was constructed 5000 years ago endows it with an almost mystical quality. I hope your visit does not coincide with the presence of other people, for one needs mental and physical space in order to appreciate Belas Knap to the full.

A stone stile releases you from the site at the northern end near a wall plaque, and sets you walking beside a wall to a stony lane where you turn left towards what is left of Wontley Farm. Further west through walled pasture begins a big sweep round Cleeve Common, first on its gentler eastern slopes then along the spectacular western escarpment. The going is firm over rough, tawny grasses patched with gorse and if you stop to examine the path you will probably find fossil sea shells here at 1000ft (350m) above the present sea level.

Having crossed the heads of two dry valleys (the latter above Postlip Hall, Church and Tithe Barn on private land), the way swings west across golf links and above the golf clubhouse before angling south-west up to the summit OS pillar and nearby topograph at 1040ft (317m) above sea level. It is the highest point in all the Cotswold Hills and the panorama in clear weather is truly memorable—a fitting climax to the walk.

If your goal is Prestbury or Cheltenham, you could continue south above Castle Rock and Cleeve Cloud to the sprawling Iron Age camp. Just beyond an intersection of old trackways you can descend the broken scarp to an isolated square stone known as Huddlestone's Table and follow a path down through bracken into the deep, sunken ruts of an ancient holloway at the northern margin of Queen's Wood. You come out into Bentley Lane and eventually meet the B4632 opposite the De La Bere Hotel at Southam.

A more direct termination of the walk follows the Cotswold Way off Cleeve Common summit to the youth hostel (or the nearby Rising Sun pub) beside the same B4632 higher up the hillside. This could possibly be more convenient for walkers being picked up by car. Either way, buses connect with both Cheltenham and Winchcombe.

WALK 23: *THE WESSEX RIDGEWAY*
From Avebury to the Uffington White Horse

A long, gently undulating hike, predominantly along a chalk down escarpment. The going can be muddy at times and is exposed to wind and weather. Sites of prehistoric interest occur widely along the way. **Start:** Avebury. **Finish:** Uffington White Horse. **Distance:** 22 miles (35km)—allow 8 or 9 hours but the hike could be split into two shorter days. **Location/Access:** Avebury lies in Wiltshire on the A4 between Chippenham and Marlborough. Uffington lies in Oxfordshire's Vale of the White Horse, reached by minor roads between Swindon and Wantage. Nearest railway stations—Swindon and Didcot. **Map:** OS Landranger Sheets 173 and 174.

The Countryside Commission's long-distance Ridgeway Path begins near Avebury and ends 85 miles (137km) east at Ivinghoe Beacon in Buckinghamshire. In fact, these two termini mark out the best-preserved section of a prehistoric trackway that once stretched from the Wash to the Dorset coast, a distance of over 250 miles (400km). The old track line is still traceable for much of its length, taking advantage of the relatively unwooded, well-drained chalk uplands. Trade and invasions alike throughout prehistory used this arterial route to the heart of England, enabling different cultures to confront one another for the first time. Interestingly, and as if to underline its significance, fragments of the Ridgeway appear in two of this book's other walks—as the Dorset Ridgeway and on the Peddar's Way in Norfolk.

The Ridgeway was by no means the only one of its kind. In pre-Roman times a vast and complex web of green roads and pathways already existed in Britain, some becoming the drove roads and smugglers' routes of later centuries, a few still recognisable to this day. Walkers invariably find themselves drawn to these natural cross-country routes—partly, perhaps, because the lines they adopt often avoid orthodox valley throughways long since swamped by modern roads and buildings. There may be something instinctive in all of us that relishes the advantages of elevation— the views, freedom from obstruction, firm going and good air. I suspect there is also some deeply sensed satisfaction in treading the same ground with our own feet that countless generations trod before us. Could there be an accumulation of footfall memory inexplicably absorbed by these ancient trackways, similar to the historical aura claimed by some to

inhabit the fabric of very old buildings?

The Wessex Ridgeway is worth walking in its entirety, but as with all long-distance paths some stretches are more rewarding than others. I commend this section as embracing most (though not all) of the really impressive prehistoric sites. Apart from a few climbs and descents, much of the going is easy, if a little tiring for unhardened feet. Taken in one bite, the 22 miles (35km) would occupy a long day some time between spring and autumn when daylight hours are generous. Eight hours might be par for the course, but allow extra for perusing the sites you pass. Alternatively, Ogbourne St George on the A345, at roughly the halfway stage, would provide an ideal point at which to split the journey. Overnight accommodation can be arranged there or in any of the spring-line villages strung out along the north scarp below the final stages of the walk. Be sure to carry liquid with you, for although you do pass a couple of pubs, there is no naturally occurring source of water. Protective clothing is a must for this ridgetop hike.

The official Ridgeway Path starts near a café by the A4 on Overton Hill but one can hardly ignore Avebury, a mile or two down Stone Avenue to the north-west, and it is here that I have chosen to start this Classic Walk. If you can arrange to come here early or late in the day and preferably not on a fine weekend, then do! The tiny village—hardly more than a church, manor house, pub and a few cottages but surrounded by a haunting complement of prehistoric standing stones—is best appreciated in an atmosphere of quiet calm. Even then, the niggling presence of fencing and through traffic remind you of our crowded islands and how everything of value must be protected from abuse.

The leap of imagination necessary to connect our own age with a civilisation that existed 4500 years ago is not made any easier by such distractions. But perhaps it is a price we must pay for greater personal mobility and leisure time with which to investigate our heritage. Travelling through France, I have been struck by the unrestricted access to many ancient historical sites, but I cannot deny they all too often seemed tatty and neglected.

Even before you contemplate its detail, Avebury is an immensely impressive place. Stone circles and alignments bewilder you with unanswered questions: who raised them? why? and how does one decipher the patterns? Archaeologists have called Avebury the metropolis of Neolithic England and certainly the manpower required to transport and erect the sarsens would have been prodigious.

Nothing specific is known of the religious rituals that prompted such enterprise but

clearly, earth and sky represent major elements. Around 5000BC, Neolithic farmers had reached Britain from southern Europe and had brought with them a religion of the earth encapsulated in the worship of the White Goddess—Earth Mother—typical of the Mediterranean and Near East. Some 2600 years later, an incursion of the so-called Beaker Folk from the Low Countries—hunters and warriors—introduced a religion directed skywards to the masculine sky-god of thunder. From this great meeting of peoples sprang a flourishing Wessex culture connected through trade in precious metals and through war with the whole of Europe from Scandinavia to Egypt. Its catalyst had been the Ridgeway and its ritual pivots became Avebury and Stonehenge.

Approached by curving avenues of menhirs, the great stone circle—1400ft (427m) across—is echoed by a large outer bank and ditch. Two smaller circles of about 350ft (107m) diameter are arranged within, the northern one containing three massive stones known as the Cove, opposite the Red Lion pub. In more superstitious times than our own, no buildings were put up inside this awe-inspiring pagan circle and during the Middle Ages attempts were made to bury the stones, thus, it was hoped, discharging their latent menace. Ultimately though, the stones were seen as a convenient source of building material and in the eighteenth century—before the unique value of such antiquities was fully appreciated—almost three-quarters of the total scheme was removed or broken up. That the remains are so impressive today leaves us marvelling at the scale and ritualistic magnitude of the original, intact, site. Further insights may be gained into this, along with the West Kennett long barrow and Silbury Hill, by visiting Avebury's museum.

As you set off east past Manor Farm and up on to Overton Down to swing north on the Ridgeway Path, the landscape is peopled with grey sarsen stones—glacial erratics and remnants of a harder sandstone overlay from which the Avebury alignments were assembled. Ridgeway walking begins to establish itself. It falls between our modern categories of footpath and track, being sometimes little more than worn field ruts but on other stretches a broad, hedged way or farm road. Do not be surprised to encounter cyclists, motor cyclists, horse-riders, tractors, Land Rovers and even cars, for they too enjoy access over some sections. Vehicles and walkers make unhappy bedfellows but personally I am only offended by the noisy motor cycles of trail-riders.

In a sickle-like curve, the way veers northeast as a broad stony track past isolated spinneys on Hackpen Hill. Within a mile of cross-

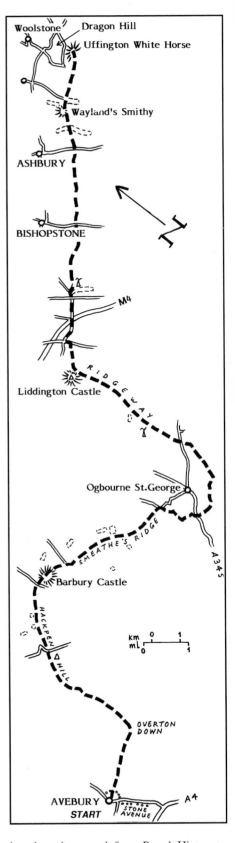

ing the minor road from Broad Hinton to Marlborough, you are approaching Barbury

The Ridgeway on Hackpen Hill.

Castle, seen in exciting profile. To your right, field patterns are frosted pale by the flinty soil of the Marlborough Downs which roll south to distant, tree-clumped horizons.

Barbury Castle has been designated a country park and provided with acres of car parking to the east which ensures the area is well visited. Designed to be defended by sling-shot, the Iron Age hill fort itself sprawls over its commanding hilltop site. Perimeter bank and ditch added to the difficulties of would-be attackers, already beset by stone missiles given extra impetus by being fired downhill. Hill forts like these may well have served as cult or tribal centres—even as markets—as well as refuges in times of conflict.

You pass right through the structure then, beyond the car park, you turn right at Upper Herdswick Farm and left down Smeathes Ridge—a most delightful descent emerging at the only street of Ogbourne St George. The official path skirts south of the village, but if a stopover is taken for refreshment or a bed, the Ridgeway is easily regained by climbing past a rubbish-filled quarry from the A345. Ogbourne's pretty colour-washed houses, its pubs and café, are likely to tempt you anyway!

With half the walk now behind you, a little forebearance is called for on the stage across Round Hill Downs, past the aerial on Whitefield Hill and on towards Liddington Castle. Particularly after a wet spell, the overlying clay will be pocked with large puddles, while impenetrable hedgerows deprive you of compensatory views for a mile or two. Presumably the going on lower ground was even harder, with dense tree cover and soggier ground during the Ridgeway's formative centuries.

Liddington Castle hill fort and its crowning OS pillar at 909ft (277m) above sea level lie a little west of the route on the north-facing scarp as you enter the Vale of the White Horse. This is Richard Jefferies country and Liddington Castle was one of his favourite

haunts. Here he would shake off 'the petty circumstances and annoyances of existence' and drink in the spirit-lifting combination of sky, earth and air. Born at nearby Coate, this well-loved nineteenth-century natural history writer drew untold inspiration from his hilltop forays and a plaque has been installed here to his memory. His was a different world: the uninterrupted sheepwalks of his day have long since succumbed to arable farming.

The Ridgeway proper, now partly a motor road, cuts due east from Barbury Castle to resume its scarp-top line here, but the Countryside Commission quite properly chose a southwards loop to maintain quality.

From Liddington Castle, the path drops to cross the M4 motorway on minor roads and reaches the Shepherd's Rest pub below Fox Hill. The tarmacadamed Ermin Way which sweeps traffic north-west–south-east was the main Roman thoroughfare from Silchester to Gloucester. Back from the escarpment now, you are once more flanked by hedges, caught between wide cultivated fields; if you did not known where you were, this could as easily be East Anglia. Delights will be reduced for a while to pathside detail—the hedgerow flora, the birds and butterflies, the clean air and the great vault of sky above your head.

Soon in Oxfordshire, you cross the B4000 and reach Wayland's Smithy, a long barrow of similar date (*c.* 3500BC) and construction to that at West Kennett near Avebury. Wayland was the Saxon god of the forge, and his 'smithy' here is an imposing 180ft (55m) by 30ft (9m) mound.

At last you regain open country for a finale of classic Ridgeway walking. In springtime, fields of oilseed rape burst into lurid yellow bloom, violating the usually delicate colour balance of the English landscape yet exotically beautiful for all that. You pass an intersection of dazzling chalk tracks and leave the Ridgeway by a stile to climb left on to White Horse Hill. An area rich in prehistoric remains, it is

capped by Uffington Castle—an astonishingly large circular enclosure from 500BC, surrounded by a bank and ditch partly strengthened by an outer bank, or counter-scarp. By the tenth century, the hill fort was known as Aescesbryg (Ashbury) and gave its name to an estate of the Kings of Wessex which included the modern parishes of Uffington and Woolstone. The site has not been scientifically excavated.

North of the OS pillar and barely decipherable from directly above, the Uffington White Horse represents this walk's culmination and in many ways acts as a central focus for all the Ridgeway's antiquities—a sort of distillation of prehistory in one extraordinary, enigmatic form.

The Horse's precise age and purpose can only be guessed at. Since the twelfth century it has been known as an important landmark and was listed among the 'Wonders of Britain'. Seventeenth-century antiquarians suggested it may have been cut to commemorate King Alfred's victory over the Danes at nearby Ashdown in AD 871, but more recent theories link the disjointed figure with similar depictions in early Iron Age art, particularly coins of the time. If this is correct, the Horse may be as old as the hill fort itself.

Throughout almost 2500 years the Horse has been periodically 'scoured' to clear its chalk segments of vegetation and debris. Over the years this work became associated with fairs, festivities and games such as cheese rolling. The Horse and its legend were greatly popularised by several writers, among them Thomas Hughes, a resident of Uffington during the mid-nineteenth century.

As you stand above the Manger—a steep-sided bowl of sheep-tracked hillside—the eye sweeps down across the foreshortened White

Horse to the flat-topped Dragon Hill. Perhaps St George did slay the dragon here, for a horse cult existed in the Iron Age and might well have given rise to the traditional story. Beyond Woolstone village, a patchwork of fields and settlements seems to reach out to infinity.

Footpaths run west above the Manger to the car park on Woolstone Hill, or down to the road junction above Woolstone.

There is a curious postscript to my account of this walk. I researched it one late April weekend and found police patrols had closed off all motor access roads to the Ridgeway as well as to the car parks. Fearing an invasion by 'hippies', the County Council had obtained an injunction sealing off the ancient trackway from these modern would-be-pilgrims. Shades of Stonehenge, I thought: curious how threads still run back through the intervening layers of history to those dim and distant times . . .

Facing page **Rochester Castle, a Norman stronghold on Saxon and Roman foundations.**
(Photo Kev Reynolds).

Below **A walker's perspective on Uffington White Horse—the distillation of prehistory in one extraordinary, enigmatic form.**

WALK 24: *KENT AND SUSSEX*
The Saxon Shore Way by Kev Reynolds

Varied, but predominantly level walking. It goes through coastal mudflats, industrialised areas, attractive towns and small villages and over agricultural land. As it follows a coastline (both contemporary and historic) that has been at the forefront of invasion threats for more than 2000 years, there are numerous fortifications along the Way. In places there could be some difficulty with route-finding. **Start**: Gravesend. **Finish**: Rye (Sussex). **Distance**: 143 miles (230km)—allow 7–9 days. **Maps**: OS Landranger Sheets 177, 178, 179 and 189.

The shape and extent of Britain's coastline is constantly changing. In places huge cliffs, weakened by an ever encroaching tide, crumble and collapse into the surf; new bays and coves are scooped out while elsewhere one-time estuaries become clogged with silt and marshes take the place of tidal rivers. In due course those same marshes are drained, either by natural causes or by the works of man, and the landmass increases. Every schoolboy knows that the coastline is changing, and if ever a walk was designed to illustrate this fact, it is the Saxon Shore Way.

For about 140 miles (230km) this long-

distance route works a meandering course round the heel of England, beginning on the south bank of the Thames at Gravesend in Kent, and ending in the sea-lost harbour town of Rye in Sussex. The shore it follows is not always evident, however, although it was when the Saxons ruled this part of the realm following the withdrawal of the legions of Rome. At times the sea is several miles away—out of sight, if not out of mind—as the trail crosses rich agricultural land where once ships sailed and fish swam, but tractors now turn the black soil for clouds of wheeling gulls.

Along its route the Saxon Shore Way links

a number of historically interesting sites. These include fortifications erected a thousand years and more ago by Romans, Saxons and Normans. There are castles dating from the fourteenth and sixteenth centuries and pillboxes from World War II ranged along the Royal Military Canal of Romney Marsh. The Way passes England's second oldest cathedral, and visits other places of worship where the weight of centuries is etched in stone and saints in stained glass mark the passing of generations in silence. There are creeks where a century ago sailing barges plied a trade in paper; the shipyard where *HMS Victory* was built; and at

Appledore the site where the Danes landed in AD 893 and moored 250 longships, while today the only waterway is a placid canal whose banks are lined with sheep. There are literary connections too, and much of interest for the birdwatcher. Along the Way there's Britain's largest heronry, and on the Swale an amazing sight in winter as some 20,000 waders feed along the mudflats.

The Saxon Shore Way offers an ever varied experience and, to the perceptive walker keen on past as well as present, a novel view of the foundations on which this England stands.

Days 1–4: Gravesend to Herne Bay (71 miles/114km)

It begins where the Wealdway also begins, on the banks of the Thames at Gravesend, a town whose history belongs to the river. For here ships emerging from the estuary take on a pilot to give them safe passage to the Port of London, and it was here in 1377 that the French arrived to burn and sack the town—as they did Rye too, at the other end of the walk. Two hundred and forty years later, in 1617, Pocahontas, the ailing daughter of an American Red Indian chief, was brought ashore in Gravesend to die. Her statue stands in the churchyard of St George, not far from the entrance to the Tilbury Ferry where the walk traditionally begins; as unlikely a beginning to a long walk as may be imagined.

Heading east towards the low, grey, melancholy nub of the Hoo peninsula, the first two hours take you past the remains of the nineteenth-century gun forts of Shornemead and Cliffe, and on then to Cooling. Cooling comes as a surprise, for where else in this wind-blown corner might you find palm trees growing? There's a castle there, the fortifications of a manor house built by John de Cobham as protection against coastal raids in the late fourteenth century. Within the broken walls you can see palms bent against the wind—strangers in this alien land. When the sound-looking twin drum towers at the castle entrance were erected, the Thames washed close by, but now two miles (3km) and more of Cliffe and Cooling Marshes separate them from the oil tankers that serve refineries in Essex on the far shore.

Then, just a short distance beyond Cooling Castle, you come to the parish church in whose graveyard will be found a sorry collection of thirteen lozenge-shaped stones marking the graves of one family's children. Dickens knew this part of Kent well (he lived not far away at Gadshill near Higham) and captured the sadness of these graves and this mist-wreathed marshland in the opening chapter of *Great Expectations*.

From Cooling you go to High Halstow and

Britain's largest heronry—a reserve of the RSPB—and across to the Medway Estuary, the outlet of Kent's major river, to see another fortress, that of Upnor Castle. Overlooking Chatham's dockyard, Upnor Castle was built in 1559 in order to protect its important neighbour, but the first time it was put to the test, when the Dutch fleet under Admiral de Ruyter attacked Chatham in 1667, its guns proved ineffective. Today the castle, appearing rather handsome and homely beneath a canopy of leaves, is open to the public.

Crossing the Medway the route leads into Rochester, that city of inelegant outskirts but with an impressive heart where scenes from Dickens are everywhere. The site was clearly of strategic importance, for it was fortified by the Romans with a wall that enclosed an encampment of $23\frac{1}{2}$ acres. After the Romans departed the Saxons added their own brand of fortification, but the huge castle we see today belongs to the Norman era. A massive keep towers over the city. 'Fine place,' said Jingle on behalf of Dickens, 'glorious pile—frowning walls—tottering arches—dark nooks—crumbling staircases—old Cathedral too.' The 'old Cathedral' stands in the shadow of the castle, and is Bishop Gundulph's masterpiece; a worthy building that should be visited by all who wander the route of this long walk.

The southern shore of the Medway Estuary is gained outside Chatham. It's an estuary freckled with saltmarsh islands, with indented creeks and bays and oozing mudflats, with sea walls and bird life, now raucous with clamour, now industriously self-contained as waders pad to and fro, intent on the all-important business of feeding. Inland there are orchards of apple trees and at Lower Halstow an ancient little church dating from Saxon times, with a Norman lead font only discovered during World War II when an air raid disturbed the plaster that was hiding it. It's an historic region, though you'd be forgiven for passing it by unknowing, for nearby the Romans had one of their tile- and brick-making centres. (There are traces of Roman tiles in the church walls too.)

Funton Hills gives the best views on this leg of the walk. It looks out at such features as Slaughterhouse Point, Slayhill Marsh, Deadman's Island and, near at hand, Bedlam's Bottom. Each name conjures up pictures of a haunted past, but it is happily relieved by a more welcoming Raspberry Hill.

Across Chetney Marshes the Medway Estuary is at last left behind, to be replaced by the waterway known as the Swale, a narrow strip broadening to the east, which separates mainland Kent from the Isle of Sheppey. At the paper-making town of Sittingbourne,

Milton Creek forces you inland, then out again to pass Dolphin Yard Sailing Barge Museum on the way to Murston Nature Reserve and along the sea wall to Faversham. Faversham is one of the civic gems on the Shore Way. It's a town with both history and pride, with notable buildings giving the place architectural style and with accommodation coming at just the right time of day.

It's 14 Shore Way miles ($22\frac{1}{2}$km) from Faversham to Herne Bay along the edge of Nagden, Graveney and Cleve marshes, on a sea wall raised high enough to spy on the waders and wildfowl that converge here, and you share the path with muffled ornithologists hung about with binoculars. Only the chalet townships and caravan sites on the approach to Seasalter and Whitstable present a bland spectre. Seasalter's beach is a mixture of sand, shingle and shells, while Whitstable was noted for its oysters when the Romans came to Kent, and later found renewed fame when the world's first passenger-carrying railway line was opened between the town and Canterbury in May 1830. Then it's a seafront stroll to Herne Bay before heading inland once more.

Days 5–9: Herne Bay to Rye (72 miles/116km)

If the mist isn't rolling, the twin towers of Reculver rise beacon-like to the east. As you wander towards them it's interesting to speculate on the changes that have taken place hereabouts since the church they once belonged to was built. For Reculver is an ancient and important site, recognised as such by Iron Age man, and by the Romans, the Saxons, and the Normans, though it's hard to see why today. The answer lies in a meagre stream, the River Wantsum, that flows nearby.

The stream was once a major waterway—the Wantsum Channel—that effectively made Thanet an island. Of such breadth and depth was it that for hundreds of years shipping made constant use of it (it was more than a mile ($1\frac{1}{2}$km) wide when the Romans were here), but without maintenance it began to silt up in the eighth century. Silting was a slow process, and throughout the Middle Ages ships continued to sail down to Sandwich and out to the English Channel, yet by the end of Henry VIII's reign, severe storms had altered the Wantsum's course and rendered the waterway unnavigable. Today fields of cabbages lie where ships of the Roman fleet once sailed between Regulvium (Reculver) and Rutupiae (Richborough), both forts of strategic importance.

Saxon followed Roman, and in AD669 King Egbert of Kent founded a church within the walls of Reculver's fort, and this survived the twin threats of an encroaching sea and Danish

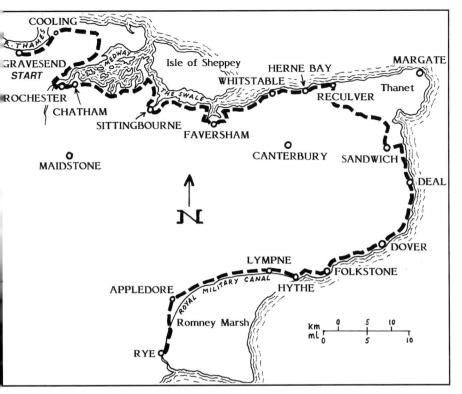

raids. In the twelfth century the Normans enlarged and strengthened Egbert's church, but as the centuries progressed, the sea took more and more land and the church was so threatened it was pulled down, the towers being saved by Trinity House as a landmark for shipping.

Heading south now to follow the course of the long-lost Wantsum Channel, the Way leads to the village of Marshside on the edge of Chislet Marshes. The village stands above North Stream, which marks the western limits of the Channel, and looks across to St Nicholas at Wade over land that once was the Channel bed.

Three miles (5km) on, the Way crosses the Great Stour at Groveferry (it has no ferry now) before heading east once more for 9 river-bank miles (14½km) to Sandwich, arguably the most handsome town in east Kent. Along the Way the three sinister cooling towers of Richborough Power Station dominate the view ahead. They are a modern landmark rising close by the point where the Saxons landed in AD449, and where Christianity came ashore with St Augustine in 597.

Before entering Sandwich you amble past the massive remnant walls of Richborough Castle. After the landing of Aulus Plautius and his Roman army in AD43, the island hill of Richborough became first their supply depot, then the main port of subsequent legions, and later gained fame as the fort that resisted Saxon invasion.

East of Sandwich the modern shoreline is regained in a stretch dominated by golf courses and big sea views. Deal and Walmer rejoice with superb castles built under Henry VIII as part of a major coastal defence system. They are solid-looking gun forts that complement the huge structure of the much older, seemingly impregnable Dover Castle, 7 miles (11km) beyond Walmer. Perched high above the gateway to England, Dover Castle is neighbour to some of the oldest buildings in the land, among them the Roman Pharos lighthouse, nearly 2000 years old, and the Saxon garrison church of St Mary in Castro built a thousand years ago largely of Roman materials.

The base of the magnificent chalk rampart of Shakespeare Cliff has been deflowered by construction work on the Channel Tunnel, sacrifice of a Heritage Coast sanctioned by the Ministry of the Environment, the loss of which creates unease among all who care for the future protection of sites of environmental importance. Beyond it the Saxon Shore Way enters Folkestone to pass one of the Martello Towers erected as a defensive measure against a feared invasion by Napoleon.

Napoleon's threat, suggested by his army's encampment across the Channel in Boulogne in 1804, was the reason for the creation of the Royal Military Canal, the last major feature of the Way. The Canal was planned as a moat around Romney Marsh, a moat that would be protected by troops and patrolled by gunboats. But it took so long to build that by the time it was finished Napoleon's threat had long diminished and its only use since has been for recreation.

Above the Canal a line of gentle green hills tell of one-time cliffs, not of chalk but of greensand. These cliffs would have been washed by tides in Saxon times, before the flat expanse of the Marsh was finally won from the sea, and along them today the wanderer gazes at the stout walls of Lympne Castle (a fortified manor house) and the remains of Stutfall Castle, another of the Roman forts met along the Way.

It's open and breezy along the Military Canal, but despite an almost Dutch-like horizon of unbroken horizontals, it makes for interesting walking. Not the least of the interest comes from a number of old, old churches—some actually on the route, others a short diversion away—that are worth visiting for themselves. Warehorne's is one; Appledore's and Stone-in-Oxney's are two more that draw you into their cool sanctuary of peace, though each has known times of unrest.

And then down from the knoll of Stone to the Canal once more for a final stretch of 4 miles (6½km) of sheep and reeds, of small canal craft and green ditches, of low-growing blackthorn and long vistas—and the nub of Rye's hilltop rising like a stunted thumb ahead. Rye, the first of Sussex after long days in Kent; a town of narrow streets full of charm and colour; a port that has lost the sea but gained in other ways. If you've energy left to climb the narrow stairs of the church and look out from the top of its squat tower, you'll find the sea is not so far away to the south; a new shore, unknown perhaps to the Saxons. But to the north-east a green table of pasture tells of land that once was sea, backed by a gentle slope of shelving where Roman and Saxon both walked with the sound of surf in their ears, where today sheep and rabbits are the only companions for wanderers of the Saxon Shore Way.

WALK 25: *NORTH DEVON—Lynmouth and the Lorna Doone Valley*

A rugged and long hike in three stages: the beautiful wooded valley of the East Lyn River, associated with the Lynmouth flood disaster; high moors and combes in Lorna Doone country; and a return along the magnificent coast path. Paths, tracks and lanes through superlative scenery.
Start/Finish: Lynmouth. **Distance:** 18 miles (29km)—allow a full day of 8 or 9 hours. **Location/access:** Lynmouth is on the A39 between Minehead and Ilfracombe on the North Devon coast. Nearest railway station—Barnstaple. **Map:** OS Landranger Sheet 180.

Much of the history we find most absorbing is separated in time from our own modern era (though there is nothing in the dictionary definition to suggest that what happened last week cannot technically be described as 'history'). However, some events in the quite recent past assume special significance for their unique interest and for the way they focused the nation's attention. One such event was the Lynmouth flood disaster of 1952. Since this catastrophe and the historical associations with R.D. Blackmore's romantic novel *Lorna Doone* might on the surface seem unlikely bedfellows, let me offer two more connections within the context of this book.

Lorna Doone country is centred on the valley of Badgeworthy Water which, swelled by its tributary streams, flows into the East Lyn River at Malmsmead. Thereafter on its way to the sea at Lynmouth, the East Lyn is joined by many other streams which drain the hills of Exmoor Forest 1500ft (457m) above sea level. As we shall discover, the nature of these moorland watercourses is inextricably linked with both the Lynmouth floods and the Lorna Doone story whose locations are only a few miles apart.

The second connection concerns the landscape on these northern slopes of Exmoor. By any yardstick it is superb walking country—a sublime mixture of steep-sided combes, hillsides clothed with sessile oak and carpets of wild flowers, upland streams babbling over rocky waterfalls, rolling expanses of heather moorland and a dramatically beautiful coastline. It is well nigh impossible to explore one story without being drawn into the other, so indelibly are they etched into the region's topography and folk memory.

Forty years or so have passed since the cataclysm which made Lynmouth a household name and inspired offers of help from across the world. The town has settled back into a comfortable role hosting visitors who flock here

by the thousand in cars and coaches during the holiday season. It is a not unfamiliar role. Throughout the early 1800s when tours of continental Europe were disrupted by the Napoleonic Wars, the wealthy looked to their own country for alternative destinations. In those days, Lynmouth was but a humble fishing village set at the conjunction of remote countryside and an often restless sea. Before long, its romantic appeal—a kind of antidote to fashionable sophistication—was recognised by discriminating members of society. Poets in particular were enthralled by Lynmouth and Lynton's lyrical situation. Coleridge and Wordsworth came here, as did Southey, whose description of what he saw still holds true: *'Two rivers join at Lynmouth. Each of these flows down a combe rolling over huge stones like a long waterfall; immediately at their junctions they enter the sea; and the rivers and the sea make one sound of uproar. Of these combes, the one is richly wooded, the other runs between two high, bare strong hills. From the hill between the two is a prospect most magnificent.'*

Percy Bysshe Shelley resided at Lynmouth with his young bride for nine weeks in 1812, avoiding as best he could the young girl's outraged parents! But his exploits finally put Lynmouth on the map and the area became known as the 'Switzerland of England'. More significantly, after 1869 and the publication of Blackmore's *Lorna Doone*, romantic associations were again kindled. Thousands came here to discover for themselves the places and atmospheres of the Doone story and to patronise local gift shops, restaurants and hotels. Lynmouth even earned itself a reputation as a honeymooners paradise!

Doone Country continues to draw in tourists from America and Europe for whom Exmoor has become a required destination—on a par, perhaps, with Tintagel Castle and Stonehenge. Interestingly, this obsession with Lorna Doone is not shared by local people, and (refreshingly) a major cottage industry has not developed around the story as one might have expected.

And so the foundations of tourism were laid in the last century. Horse-drawn coaches connected Lynmouth with Barnstaple and Minehead, though passengers had to walk up the steeper hills! By the turn of the century a narrow-gauge railway line had been laid between Lynton (Lynmouth's higher-level twin) and Barnstaple, but it failed to fulfil its commercial promise. Acquired by the London and South West Railway Company in 1923, it continued to run at a loss and finally closed in 1935.

Sir George Newnes, a devotee of Lynmouth's scenic beauty and a co-sponsor of the doomed railway link, also built a 500ft (152m) water-ballasted cliff railway which vastly improved communication between Lynmouth and Lynton and is enduringly popular with today's holidaymakers.

Difficult access has always militated against the full-blown exploitation of Lynmouth as a resort: many regard this thankfully! Even today the approach roads are steep and tortuous. The area's particular characteristics were to prove its undoing during the exceptionally wet August of 1952.

When a cloudburst of phenomenal severity occurred at around 8.15pm on Friday 15 August the 39 sq. miles (101 sq. km) of blanket-bog and heather-covered peat constituting Exmoor Forest were already saturated with moisture. It is estimated that some 5in (125mm) of rain fell in a single hour and that the 24-hour total measured a staggering 9in (229mm)—in excess of three months' normal rainfall in one day!

If you undertake this walk in ordinary weather, you may be struck by the gentleness of Exmoor's streams; they are seldom more than trickles, while even the East and West Lyn rivers themselves appear tamely shallow. However, swollen with such prodigious quantities of floodwater on that fateful day, mere rivulets became raging torrents, sweeping down boulders, mud, trees and even livestock from the moorsides. Road bridges formed temporary dams against which this debris accumulated until they, too, succumbed, adding their masonry to the deadly surge.

Waves of destruction tens of feet high hurtled down towards the narrow, rock-faced combes through which the East and West Lyn rivers converge on Lynmouth. Riverside buildings were either washed away or smashed apart by massive boulders. In total darkness following the failure of the electricity supply at about 9pm, many individual epics of survival were endured by residents as they made their decisions to see it out or to evacuate their homes. With no comparable flood in living memory, some were tempted to stay put, believing the waters would recede as quickly as they had risen. Only occasional flashes of lightning lit the dreadful scene.

In Lynmouth itself, the devastation was even greater. That night saw many dramatic rescues as firemen struggled to bring out those trapped within unstable buildings besieged by 20ft (6m) of floodwater. Some buildings, among them the Beach Hotel, disappeared altogether, as did sections of road, bridges, the harbour's Rhenish Tower and service installations such as water mains, electricity and telephone cables. Thirty-four people lost their lives before the floodwaters subsided.

Dawn next day revealed the full extent of the damage. Where the East and West Lyn had once met was now submerged beneath an estimated 100,000 tons of boulders, while a tangled mass of trees, telegraph poles, crushed cars, masonry, furniture and miscellaneous rubble was piled to a depth, in places, of over 25ft (7½m). The river mouth had widened to several times its former span and hundreds of uprooted trees protruded from the mud-brown sea offshore.

Elsewhere in the region the deluge's severity was reflected in the destruction of 28 bridges and the scouring of gullies as deep as 8ft (2½m) in hillside lanes. People died in harrowing circumstances caused by the flood's sudden and overwhelming force.

Naturally a combined rescue operation was immediately mounted and became the largest ever seen in peacetime Britain. Voluntary, military and government services were all represented to ensure the personal welfare of surviving residents and the reinstatement of essential services. Heavy earth-moving equipment played a vital part in clearing the river bed and demolishing unsafe buildings. Of wrecked motor vehicles, 121 were recovered but 38 were never found at all. In due course, temporary, then permanent, bridges were built, caravans were brought in for the homeless and at last some semblance of order was restored. Then a young lad, I was taken to see the immediate aftermath by my parents. The chilling memory is of monstrous rocks, tree trunks and silt choking the river bed, either side of which those houses still standing were ripped open as if a bomb had exploded.

The nation, and soon many countries of the world, responded to the disaster with heartfelt messages of sympathy and much practical help. A national appeal—the North Devon and Somerset Relief Fund—was launched on 17 August 1952 and had accumulated £1,336,425 before the funds were drawn upon—an enormous sum in those days.

On 13 September that year, Lynmouth formally declared itself 'open for business'. The ensuing years have seen extensive engineering work on the river banks and the clearance of boulders upstream to ensure that such an inundation cannot occur again. Uninformed visitors would be unlikely to guess that the disaster had even happened but clues remain and the Flood Memorial Hall provides a permanent reminder. (For fuller details of the disaster, see *The Lynmouth Flood Disaster* by Eric R. Delderfield, available locally).

The walk itself, which begins here, is a lengthy and moderately strenuous one but is well supplied with refreshment places and short-cut options. Even devoid of the historical threads which weave its shape, it is as fine and varied a hike as you could wish for.

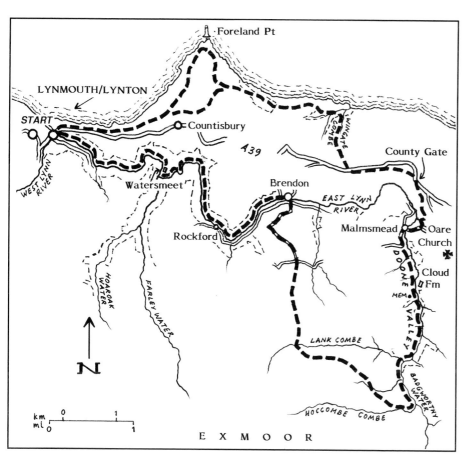

corner you keep to the right-hand trod, a grassy track through heather which ascends easy slopes ahead. Beyond a farm track on Tippacott Ridge you crest a rise and reach the Malmsmead–Brendon Common track.

Immediately before you lies the head of Lank Combe—a valley of central significance in the Lorna Doone story, of which more later. You dip down over Lankcombe Ford and follow the stony track which heads east along the combe's rim; it gives up the ghost over rough pasture, squelchy after rain, but a post will aid navigation in mist.

Once on the tops, Exmoor's landscapes are gloriously expansive—broad whalebacks clad with course grasses and heather and populated with sheep. Wooded combes which, tentacle-like, bite into the upland massif, are lost to view so that one's impressions are of a moorland wilderness swelling voluptuously to the dark heights of Dunkery Beacon, 1703ft (519m) above the sea.

At a wall gate you begin the descent of a broad ridge, regaining a good trackway and crossing a minor stream at a paint-flashed rock. An old bank and stunted trees lead down into Hoccombe Combe, its bed split by a long hillock.

Early Ordnance Survey maps and guidebooks erroneously sited the Doone Valley as here in Hoccombe Combe. Over 60 years of research by Sir Atholl Oakeley has established its proper location in adjacent Lank Combe, soon to be encountered. The ruin on your left was a nineteenth-century shepherd's shelter built of foundation stones from a twelfth-century hamlet of the Brethren of St John of Jerusalem, a community of hermits; the shelter was blown up by the Army in 1945. Other overgrown foundations are still discernible but any connection with the Doones' timber dwellings were always bogus.

The Lorna Doone story—one of romance and violence—was part of North Devon folk history long before Richard Dodderidge Blackmore immortalised it in his book. Indeed, W. Wortner, RA, had painted a portrait of Lorna Doone 18 years before the book appeared. Sir Atholl Oakeley's painstaking research has uncovered how Blackmore obtained the story, the exact locations of places and events, as well as the Doone family lineage (which ultimately led to the book becoming a best seller). There is no space here of course for a detailed resumé—refer instead to Sir Atholl's own fascinating booklet, on sale locally.

Down at Badgeworthy Water you turn left, contouring prettily in and out of trees to the meeting with Lank Combe. Here, definitively, is the waterslide which features prominently in Lorna Doone and forms the lower entrance

Taking to the left (north) bank of the East Lyn River, a tarmac lane then a well-walked, undulating track lead you along the lower edges of Wester and Horner's Neck woods. There is a path along the other bank too, and several footbridges, so you can choose your own course as the river swings in a great 180-degree arc to reach Watersmeet House.

Attracted by the romantic scenery and having inherited a family fortune, the Rev. W.A. Halliday built this 'rustic cottage' in 1832 to his own design. He and his wife Catherine enjoyed it as a family springtime retreat and fishing lodge throughout their lifetimes, after which it was leased to the Newcombe family, bakers and confectioners who began serving teas in 1901. Passed to the National Trust in 1934, that tradition lives on and it is hard to imagine a more delightful spot at which to savour a drink and a snack.

Before leaving, do cross the footbridge to view the waterfalls where Farley Water joins the East Lyn. Steep ground here is typically north Exmoor and illustrates graphically the funnelling effect to which serious floodwater is subjected.

You now take the Fisherman's Path to Rockford, still on the north bank of the East Lyn. Passing above an old limekiln, the way

is quite rugged for a while, until the deeply wooded combe opens out at Ash Bridge. Less than a mile ahead and reached by footbridge lies Rockford hamlet, its inn perhaps of more than passing interest and one that welcomes walkers! Nearby is a shop selling traditional craftwork.

Easy riverside walking upstream to Brendon continues the theme of beautiful cascades and salmon pools caught between picturesque boulders. Watch out for a restored 21ft (6.4m) water-wheel on the opposite bank; it was built in 1870 by a local carpenter and wheelwright to power his woodworking machinery.

It is time at last to leave the sylvan charms of the East Lyn River for a moorland crossing to the Doone Valley. To achieve this, you cross the road bridge and take to the narrow Cross Lane climbing south up to a T-junction at Cross Gate. I hesitate to incorporate tarmac into any itinerary, for most walkers (myself included) find the surface anathema. However, by-roads such as this receive so little use and provide such a clear line of march that all the usual reservations are groundless. You emerge on the moortops and should continue forward over heather towards a field bank. A walker's signpost will confirm your destination, though I found paths hereabouts confusing. At the field to the Doone Valley. A path runs up from the footbridge, above the rock slabs past the 'Grass Sward' where 14-year-old John Ridd met 9-year-old Lorna Doone on St Valentine's Day 1675, and on into the Doone Valley 'carved from the Mountains in a perfect oval'. Here was the Doones' lair, a streamside hamlet of timber dwellings, and higher still is the combe's rocky entrance known as Doone Gate. You can walk up, returning over Great Black Hill to regain the valley track beneath the sessile oaks of Bagworthy Wood.

The onward way to Malmsmead is worn broad by the passage of countless visitors who, since 1969, have passed a memorial stone to Blackmore, erected by the Lorna Doone Centenary Committee.

From Cloud Farm, over the river, a track will take you to St Mary's Church, Oare, where Lorna Doone was shot by Calver Doone during her marriage to John Ridd. Opposite stands Oare House, the Ridds' home called Plovers Barrows. Reaching Malmsmead by lane, this detour would add about a mile (1½km) to the route.

Joining a country road, you turn down left to Malmsmead. Lorna Doone Farm, where, as Malmsmead Farm, Nicholas Snowe lived, has always been the base for explorations of the Doone Valley. Despite a seasonal influx of cars and coaches and its conversion to a gift shop and tea room, it appears supremely picturesque when viewed from across the ancient, narrow road bridge by the ford.

In fact, over the bridge and about 300 yards towards Oare stands a footbridge spanning Oare Water. A muddy, walled path ensues as you pick up the bridleway rising to County Gate, a car park and National Park information centre beside the A39. From here begins the third and final component of this varied hike—an encounter with a splendid section of coast path back to Lynmouth.

Following signs for Wingate Combe, you cut across Cosgate Hill and rejoin the roadside verge for about 800 yards (750m), where a gate on the right yields the key to a waymarked descent—quite rough underfoot in places. Down in wooded Wingate Combe you turn left on to the coast path proper, soon emerging on to open heights above dizzy drops to a bouldery beach. Eventually you reach a metalled drive from Rodney in Kipscombe Combe, continuing on the access road to Foreland Point lighthouse. Although the official coast path turns up left round Butter Hill to Countisbury, the more adventurous might appreciate the steep and stony path from the lighthouse entrance round Foreland Point itself.

You could detour to Countisbury's Blue Ball pub but it is downhill all the way to Lynmouth

and sights will probably be firmly set upon journey's end after a long day. As you undulate on grassy ledges below the A39, you cross the ramparts of Wind Hill, one of the most important Iron Age promontory forts in the region.

Little by little you converge on the A39 and are ultimately forced to join it where Countisbury Hill is steepest! One stormy January night in 1839, Lynmouth's lifeboat, the *Louisa*, prevented from launching at her home port by mountainous seas, was hauled up Countisbury Hill and over the moors to Porlock Weir in a mission to save the *Forrest Hall* which was in difficulties on Hurlstone Point. Eighteen horses were needed to manhandle the 3½-ton vessel, wild weather and numerous obstacles adding to the crew's problems. The rescue took 10 hours but was successfully accomplished— an extraordinary feat considering the odds.

A waymarked path off right into woods rescues you from the traffic and zig-zags down behind the Manor House to Lynmouth's seafront and harbour.

Facing page **Chevening Church, near the North Downs' Darent Gap.**
(Photo Kev Reynolds).

Lorna Doone Farm (now a shop and tearoom) is the traditional base for an exploration of the Lorna Doone Valley.

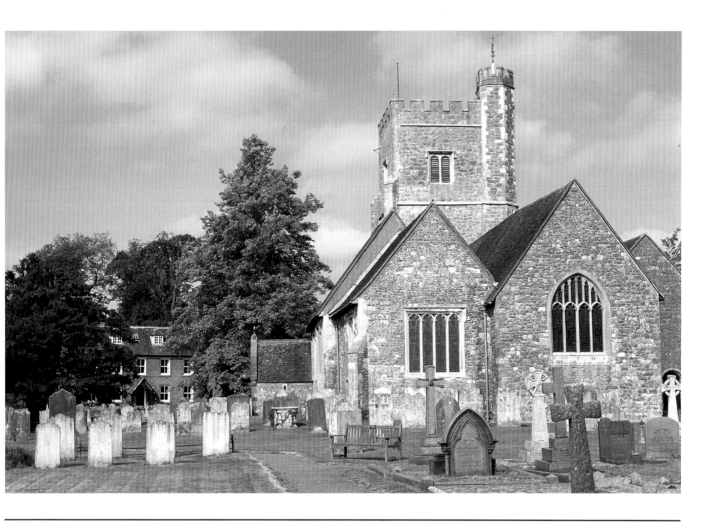

WALK 26: *THE SOUTH-EAST*
The Pilgrims' Way by Kev Reynolds

Mostly on metalled lanes, but there are stretches of footpath and trackway. There are few steep ascents or descents. For much of the way the walk absorbs places of interest from all periods of history and it is this that gives the Pilgrims' Way its essence and its charm. It is also worth diverting from the true path in places to visit neighbouring sites of historic or architectural interest. **Start:** Winchester. **Finish:** Canterbury. **Distance:** 118 miles (190km)—allow 6–7 days. **Maps:** OS Landranger Sheets 185, 186, 187, 188, 189 and 179.

With the words: 'Will no one rid me of this turbulent priest?' Henry II sealed the fate of his Archbishop of Canterbury, Thomas à Becket. On 29 December 1170 four knights, riding from Saltwood Castle near Hythe, murdered Becket in his own cathedral and thereby sowed the seeds of a pilgrimage the like of which England had never known before. Within a short span of time Canterbury, and in particular Becket's shrine, had become the most important place of pilgrimage in Christendom after Rome.

That pilgrimage was made from various corners of medieval Europe as well as Britain,

but although there is no conclusive evidence to prove that the trackway leading from Winchester to Canterbury and commonly known today as the Pilgrims' Way was in fact traced by pilgrims, it is considered likely that it would have been. Certainly this is thought to be the route taken by a penitent Henry himself some 3½ years after Becket's martyrdom. Winchester was then the secular capital of Henry's England while Canterbury, then as now, was the ecclesiastical centre.

It was not until the eighteenth century that the name Pilgrims' Way was given to the route, which runs mostly along a terrace of the

southern slopes of the North Downs, although it was no doubt used for centuries before that. Today that track is a combination of metalled lane, green road and footpath. It runs for almost 120 miles (190km) between the chalk of the downs and the heavy clay of the Weald, sometimes sharing the route of the North Downs Way, but often running parallel to it. It enjoys fine vistas of a green but threatened land. It ambles among blackthorn, box and beech, among hedgerows draped with old man's beard and by orchards lush with apple and cherry. It visits villages clinging to antiquity, passes ecclesiastical palaces and sites of prehistoric interest. And it never fails to remind the wanderer that the past is in severe danger of being submerged by an over-indulgent present.

Days 1–3: Winchester to Dorking (51 miles/82km)

Winchester itself is worthy of pilgrimage. Indeed, the canonised ninth-century bishop St Swithun was buried in the cathedral here, and both before and after Becket's martyrdom his shrine was also visited by pilgrims from home and abroad. Today the city makes a majestic conclusion to another pilgrimage by long-distance walkers following the South Downs Way from Eastbourne.

The Pilgrims' Way, however, heads northward out of town to follow the course of the Itchen upstream to Kings Worthy where you bear east to Martyr Worthy, Itchen Abbas and Itchen Stoke. It is here that the Way crosses the river, with a footpath taking you between streams and on to Ovington with its pub, tempting among trees with refreshment on a bright early summer's day.

New Alresford is next, slightly off route and lying downhill to the left. Early wanderers of the Way would no doubt have seen this small market town being built, for it was laid out in 1200 by Winchester's Bishop Godfrey de Lucy (there was a palace for the bishops at Sutton—or Bishops Sutton—nearby). At the same time he created a 200-acre lake as part of a scheme to make the Itchen navigable to Southampton for the export of South Downs wool to the Flemish cloth industry. This navigation lasted until the middle of the fourteenth century. As for the dammed lake, its size has been reduced to 60 bird-busy acres and is known today as Old Alresford Pond.

Much of the route from New Alresford to Farnham follows the frantic A31 road; there are exceptions, but these are few and far between. On the way you cross a watershed; on one side the Itchen flows south, on the other streams feed the Wey which meanders on to Guildford and the Thames. On the approach to Alton you come to Chawton where Jane Austen spent the last seven years of her life, writing *Mansfield Park*, *Emma* and *Persuasion*. But the 9 miles (14½km) from Alton to Farnham make for grim walking, and since there is room for speculation as to the original course of the Pilgrims' track, it might be preferable to forsake the official route and instead head north, climbing on to the ridge of downland to pick up a cross-country route at Shalden and then by lane and footpath to Well. At Well you can join the Harrow Way and follow this eastward to Farnham, once the greatest corn market in England apart from

London.

Farnham is still a solid, respectable town, and an old one at that. It has the remains of a twelfth-century castle overlooking the town from a hilltop site where the Danes were defeated by Edward, son of King Alfred, in AD893. The castle was another residence of the peripatetic bishops of Winchester until as recently as 1927.

Once at Farnham the walker has the North Downs Way for company. It is a modern trail that nonetheless also has its roots deeply bedded in history—or perhaps that should be prehistory, for our Mesolithic forefathers would have used the crestline of the downs as their route of migration, while medieval journeymen chose the lower terrace for their pilgrimage.

East of Farnham the narrow, steep-sided ridge of the Hog's Back is one of the best-known features hereabouts, but the Pilgrims' Way now firmly establishes its intentions and avoids the crest. Instead it edges the slope, sometimes tree-lined, sometimes open and enjoying expansive views south across acres of heath, meadow or woodland. There are villages like Seale and Puttenham to visit, the first with a church built at the time of the first pilgrimages, the second a pretty place whose church has a decorated south porch dating from the same year that Becket was martyred.

Guildford is by-passed to the south with a footbridge leading across the River Wey. The route then cuts along the edge of Chantries Wood and climbs to the lovely viewpoint of St Martha's Hill, surprisingly topped by an isolated church, far from the parish it was built to serve.

St Martha's is not on the North Downs, but on the Greensand Ridge which forms an inner lining to the chalk of the downs. From it there are splendid views south into the Weald and east along the jutting wooded prows of the ridge. Up there, at 573 feet (175m) above sea level, you wander among pine and birch whose roots are straining in the hilltop sand, then plunge down to the north side of Albury, a neat village in the valley of the Tillingbourne stream caught between the North Downs and the Greensand Ridge. Edging Albury Park you come to Shere then cross the valley to follow a series of footpaths that skirt the downs in that intermediate region bordering chalk and clay. With Ranmore Common high above and Box Hill ahead, the Pilgrims' Way comes to Dorking and the crossing of the River Mole.

Days 4–7: Dorking to Canterbury (67 miles/108km)

The Mole is imaginatively named, for although Milton, Pope and Spenser all gave poetic credence to its supposed burrowing tendencies, it

is unlikely that this river ever lost itself by tunnelling through the downland chalk. Milton called it '. . . sullen Mole that runneth underneath', yet over untold centuries the river has carved a deep cleft through the downs, and it was through this cleft that the Romans pushed their Chichester to London Road—Stane Street. In true romantic style it is possible today to cross the river on a series of trusty stepping stones, then either climb on to southern England's favourite viewpoint, Box Hill, or traverse the slopes to Boxhurst and Brocken Warren Wood where the trackway is a distinct terrace marked out by yew trees.

Several large chalk pits have been quarried from the hillside, betraying the line of the old road again, but then because of the steepness of the slope the Way climbs to the crest of the downs over Buckland Hills, Colley Hill and Reigate Hill, skirting above London's notorious orbital motorway, the M25. Nothing could better illustrate the contrast between the domination of travel today by the internal combustion engine and the ways of old when pilgrims trod the trackways, meadows and woodlands with only the song of birds to disturb the rhythmic plod of feet on bare earth. We trade tree views for a concrete ribbon winding far ahead with its thunderous tail of traffic hurtling towards tomorrow.

It's unnecessary to go down into Reigate for the Pilgrims' Way remains on the northern side of town to pass alongside Gatton Park, a one-time rotten borough whose 23 houses were until 1832 represented in Parliament by two MPs! Merstham comes next, but this one-time quarry village is almost marooned in concrete and the passage through is one of the worst stretches of the whole walk, for the modern-day pilgrim has to cross two motorways and two railways, and the resumption of the old road on the crest of the downs comes with a sigh of relief that would be audible but for the distant roar of traffic below.

The motorway acts as a moat to the castle of the North Downs and mimics the line of the old road for many a long mile across east Surrey and into Kent. But the Pilgrims' Way regains its lost tranquility, diverts round Titsey Park and resumes again by the trim little Church of St James where the ancient trackway has been metalled into a lane of great charm. This lane becomes the most consistent line of the route to Canterbury. Only where large private estates have clawed the land does the Way divert from its now established course, and you can swing along easily and joyfully between hedges of honeysuckle and deadly nightshade, shoulder-high in cow parsley while the North Downs outline your route a day or so ahead.

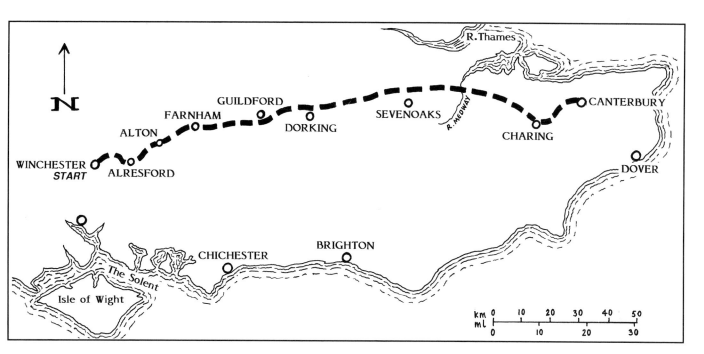

Without knowing it, you cross out of Surrey and into Kent, away from towns and villages and with only a handful of farms and farm-workers' cottages to line the walk. Westerham is a mile or so off, but the metalled lane continues at the foot of the downs until, like Titsey, Chevening Park gets in the way and it becomes necessary to make another diversion. Chevening House is just seen across a meadow—a seventeenth-century mansion that was in the Stanhope family for more than 200 years, but is now the official country residence of the Foreign Secretary or, should he choose not to make use of it, the Chancellor of the Exchequer.

The Darent Gap clefts the North Downs, with the M25 scurrying towards the Dartford Tunnel. Away from such madness lies Otford, an unpretentious village with a long history. The Romans were here 2000 years ago, and after them Offa, King of Mercia, who fought a battle with the men of Kent in AD774. Offa's battleground was again in use in 1016 when the Danes were routed by Ironside, and some 500 years later Otford was again the scene of historic events when Henry VIII came through with his entourage of 5000 on the way to France and the Field of the Cloth of Gold. At that time Otford boasted one of the grandest palaces in Kent—an archbishop's palace that grew from a modest manor house in Becket's day to a palace of size and style so grand that Henry VIII took it from Cranmer. However, Henry never stayed there long for he complained it made him 'rheumaticky' and he preferred instead Knole a short distance to the south in Sevenoaks, so he gave Otford to Princess Mary as a country residence.

The remains of the archbishop's palace may still be seen in Otford near the Church of St Bartholomew opposite the village duck pond. This in itself is of note, for it is said to be the only area of water in England designated a listed building. (It was actually mentioned in an eleventh-century document, so we may picture pilgrims of old resting beside it on their long journey to Canterbury.)

From Otford to Wrotham the line of the old road is almost completely undisturbed. It traces the foot of the downs again, mostly metalled but with a stretch of footpath to finish. Like Otford, Wrotham also had an archbishop's palace, but this was pulled down in 1349 in order to provide the stone to build another on the banks of the Medway in Maidstone. The village was a staging post on the London road (hence the need for a palace here) and it is said that whilst travelling through in 1536 Henry VIII learned that Anne Boleyn's execution had been carried out. Set in a wall opposite Wrotham Place a stone commemorates the murder of Lieutenant-Colonel Shadwell by a deserter during the Napoleonic Wars.

East of Wrotham the Pilgrims' Way resumes on the far side of the M20. A continuing narrow lane contours the hillside, but then breaks away sharply to the right to descend to Wrotham Water and the village of Trottiscliffe. Instead of following the lane, the track continues ahead as far as another crossing road with a lane directly ahead that runs below Trosley Country Park. It would be a shame to miss Trottiscliffe Church, though, so it is

worth dropping to it by way of a field path. The church is set in a hollow next to a farm half a mile from the village. The farm occupies the site of yet another former bishop's palace, while the church itself contains a magnificent pulpit taken from Westminster Abbey. Half a mile to the east, and again a little below the actual Pilgrims' Way, will be found the Coldrum Stones, remnants of a Neolithic long barrow in which were found the skeletal remains of 22 people and a number of animal bones. Back on the Way once more, footpaths and lanes lead to Snodland (as Dickensian a name as one might hope to find on this walk) and Kent's major river, the Medway. There used to be a ferry at Snodland, but this is long gone and one is faced with either heading north to cross the river by the M2 bridge, or south to Aylesford. Aylesford's bridge is a splendid medieval stone structure, one of several such along the Medway (others are found at East Farleigh, Teston and Yalding) and it leads into a village of considerable charm and history. That history claims that the Danish invaders Hengist and Horsa 'fought against Wyrtgeorm the King at a place which is called Aegelsthrep, and . . . Horsa was slain, and Hengist after this obtained the Kingdom'. This was in AD455.

On the downs high above Aylesford there stands another Neolithic tomb, grander than the Coldrum Stones but inappropriately caged by iron bars. This is Kits Coty House, the most famous (and consequently the most vulnerable to graffiti) of all the Medway group of Neolithic monuments. With the Pilgrims' Way running below, a short and steep diversion will be needed to visit Kits Coty.

From Boxley to Hollingbourne a narrow metalled lane takes the Pilgrims' Way for a little over 5 miles (8km) among hedgerows and through leafy tunnels, the wall of the downs rising on the left, the broad sweep of the Weald stretching off to the right. Some fine panoramas are to be enjoyed along here; poppies at your feet, jackdaws overhead and rabbits gambolling in the meadows to either side.

Hollingbourne was visited by Cobbett who appreciated the view over what he called the Garden of Eden. If you can dodge the trees that screen the view you may catch sight of Leeds Castle, considered by Lord Conway of Allington to be the loveliest in the world. No modern-day pilgrim should miss the opportunity to pay it a visit. There are footpaths that give daily access to the grounds, even when the castle itself is closed to the public.

Now the old road out of Hollingbourne is practically unmetalled to Charing, a mixture of footpath, bridleway and track offering long views in which you pick out isolated farms, village clusters and, if the light is good, a distant glimmer of the Channel. Charing is obviously old and interesting. By the church a huge barn was once the great hall of another of those archbishops' palaces seen along our route. Both Henry VII and Henry VIII were entertained here, and Charing, like Otford, also passed into the greedy hands of the crown by way of Cranmer.

The Way draws close to Canterbury. After all the miles and all the days of walking, one senses an approaching presence, but there are still good things in store. One is the route through Eastwell Park, tripping over pheasant and guinea fowl, with the broad expanse of a 40-acre lake spreading to the right and on its bank the crumbling Church of St Mary's, now in the care of the Friends of Friendless Churches, where lies the body of Richard Plantagenet, son of Richard III.

Heading north-east the home leg of the walk overlooks Godmersham Park across a slope of greenery, then into Chilham, perhaps the loveliest village met since leaving Winchester. On its hilltop crown it is heaven in timber and stone, but it must be hell to live there with its steady stream of visitors. There are charming streets, a beautiful church where no doubt medieval pilgrims would have prayed, and a Jacobean manor house in whose grounds jousting competitions and falconry displays are held.

Six miles (9½km) separate Chilham from Canterbury, the first part on a lane, the next on a string of footpaths among orchards. Then suddenly you're among houses and busy roads, crowds again and a great tide of humanity drifting inevitably—as inevitably as the crowds of early pilgrims—to Christ Gate and the precincts of Becket's cathedral. No sight ever greeted a pilgrim, ancient or modern, with more certainty of grace than that.

Below **The Coldrum Stones—remains of a Neolithic long barrow.**

Facing page **Canterbury Cathedral— England's finest—where so many pilgrimages have ended.**
(Photos Kev Reynolds).

WALK 27: *DORSET—Cerne Abbas, Maiden Castle and Abbotsbury*

A long walk on undulating paths and tracks over the Dorset Downs from the Cerne Abbas Giant to the Channel coast. The route would be exposed in rough weather. No refreshment points in the second half. **Start:** The Cerne Abbas Giant. **Finish:** St Catherine's Chapel, Abbotsbury. **Distance:** 17½ miles (28km)—allow a full day's walking. **Location/access:** Cerne Abbas is just off the A352 approximately 7 miles (11km) north of Dorchester. Abbotsbury is on the B3157 coast road about 9 miles (14½km) west of Weymouth. Nearest railway stations—Maiden Newton, Dorchester and Weymouth. **Map:** OS Landranger Sheet 194.

Facing page **Quaint Tudor houses in the pretty village of Cerne Abbas.**

This exhilarating, breezy walk links some of Dorset's best-known historical landmarks and ends—where better—at the English Channel coast. Because it is not a circular route, arrangements must be made for being dropped and picked up. Whilst this is usually less convenient, there are ample compensations in that you are continually encountering fresh countryside and have a well-defined goal to aim for at the end of the day. Equally feasible would be to split the route into two parts and include a visit to Dorchester.

Of course, each historical feature could be seen separately by car and many visitors will be content to do so. However, the process of travelling from one to the next on foot not only allows you time to ponder their significance and anticipate their presence from afar, but sets them and the Dorset landscape in a uniquely human perspective: viewed through a car window this is never achieved for you miss the wayside detail, the contemplative pace.

Cerne Abbas is one charming Dorset village among many, but its attributes extend even beyond its flint and timber cottages, its tea rooms and antique shops, and its fictional portrayal as Thomas Hardy's Abbots Cernal. For above the village, cut into chalk hillside, looms the famous Cerne Abbas Giant.

Like other similar hill figures in southern England, northern Europe and Scandinavia—all of Bronze Age or early Iron Age origin—this rampant (some would say rude!) male colossus brandishing a club probably represents a tribal fertility symbol. Another theory connects his resemblance to Hercules with the Romano-British era around AD200. A local version names the giant Helith after a pagan god worshipped in Dorset at the time of St Augustine's legendary visit to Cerne Abbas in the sixth century. Immediately above the Giant, bank and ditch define the Trendle, a straight-sided earthwork thought by some to have been the site of a temple or shrine associated with the Hercules cult.

The majority of hill figures are best viewed from the air—a thought-provoking characteristic! Satisfactory vantage points are often hard to come by and the Cerne Abbas Giant location is no exception. There is a viewing lay-by beside the A352 Sherborne–Dorchester road, while various hilltops to the west could be explored for a less foreshortened (if more distant) perspective if time is no object.

For a thorough close-up, take a path through the churchyard on to Giant Hill. Only at close quarters does the immense scale of this primitive monument become apparent. The Giant measures 180ft (55m) in height and is outlined by trenches some 2ft (0.6m) wide excavated down to the chalk bedrock; the outline is scoured periodically by local people to maintain definition. You used to be able to wander at will over Giant Hill, but erosion was a growing problem and the National Trust, the present custodians, have fenced off the site.

Before embarking on the walk, an hour's browse around Cerne Abbas village is to be recommended for there is much to see. Signs of a once flourishing leather industry have all but vanished, but had the railway line run through here instead of a few miles to the west, Cerne's history may have proved less tranquil.

North of the village stood Cerne Abbey, founded in the ninth century and thriving under the Benedictine Order from AD 987 until the Dissolution of the Monasteries in 1539 when it passed into private ownership. Over a thousand years of eventful history have included its plundering and burning by King Canute (he later restored the church on being converted to Christianity), and visits by King John, King Henry III, Elizabeth the Queen Mother and Winston Churchill.

Parts of the fine Abbey House date right back to the foundation. Over the years it has been altered and enlarged but it incorporates many stones from the original Abbey buildings. In 1959, Lord Digby was presented with a Civic Trust Award for extensive restoration of the house but, being a private home, it is not open to public visits.

Behind stands the Abbot's Porch, an evocative ruin overhung romantically by trees. Built in 1509 by Abbot Thomas as part of his living quarters, it led from the Abbey's outer to its inner precincts and remains of connections to other buildings can be seen at the rear.

Nearby stands the Abbey Guest House, or Hospice, put up by Abbot John Vanne and part of the original Abbey complex. Margaret of Anjou held conference here in 1471 before the Battle of Tewkesbury. As one of few surviving examples of monastic guest houses in the west country, its architectural importance is undeniable, but it too—alas—is not open to the public.

East of the Abbey site is a graveyard containing St Augustine's Well—a tree-ringed pool which, according to twelfth-century William of Malmesbury, gushed from the ground when the saint struck it with his staff to refresh his entourage and to baptise local converts.

Down past the loftily towered church, Tudor houses overhang the street and lead you to the

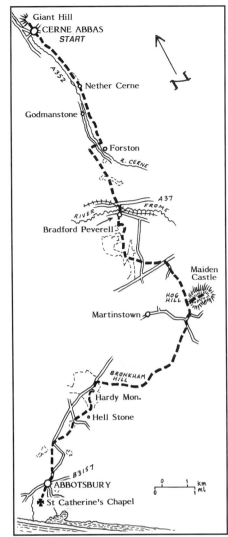

village centre. If you turn left, then right and right again, you will enter a residential loop road, south from which, at Chescombe Close, a gate and field path set you on your way.

Round by trees beneath Black Hill, a mile or so of pastoral walking between the River Cerne and steep hillside brings you past Pound Farm, over sheep-grazed fields, along the edge of woods above a string of small lakes, and out to Nether Cerne hamlet. Straight ahead you fork right to pass close above the diminutive settlement. The little thirteenth-century All Saints Church, sadly no longer used, is maintained by the Redundant Churches Fund and is flanked by pretty lawns, a seventeenth-century manor house and a few cottages—a capsule of rural tranquillity that motorists on the nearby A352 would never guess existed.

Still heading resolutely south in the Cerne valley, your footpath soon arrives opposite Godmanstone where a footbridge provides access to the Smiths Arms Inn; reputedly the

Facing page **The Abbot's Porch once connected the outer and inner precincts of Cerne Abbey.**

smallest in England, it is—unusually—named on the OS map. Another short section climbs and drops to Forston Farm where leave is taken of the River Cerne for a crossing of Charminster Down. Over the A352 you climb up field edges past barns and turn left alongside a hedge towards a thin copse above Brooklands Farm.

These may be downs but gone are the days of unenclosed sheep runs and virgin grassland. Instead, the rolling hills bear patchworks of colour and texture as land is given over to crop cultivation. In bright spring weather, the play of sunshine and cloud shadows over these mosaics of colour, accompanied by a clean breeze and the music of birdsong, are guaranteed to lift the spirits of the most phlegmatic among us!

Avoiding private gallops, the bridleway makes a beeline for Bradford Peverill clearly visible ahead on the line of an ancient Roman road to Dorchester—the Roman city of Durnovaria. You turn left, cross the A37 and soon turn right to the village, passing under the railway and over the River Frome.

A lane past the elegant St Mary's Church leads to bungalows, a barn and, incongruously, a scrap dump. There the main track ahead swerves uphill then levels off at New Barn Cottages. At the next tree belt, a 'No Footpath' sign directs you off the estate track and down through a shallow valley. Once into the ensuing copse, you rejoin the track, turning left but leaving it again for a footpath diagonally left off a bend. Through trees then a crop field, this rises to an unclassified minor road. Immediately opposite, yellow waymarked stiles define a single-file course directly over grain fields to a house by the A35, across from which a handgate leads into a short stretch of pre-bypass road.

Already the long profile of Maiden Castle sprawls on the forward horizon and there are glimpses of the Hardy Monument to the southwest. Although the Dorset Downs are overlaid with ancient tumuli, field systems, dykes, barrows and other earthworks, many are only discernible at close quarters or else have been levelled by ploughing. The proximity of Maiden Castle draws you compulsively towards it.

Off the road corner you swing left into a delightful hedged bridleway along field edges. So massive is the Maiden Castle site that one's perception of distance is distorted and it takes

Nether Cerne—a capsule of rural tranquility.

The Dorset Downs in springtime are a mosaic of colour and light.

longer than anticipated to reach it. Once there, it is not easy to get to grips with it, let alone photograph it! If you've half an hour to spare, it is possible to scramble up the tiers of defensive banks which enclose 47 acres of Hog Hill. Complex earthworks guard the entrances; a zig-zag through can best be found at the west gate where this walk flanks the site. Only by exploring on foot will the form and antiquity of this extraordinary hill fort be fully experienced. It is one of the most important examples in the whole of Europe—in the words of Thomas Hardy, 'a stupendous ruin'.

Its story begins around 3000BC when Neolithic man created a modest enclosure of some 10–15 acres (no longer visible); excavations have unearthed knives, axe-heads, flint tools, bone implements and basic hand-made pottery from this period. From about 1750BC until the fourth or fifth century BC, the hilltop was deserted. Then, however, Iron Age tribes appear to have established farming communities and extended the enclosure, defending it with a single large rampart and ditch. They lived in timber huts and evidently thrived, for archaeological finds suggest they manufactured cloth and built walls using limestone quarried from Upwey, 2 miles (3km) to the south. The surrounding land was cultivated, sheep and cattle provided food and clothing materials, and the population swelled to an estimated 5000.

Across the Channel in Brittany during the

first century BC, the stone-sling was being developed as a weapon of war—an innovation that would soon spread to south-west Britain. With their existing defences now inadequate, the Maiden Castle township and other hill-fort communities were forced to construct multiple ramparts and ditches. Rounded pebbles were collected from nearby Chesil Beach, for the sling was as effective in defence as in attack and for a time Maiden Castle was at its most impregnable.

All that soon changed with the Roman occupation of Britain. Under Vespasian, one of Rome's great generals, the 2nd Legion swept over from the east in AD44. Attacking Maiden Castle's more vulnerable east gate, Vespasian's troops fired ballista bolts (spear-like arrows propelled from a large crossbow) then stormed the fortification. Men and women of all ages were mercilessly killed in this savage subjugation of the Durotriges tribe and the site became a sort of military cemetery as the survivors buried their dead with the pagan rituals prevalent at the time. Finds from Sir Mortimer Wheeler's major excavation of 1934–37 are imaginatively displayed in Dorchester's Dorset County Museum and graphically illuminate this unfortunate episode.

With the main Roman settlement established in Dorchester (Durnovaria and, later, Hardy's Casterbridge), subsequent human occupation of Maiden Castle dwindled to insignificance. Four centuries later a Romano-British temple

Tiers of defensive banks enclose the extraordinarily large and complex Maiden Castle hill fort.

was built—a confused hybrid suggesting that Celtic paganism co-existed with Christianity, the official religion of the Roman Empire. The square foundation plan is still discernible and various finds can be seen in Dorchester Museum.

The onward walk resumes from the western edge of Maiden Castle, dropping down a little grassy valley to the gated minor road from Winterbourne Monkton. You continue ahead to the B3159 and fork right on to a farm lane and a bridleway south-west over Four Barrow Hill. Within a mile you meet the inland variant of the Dorset coast path (designed to by-pass the Weymouth conurbation) and turn right along the Dorset Ridgeway.

There is a 'top-of-the-world' feeling as you stride out westwards on this spine of chalk downland parallel to the coast. Over Corton Down and Bronkham Hill the way is flanked by innumerable tumuli but by now the Hardy Monument is beckoning from Blackdown Hill.

Many visitors assume that this 70ft (21m) high tower commemorates Dorset's famous novelist Thomas Hardy, learning with a tinge of disappointment that in fact it is dedicated to Sir Thomas Masterman Hardy in whose arms Nelson died at the Battle of Trafalgar. Born in 1760, Hardy was brought up at nearby Portesham, for which he held a lifelong affection. His seafaring career, begun at 12 but interrupted for three years' schooling, was to be eventful and distinguished, culminating in a long association with Nelson whose Flag Captain he became. After active service, Hardy was made Governor of Greenwich Hospital where he championed the cause of the under-privileged lower-deck sailor.

Although visible from many parts of Dorset and out at sea (a fitting landmark), the monument has the architectural charm of a factory chimney! Nevertheless, its situation as a superb panoramic viewpoint is hugely popular with car-borne visitors.

Gravelly workings then a wooded groove take you down south to open ground and a path on the right (signed 'West Bexington'). Halfway up the ensuing field you can detour left to the Hell Stone, an impressive Neolithic dolmen on high ground. Originally a burial place for the bones of the dead 6000 years ago, its earth covering has been washed away by centuries of erosion. More significantly, the stones were wrongly reassembled in 1866 by over-enthusiastic amateur archaeologists!

Regaining the inland coast path at the valley head, you cross the Portesham road and branch right—muddily at first—past barns and

a copse on to a field path with wonderfully wide-ranging views over to Weymouth and the tapering wedge of Portland Bill. On your left appears a rather forlorn fenced-off stone circle, excavated in 1965, whereafter yellow way-marks indicate your line ahead to a minor road above Abbotsbury. A hundred yards along to the left, you fork off right, following a fence to a walkers' signpost on White Hill. Here the coast path variant heads west but, with a conclusion at Abbotsbury in its sights, this walk continues south-west on a thin trod which soon grows clear at the rim of Abbotsbury Plains. The village is laid out before you and a simple beeline towards St Nicholas's Church brings you down to the road just short of the first houses.

To do Abbotsbury justice requires the better part of a whole day. Because there is so much to see—the famous Swannery, Sub-Tropical Gardens, St Catherine's Chapel, the Abbey ruins and the magnificent tithe barn—regular inundations by a veritable sea of visitors can be expected during the summer months. It is better to arrive early or late in the day, or out of season. If you're gasping for refreshment, there is no shortage of tea rooms and, thus fortified, you will enjoy the culmination of this outing all the more!

A path south of the church leads out to the site of the old Abbey. Built around AD 1000 by Orc, a senior member of King Canute's household, it was soon monopolised by monks

from Cerne Abbey and flourished for a further five centuries until the Dissolution during Henry VIII's reign. The ruins passed to Sir Giles Strangways who built a mansion using the Abbey stonework. The Royalist-held church and mansion were stormed by Round-heads during the Civil War in 1644 and the mansion was blown up in the midst of battle, killing all within. The archway we see today is all that remains.

Below you, across a leafy, duck-frequented pond, stands Abbotsbury's *pièce de résistance*—a splendid fifteenth-century tithe barn. Despite the unfortunate lack of car parking restrictions immediately in front of the building, its cathedral-like presence dominates the scene. Mellowed by 500 years of weathering and used today to store reeds for roof-thatching, the barn measures 272ft (83m) long by 32ft (10m) wide and is supported by close-set buttresses between its two porched entrances. It is one of Britain's very finest examples of tithe barn architecture.

The reconstructed Hell Stone dolmen and, in the distance, the Hardy Monument.

You could ascend Chapel Hill to the west from here, but I recommend returning to the village centre, past the Victorian schoolhouse and the old Ilchester Arms Hotel. A little further on, a lane to the left provides access to a footpath to the hilltop St Catherine's Chapel, 250ft (76m) above the sea. It seems to exert a magnetic attraction for visitors to Abbotsbury, many of whom—whatever their disposition or level of fitness—make the uphill pilgrimage amidst unfolding views. As befits its exposed position and fourteenth-century origins as a landmark and Mariners' chapel, the 50ft (15m) long edifice appears squarely massive, thick walled and heavily buttressed. Fencing channels you to an entrance on the south side, but all around are tremendous vistas, not only back over Abbotsbury itself and the Dorset Ridgeway, but along the coast and out to a watery horizon.

Facing page **A first glimpse of Levant Mine ruins from the clifftop at Pendeen Watch.**

Abbotsbury's tithe barn is one of the finest examples in Britain.

WALK 28: *NORTH CORNWALL*
Coastal Tin and Copper Mines

A walk through the extensive remains of nineteenth-century tin and copper mines. Though not a long walk, underfoot conditions are rough and there are one or two appreciable gradients. **Start:** Pendeen Watch car park. **Finish:** Cape Cornwall car park. **Distance:** 4½ miles (7km) excluding detours—allow about 3 hours. **Location/access:** Both ends of the walk are reached from the B3306 coast road between St Ives and St Just, not far north of Land's End. **Map:** OS Landranger Sheet 203.

It is not often appreciated that during the nineteenth century Cornwall was one of the foremost industrialised regions of England. Our present-day perceptions of this far-flung arm of land, besieged on three sides by ocean and remote from the country's cultural and commercial centres, are invariable coloured by its reputation as a holiday area.

It is a place of surfing beaches, picturesque fishing harbours and dramatic clifftops—mildly exotic with a hint of Celtic 'foreignness'. Yet prior to the development of tourism, many parts of this rural county were bustling with industrial activity. Mining brought welcome work for a population otherwise dependent upon the vagaries of agriculture and fishing and left, as a legacy, unique landscapes studded with abandoned mine buildings. In their own way these landscapes invoke the essence of Cornwall more powerfully than the scenic attractions and amenities by which the holiday-maker is lured to this outpost of Britain.

Great wealth was won from beneath the Cornish soil during the late eighteenth and nineteenth centuries and, while the markets held, the region was a world leader. Tin and copper were the most highly prized ores, laid down eons ago within Cornwall's granite spine as mineralising vapours and solutions from deep below the earth's crust which crystallised to form mineral deposits called 'lodes'. In smaller quantities, silver, gold, nickel, cobalt, zinc and iron also exist, while similar geological processes formed china clay (now mainly extracted in South Cornwall) and gabbro, quarried for road stone.

Small-scale exploitation of exposed ore-bearing granite dates back some 6000 years to Bronze Age man and it is well known that the Romans used these metals of Cornish origin. Early methods of obtaining alluvial tin included streaming—washing ore from river bed deposits—and using crude explosives, or heating at surface level. Mining as such probably began on coastal cliffs where mineral veins were exposed naturally. Adits, or galleries, were driven in to work the ore-bearing rocks but once tunnelling became necessary, water posed a real problem.

To pump it out, first manpower then horse-power and eventually steam were employed, the latter generating major innovations in machinery—particularly the beam engine for pumping, winding and crushing ores. The swashbuckling Captain Richard Trevithick pioneered the use of high-pressure steam in Cornish mines and was instrumental in building the very first steam-driven vehicles—an exciting development which led, through his associations with George Stephenson, to the famous first steam locomotive—'Rocket'.

Despite the introduction of mechanical advantages, miners still faced an extremely hazardous and gruelling life underground. Accidents—even fatalities—were common and the work itself back-breakingly hard, illuminated only by helmet candles. Men were sustained by the legendary Cornish pasty whose thick, crusty ridge was discarded after being soiled by hands contaminated with toxic substances such as arsenic.

After the mid-1800s when foreign competition had depressed the world price of copper and tin, many mines were closed, their workers forced to seek work elsewhere—often overseas. Already doomed by the end of World War I and further decimated by the great 1930s slump, profitable mining in Cornwall had shrunk to a two-mine operation—Geevor and South Crofty—by 1945.

Today, the acres of spoil have become colonised by gorse, heather, brambles and bracken. Masonry crumbles beneath the onslaught of wind and rain but because mine engine-houses were built so solidly—especially the bob wall upon which the beam rested—many have survived. Chimney stacks, too, are in evidence—characteristically round in section, stone built and topped with brick. Other buildings have either fallen to their foundations or been converted into dwellings.

In places, mine ruins have been renovated for safety and posterity, but wherever you explore as a walker you are ideally placed to inspect the close detail of a bygone industry. (NOTE: Abandoned mines are dangerous—beware of hidden shafts and unsafe masonry).

Geevor (pronounced with a soft 'G') offers tours of its surface workings for visitors and its excellent Tin Mining Museum is well worth looking round—perhaps before setting out on this walk. There is a café, a shop and a children's play area here too. The tin market crash of 1986 caused nearly 300 men to be laid off and the mine was left on a care-and-maintenance basis: effectively, operations were frozen in the hope of a recovery in tin prices.

The majority of nineteenth-century tin and copper mines in the Penzance district were situated along the north coast, especially around St Just and Pendeen, but were never served by a mineral railway. Most ores and coal were taken by road to and from Penzance harbour, the coast proving too inhospitable for shipping. Indeed, the unacceptable frequency of wrecks on these lethal rocks and reefs finally prompted the building of Pendeen Watch Lighthouse in 1900 and it is from here—at the lane-end car park below Boscaswell—that the walk begins.

A stone coast path sign opposite a row of white cottages a quarter of a mile (400m) up

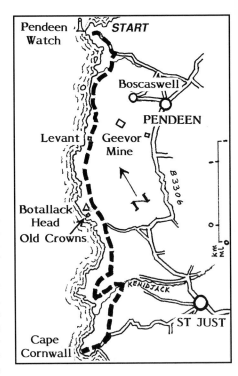

the Boscaswell lane sets you off across a marshy valley to Levant Mine. It really is a sorry sight today but was once one of Cornwall's great tin and copper mines, its workings extending a mile (1½km) out beneath the Atlantic (despite this it was exceptionally dry!). A 30ft (9m) whim engine, saved from the scrapman in 1935 and now maintained by the National Trust, can be viewed inside a tiny engine-house on the cliff edge at Skip Shaft.

On 20 October 1919, a hinge sheared at the top of Levant's beam engine used to transport miners up and down the shaft. At each 12ft (3½m) stroke, men would step on and off platforms set in the shaft side, thus making vertical progress, but on this occasion the entire man-engine collapsed sending 31 miners to their death and seriously injuring many more. It was Cornwall's worst mining disaster. Re-equipped, the mine limped on for a few more years before finally succumbing during the Depression years. Nearby Geevor subsequently re-opened the Levant workings to exploit its remaining reserves.

Passing three chimneys and a miscellany of ruins and derelict installations, the stony track continues ahead towards the OS pillar on Botallack Head. A little further on you veer right at a finger post to emerge above the two dramatic engine-houses on Botallack Mine's Crown section. Restored by the Carn Brea Mining Society in 1985 and much photographed by visitors, they crouch on a shoulder of cliff barely safe from the wash of rough seas. In its heyday, Old Crowns Mine was regarded as a wonder of the world. On 24 July 1865, its 1360ft (414m) depths were plumbed by the intrepid Duke and Duchess of Cornwall (later King Edward VII and Queen Alexandra) who were lowered down the diagonal shaft in a wheeled skip. Five years earlier the author Wilkie Collins had written an account laced with awe and terror following his own experiences of a descent!

Botallack Mine employed 500 people and early photographs show the cliff festooned with steam engines, timber supports and associated paraphernalia. By 1895, however, with tin prices at an all-time low, production had ceased and the Crowns section was being dismantled.

Yet more ruinous winding houses, overgrown heaps of stones and old walls lead on to where you join a path from the left by another impressive ruin. Bearing off right across gorse at a coast path waymark, the scene inland towards St Just leaves you in no doubt about the settlement's industrial roots. Rounding a corner, you are suddenly confronted by the earth ramparts of Kenidjack cliff castle, with Cape Cornwall beyond and, if visibility allows, a sighting of the Longships Lighthouse and rocks off Land's End.

Keeping left of the Iron Age earthworks, the way drops to a track heading inland and after a hundred yards forks down right over a stile and along a grassy pathway. (It is possible to cross the Kenidjack valley at its mouth but the going is steeper and rougher). In summer, the nearby cottage may provide refreshments and if time permits, you could explore more of this small valley. Its floor is rich in industrial remains. Here stood tin stamping mills, dressing floors and an arsenic works whose stack and flues are still extant. At the lower end is a large masonry pit which, in the 1860s, held a 52ft (16m) water-wheel. Thirty years before that, the Kenidjack valley boasted Cornwall's largest water-wheel—a full 65ft (20m) in diameter.

The walk now crosses a footbridge amidst luxuriant vegetation and zig-zags determinedly up through drifts of bluebells in springtime. Back at the coastline above Porth Ledden you meet a road and turn right down to the Cape Cornwall car park.

This promontory—the only cape in England and Wales—lies fractionally east of Land's End's latitude and in previous centuries was mistakenly considered to be England's most westerly point. Crowning the pyramidal summit is a fine brick chimney—a conspicuous feature from afar, like some futuristic beacon. The draught it created for a whim engine lower down to the south proved so ferocious that it was necessary to build a shorter

Cape Cornwall's mine chimney—a landmark and relic from a former industrial era.

Overleaf **Walkers on the coast path above Old Crowns Mine, Botallack Head.**

version on the hillside! Production ceased around 1873 and the old boiler-house and count-house are now dwellings.

Small mines like Cape Cornwall ran in an almost unbroken chain back along the coast to Morvah, Zennor, St Ives and Lelant. A few larger concerns developed here and there— Levant and Botallack for example, and St Just United which occupied Priest's Cove just south of the cape. Engine-houses, sheds and winding gear, terraced into the slopes towards Carn Gloose, served workings deep beneath the sea. St Just was distinguished in 1869 by becoming the first limited liability company in Cornwall to pay a dividend.

There is little to see above ground today, but it should be remembered that, in common with all similar mining operations, the shafts and levels where men laboured to extract ore-bearing rock represent the extensive but invisible heartland of the industry. The dangers faced by those early miners are hard to overstate. Technology was advancing quickly but machinery was often inadequately guarded and was subject to failure. Safety procedures were not always enforced so accidents were common

and the very process of tunnelling deep underground carried its own inherent risks of roof-fall, flooding and bad air. Down in the workings, more than anywhere else, hardships were endured, mishaps survived and lives tragically lost in this most perilous of human endeavours.

Should you want a circular walk (the total distance would still be under 10 miles (16km), a return to Pendeen Watch could be made by linking stretches of the B3306 coast road with field paths and lanes via Botallack and Boscaswell.